The Preacher's Paperback Library
Edmund A. Steimle, Consulting Editor

The Preaching of Chrysostom

Homilies on the Sermon on the Mount

Edited and with an Introduction by

JAROSLAV PELIKAN

FORTRESS PRESS • PHILADELPHIA

Library of Congress Catalog Card Number 67-13057

3682A67 Printed in U. S. A. 1-4007

ABOUT THE PREACHER'S PAPERBACK LIBRARY

The renewal of the church in our time has touched many aspects of parish life: liturgy and sacraments, biblical and theological concern, the place of the laity, work with small groups. But little has been said or done with regard to the renewal of the church in the pulpit.

The Preacher's Paperback Library is offered in the hope that it will contribute to the renewal of the preaching ministry. It will not stoop to providing "sermon starters" or other homiletical gimmicks. It will, rather, attempt to hold in balance the emphasis which contemporary theologians and biblical scholars lay upon the centrality of proclamation and the very practical concerns of theological students and parish pastors who are engaged in the demanding task of preparing sermons of biblical and theological depth which also speak to the contemporary world.

To that end, the series will provide reprints of fundamental homiletical studies not presently available and contemporary studies in areas of immediate concern to the preacher. Moreover, because the study of sermons themselves can be of invaluable help in every aspect of the preparation of the sermon, volumes of sermons with introductory notes will appear from time to time. The sermons will include reprints of outstanding preachers in the past as well as sermons by contemporary preachers who have given evidence both of depth and of imaginative gifts in communication. It is our hope that each volume in The Preacher's Paperback Library, prepared with the specific task of sermon preparation in mind, will contribute to the renewal of the preaching ministry.

In determining which of the outstanding preachers of the past should be included in The Preacher's Paperback Library, the name of John Chrysostom was an obvious choice. He is, by common consent, the most renowned preacher in the history of Christendom. Not so obvious was why he should be included other than as an historical curiosity.

Professor Jaroslav Pelikan, an historian sensitive to the importance of preaching in the history of the church, gives cogent reasons in his Introduction for the inclusion of Chrysostom in this series. Professor Pelikan makes clear that to study the sermons of Chrysostom is to engage in the same crucial problems which haunt the preacher today: the hermeneutical problem, the problem of the relation of the church to the world, the problem of the interaction between rhetoric and Christian proclamation, and the perennial problem of the interpretation of the Sermon on the Mount for a people as far removed today from these "counsels of perfection" as the people addressed by Chrysostom.

For the knowledgeable student, this volume with its scholarly Introduction provides a brief but valuable contribution to the literature about Chrysostom and to the history of preaching. For the novice, it provides an introduction to one of the fathers whose significance for the task of preaching in each succeeding generation has not dimmed, even for the task of preaching in a "world come of age."

EDMUND A. STEIMLE

Union Theological Seminary
New York, New York
Ash Wednesday, 1967

ACKNOWLEDGMENTS

A theological scholar who is occupied with the history of Christian doctrine does not often have a sense of direct relevance to the task of the preacher. He may try to be a responsible preacher himself, and he ought to be gratified when many of his students prefer the vocation of the preacher and pastor to that of the professor. But the importance of his historical research for this personal commitment to the centrality of preaching is not immediately evident.

Therefore it was a source of personal satisfaction when Fortress Press asked me to prepare this volume on the preaching of St. John Chrysostom for its Preacher's Paperback Library. For here an assignment that only a historian could undertake could be put into a form that is useful to the man who must stand in the pulpit every Lord's day. I am happy to record my gratitude to Dr. Edmund Steimle, the editor of this series, and to Mrs. Raymond Schulze, my secretary and editorial assistant.

JAROSLAV PELIKAN

Yale University
New Haven, Connecticut
St. Chrysostom's Day
January 27, 1967

CONTENTS

Introduction by Jaroslav Pelikan

1. The Study of the History of Preaching 1
2. Saint John Chrysostom 5
3. Chrysostom as Antiochene Exegete 12
4. Chrysostom as Rhetor 19
5. Chrysostom as an Expositor of the Sermon on the Mount 28
6. A Note on the Present Edition 34

Saint John Chrysostom: Homilies on the Sermon on the Mount 37

Homily XV—*Matthew 5:1-16* 39

Homily XVI—*Matthew 5:17-26* 67

Homily XVII—*Matthew 5:27-37* 96

Homily XVIII—*Matthew 5:38-48* 114

Homily XIX—*Matthew 6:1-15* 130

Homily XX—*Matthew 6:16-23* 153

Homily XXI—*Matthew 6:4-27* 167

Homily XXII—*Matthew 6:28-34* 177

Homily XXIII—*Matthew 7:1-20* 191

Homily XXIV—*Matthew 7:21-29* 214

Index 225

Introduction

1. *The Study of the History of Preaching*

THE CHRISTIAN CHURCH is constituted by the preaching of the word of God and the administration of the sacraments. This axiom of Reformation theology,[1] whose validity in one form or another would be acknowledged even by theologians standing outside the tradition of the Reformation, ought to have far-reaching consequences for the study of the history of the church. On the basis of it, one ought to pay careful attention to when and how the word was preached and the sacraments were administered, inquiring into the bearing of these activities on the faith, hope, and love of the church as the people of God. In practice, however, church history is usually written on the basis of a hierarchical and institutional definition of the church, rather than of a kerygmatic one.[2] Not the preaching of the word and the administration of the sacraments, but the careers of popes and other prelates, the relation of the church as an institution to such other institutions as the state, and the schisms and divisions of churches and denominations have determined the outline and the content of books on church history. Similarly, the church's theology has traditionally represented itself as a faithful exposition of the word of God in the Bible, but the standard interpretations of the history of Christian theology do not take that representation very seriously.[3] Therefore the histories

[1] See the comments of Wilhelm Pauck, *The Heritage of the Reformation* (2nd ed.; Glencoe, Ill.: Free Press, 1961), p. 391, n. 13.

[2] This entire issue was put into new perspective twenty years ago by the programmatic essay of Gerhard Ebeling, *Kirchengeschichte als Geschichte der Auslegung der Heiligen Schrift* (Tübingen: J. C. B. Mohr, 1947).

[3] Cf. Jaroslav Pelikan, *Luther the Expositor* (Saint Louis: Concordia, 1959), pp. 5-31.

of speculative systems far outnumber the histories of biblical exegesis.

It is, to be sure, far easier to lodge that complaint against the manuals of church history and of historical theology than it is to come up concretely with a narrative interpretation that is actually shaped by the centrality of preaching. At first examination, it seems that there exists an abundance of source material for such an interpretation. In the collected works of such a theologian as Augustine, the volumes of sermons bulk large;[4] the deposits of manuscripts in monasteries and libraries are often dominated by the homilies which formed so important a part of the required reading of monks and clerics;[5] and among the Puritans, where printed sermons were favored as reading matter for laymen, the mass of such books proliferated even beyond that of earlier times.[6]

Closer scrutiny of this source material, however, uncovers some of the thorny methodological difficulties involved in its use. For one thing, most sermons that have been preached are now lost forever. Many of the sermons that are available in various collections—perhaps most of them—appear in a form that does not correspond exactly to their state when they were delivered. Some of them were written down by listeners and then edited for publication; from careful studies of how this was done by George Rörer in the preparation of Luther's sermons and lectures, we have reason to be suspicious of any interpretation based only on such sources.[7] Some sermons were delivered *ex tempore* and then written down or dictated by the preacher for wider circulation; this seems to have been the

[4] F. van der Meer, *Augustine the Bishop,* trans. Brian Battershaw and G. R. Lamb (New York: Sheed and Ward, 1961), pp. 405-67.

[5] Jean Leclercq, *The Love of Learning and the Desire for God: A Study of Monastic Culture,* trans. Catharine Misrahi (New York: Mentor Omega Books, 1962), pp. 94-115.

[6] On Puritan preaching, see William Haller, *The Rise of Puritanism* (New York: Columbia University Press, 1938), pp. 128-72; Perry Miller, *The New England Mind,* I, *The Seventeenth Century* (Boston: Beacon Press, 1961), 280-362.

[7] The work of Rörer, Dietrich, and other editors has been investigated several times, most notably perhaps in Peter Meinhold, *Die Genesisvorlesung Luthers und ihre Herausgeber* (Stuttgart: W. Kohlhammer, 1936).

procedure which Cicero followed in composing at least some of his orations,[8] and in this respect as in others Christian preachers imitated classical orators. But this makes the sermon more a written essay than an oral address, and a later scholar has great difficulty attempting to distinguish between what was actually said and what was added for effect when the sermon was transposed into the literary modality. In addition, the sermons and homilies of the fathers that were used for edification in monasteries and sometimes in churches underwent further revision at the hands of later copyists, who, with the best of intentions, smoothed out the language and even the thought of the transmitted text.[9] Thus it would seem that although one might be able to write a history of the sermonic essay as a literary form, one cannot write a genuine history of preaching.

Nevertheless, even a history of the sermon would be an extremely useful contribution to our understanding of the history of the church. This is especially true because of the use to which written sermons were put. It seems a safe generalization that in many periods of church history more sermons were being read from such compilations of traditional preaching than were being composed afresh by the preacher, whether in the study beforehand or in the pulpit itself. Even the Protestant Reformers, for all their insistence upon the responsibility of the parish minister to preach the word of God, found themselves constrained to prepare postils for the clergy as well as for the laity.[10] These became a substitute for the pastor's own sermons or at least a present help in his time of need on Saturday night. And so a history of preaching based on written

[8] This problem has been studied by J. Humbert, *Les plaidoyers écrits et les plaidoiries réelles de Cicéron* (Paris: Les Presses Universitaires de France, 1925), pp. 252-76.

[9] As Johannes Quasten has summarized the situation in the case of Chrysostom, "The manuscripts present not infrequently two editions of the homilies, the one in a comparatively smooth style, the other in a rather rough state. The former is a deliberate later revision of the latter. Thus the superiority and greater antiquity of the rough text is too evident to be called into question." *Patrology,* III (Utrecht: Spectrum, 1960), 433.

[10] Cf. Luther's preface of 1543/1544 to the *Sommerpostille, Werke* (Weimar: Böhlau, 1883 ff.), XXI, 200-203.

and printed compilations of sermons would not be simply a chapter in the history of Greek, Latin, German, or English prose, but a fairly accurate study of how the word of God was proclaimed.[11] Nor should the historian ignore the widespread practice of preaching from a manuscript of the preacher's own composition, or at least from an outline. With some deviation introduced *ad libitum,* the preacher spoke what he had written, and when one studies what he spoke and compares it with what he wrote elsewhere for publication, some extremely interesting historical observations may result. The church historian who fails to pay attention to the history of preaching, even though so much of the source material is to some extent artificial, will be impoverishing himself.

The same is true of the preacher. "How can men preach," asks the Apostle (Rom 10:15), "unless they are sent?" Part of this sense of being sent is assuredly the preacher's own consciousness of his personal vocation to the ministry of Christ's church. Another important part is his sense of commission as one who stands in the long succession of heralds of the gospel. He follows in their train, and as he studies their achievements and failures, his own vocation comes into better perspective. But he can also learn from the history of preaching not to expect either too much or too little from his sermons. The "princes of the pulpit" often seemed to leave their hearers undented, while some preaching that seems to us shabby or banal became a vehicle of authentic divine revelation. "Therefore having this ministry by the mercy of God, we do not lose heart. But we have this treasure in earthen vessels, to show that the transcendent power belongs to God and not to us" (II Cor. 4:1, 7). Beyond these benefits, is there not a great deal that the modern preacher may still learn from those who lived before the Enlightenment or even before the Reformation? Indeed, there are certain epochs in the history of the church and therefore in the history of preaching that commend themselves with special force to the attention of today's minis-

[11] See the recent comments on the preaching of Ambrose in Angelo Paredi, *Saint Ambrose: His Life and Times,* trans. M. Joseph Costelloe (Notre Dame: University of Notre Dame Press, 1964), pp. 257-77.

ter, as a source not only of religious inspiration but of diagnostic insight for the performance of his tasks.

Such a period is the century following the conversion of Constantine. Into that century fall the major parts of the careers of those Greek and Latin fathers who shaped the subsequent development of the church and of dogma more decisively than any group of men since the apostles: Eusebius, Athanasius, Basil, Gregory of Nyssa, Gregory Nazianzus, Ambrose, Jerome, Augustine, and John Chrysostom, to name only some of them. What official Christian doctrine became in the 125 years from the Council of Nicaea in 325 to the Council of Chalcedon in 451, it has remained to the present day. Underlying the codification of the dogma was the establishment of the church as Christendom, dominating the culture and allied with the state. Preaching had been a witness to the truth of the gospel, directed to the faithful on the inside for their edification and to the unbelievers on the outside for their conversion. Now that Christianity was socially respectable and eventually even fashionable, the unbelievers began to appear inside the church also; and preaching was obliged to undertake the responsibility of instructing in the rudiments of Christian doctrine those who had been baptized without any such instruction, of training them in at least the minimum requirements of the Christian ethic, and of maintaining the ecclesiastical establishment, whether with the help of the secular arm or against interference from it.

2. *Saint John Chrysostom*

By common consent, there was no preacher in that *saeculum mirabile* more admirable than John Chrysostom, whom Pope Pius X in 1908, speaking in this instance for most Christians, designated as "patron" of Christian preachers.[1] This is not the place for a full-length biography of Chrysostom.[2] The date

[1] *Acta Sanctae Sedis,* XLI (1908), 594-95.

[2] The standard modern biography is that of the Benedictine scholar, Chrysostomus Baur, *John Chrysostom and His Time,* trans. M. Gonzaga (2 vols.; Westminster, Md.: Newman Press, 1959-60), from which I have drawn much of the biographical information summarized here.

of his birth is rather uncertain, but there is some reason to place it at 354, which also happens to have been the year of Augustine's birth.[3] In his best-known treatise, *On the Priesthood,* John quotes his mother's words to him when he was contemplating the religious life: "My child, it was not the will of Heaven that I should long enjoy the benefit of thy father's virtue. For his death soon followed the pangs which I endured at thy birth, leaving thee an orphan and me a widow before my time."[4] Nevertheless, he eventually did become a monk, and one of such rigorously ascetic devotion that he broke under the regimen and returned to Antioch. There he was ordained into the priesthood in 386, and for the next eleven years preached his way through most of the New Testament and parts of the Old. (It is to this period of his career that we owe the homilies presented here.)

In 397 the preacher became patriarch of Constantinople, and from that time on his life, which even in Antioch had been anything but sheltered, was a turbulent and even a tragic one. He was driven into exile by the combined opposition of the patriarch of Alexandria, Theophilus, and the empress, Eudoxia; the former had been alienated by many of John's activities, but especially by his acceptance of monks who had been excommunicated by the Alexandrian patriarch, while the latter believed the reports that Chrysostom had denounced her as a Jezebel. Although this exile was cut short by the protests of loyalists in Constantinople, the patriarch was exiled again in the following year, 404. To this final exile in Armenia, we owe a large collection of his letters, many of them now available in a fine modern edition;[5] they are sources of valuable information both about him and about the internal conditions of the church. When he was forced to transfer his place of

[3] Chrysostomus Baur, "Wann ist der heilige Johannes Chrysostomus geboren?" *Zeitschrift für katholische Theologie,* LII (1928), 401-6.

[4] Chrysostom *On the Priesthood* i. 5.

[5] Jean Chrysostome, *Lettres a Olympias,* ed. Anne-Marie Malingrey ("Sources chrétiennes," XIII [Paris: Éditions du Cerf, 1947]), with an informative introduction on the historical situation (6-32), on the relation between Chrysostom and Olympias (32-66), and on the Stoic and Christian ideas of suffering (66-85).

exile from Armenia to the remote frontier at the foot of the Caucasus in Pityus, the fearsome journey proved to be too much for John. And on September 14, 407, he died, near a village which today bears the name Bizeri, in the valley of the Iris. His dying words are said to have been: "Glory to God for all things. Amen."

For our purposes in the present volume, it is Chrysostom as a churchman and preacher who is the most important. There are several suggestions in the text of these homilies that give us a hint about changes that had come in the life of the church within the empire, and about Chrysostom's attitude toward these changes. In the final homily, for example, he contrasts the authentic security of the life of faith with the illusory security of wealth and power. "For there is not," he says, "nay there is not another life we may find free from all evils, but this alone. And ye are witnesses, who know the plots in king's courts and the troubles in the houses of the rich. But there was not among the apostles any such thing."[6] The emperor at the time was Theodosius the Great, whose achievements in establishing Christianity consolidated the work of Constantine and prepared for that of Justinian. Although Chrysostom, like other clerics, was in many ways the beneficiary of those achievements, this did not blind him to the contrast between the imperial church and the apostolic church. Before his life and ministry were over, he would have ample occasion for further reflection on that contrast and on the effect of "plots in king's [and queen's!] courts" upon the security of the Christian church and the freedom of its proclamation.

Another by-product of ecclesiastical establishment to which Chrysostom the churchman often called attention, also in these homilies, was the incursion of hordes of uncommitted new members into the church and the catastrophic breakdown in church discipline that this presaged. Warning that he would "have no rich man, no potentate, puffing at me here, and drawing up his eyebrows," Chrysostom denounced those who came to his church because its liturgy was a dramatic spectacle or

[6] Chrysostom *Homilies on the Gospel of Saint Matthew* xxiv. 3. Henceforth, in referring to those homilies, they shall be cited merely as *Matt.*, referring to the number of the homily in lower-case Roman numerals and to the number of the section in Arabic numerals.

because his preaching was an exciting form of rhetorical display. He was not a man of infinite patience, and he did not suffer fools gladly; now he had "fairly given up in despair," for the members of the church were "still clinging to the former rude beginnings." If they persisted, he threatened, he would "forbid you for the future to set foot on this sacred threshold, and partake of the immortal mysteries" of the divine liturgy. "For it is better to offer our accustomed prayers, with two or three, who keep the laws of God, than to sweep together a multitude of transgressors and corrupters of others."[7] Despite such attacks and threats, neither liturgical decorum nor moral uprightness seems to have improved.

Therefore even so formal and stylized a series of homilies as this contains repeated admonitions to observe both liturgical decorum and moral uprightness. There were evidently some Christians who "shamelessly associated with all, and make the awful things [of the liturgy and the sacraments] contemptible." Addressing himself to such Christians, Chrysostom warned that the church still celebrated the mysteries behind closed doors and still forbade attendance at them by the uninitiated.[8] This was "not for any weakness of which we have convicted our rites, but because the many are as yet imperfectly prepared for them."[9] Both the origins and the extent of the *disciplina arcani* have long been debated by patristic scholars, but such comments as these substantiate the liturgical evidence of the church's continued effort to hold the line against the growing pressure of those who had become Christians the easy way.[10] But these homilies also show that the effort was not altogether successful. There was, the preacher warned, great "disrespectfulness" among Christian worshipers; "when prophets are chanting, and apostles singing hymns, and

[7] Chrysostom *Matt.* xvii. 6.

[8] Cf. *Ibid.* xvi. 12 and xix. 9.

[9] *Ibid.* xxiii. 3.

[10] See the summary of the evidence by O. Perler, "Arkandisziplin," *Reallexikon für Antike und Christentum,* I (Stuttgart: Hiersemann Verlags-G.M.B.H., 1950), 667-76, including several references to Chrysostom; see also the evidence on the *redditio symboli* assembled in *St. John Chrysostom: Baptismal Instructions,* ed. Paul W. Harkins ("Ancient Christian Writers," XXXI [Westminster, Md.: Newman Press, 1963]), 222-23, n. 39.

God is discoursing, we wander without, and bring in upon us a turmoil of worldly business." This he contrasted with the great reverence shown at the worldly theaters when the customary letters of the emperor were being read. The audience was silent, and if anyone presumed to interrupt this silence, he was severely punished. Here in church it was the very letters of heaven that were read, and yet the audience was indifferent. Nor was its decorum any better during the liturgy. "As though in the midst of a forum," he complained, "we make an uproar and disturbance, and spend the whole time of our solemn assembly in discoursing of things which are nothing to us."[11]

So far had such disrespect gone that the solemn regulations of the church regarding fasting were also being flouted. In the Sermon on the Mount Jesus condemned those who fasted ostentatiously, but the new breed of Christians had gone these hypocrites one better, "not merely fasting and making a display of it, but neglecting to fast, and yet wearing the masks of them that fast, and cloaking themselves with an excuse worse than their sin." When they were called to account for their hypocrisy, they claimed that they were doing this to avoid giving offense. Thus they were afraid of offense, but unafraid of blasphemy![12] As Stiglmayer has suggested, such references and allusions in Chrysostom's homilies—particularly those that were composed later than the present series—can be used as a source for the social history of the metropolitan centers of the classical world.[13] They are, of course, especially important for the social history of the church, but they also reveal a great deal about general conditions. The most distinguished of present-day historians of Antioch has noted that "Chrysostom's works complete our knowledge of Antioch at this time as much by the background they supply indirectly as by the specific facts they mention."[14]

[11] Chrysostom *Matt.* xix. 12.

[12] *Ibid.* xx. 1.

[13] J. Stiglmayer, "Antike Grossstädte im Spiegel der Chrysostomus-Homilien," *Stimmen der Zeit*, LVIII (1927), 170-85.

[14] Glanville Downey, *A History of Antioch in Syria from Seleucus to the Arab Conquest* (Princeton: Princeton University Press, 1961), p. 42.

One aspect of church life at the end of the fourth century is of particular importance for an understanding of the *Tendenz* in these homilies. Although the various Arian positions were still the most virulent heresies of the time, Chrysostom is especially concerned in his exposition of the Sermon on the Mount to refute another heretical tradition, that of Gnosticism and its descendant, Manichaeism. At the very beginning of the first homily on the Sermon on the Mount, the preacher describes Jesus as stopping "the shameless mouths of heretics, signifying by this his care of both parts of our being, that he himself is the Maker of the whole creation."[15] Against the Gnostic and Manichaean disparagement of the body as the prison of the soul, he thus defended the biblical insistence that both the body and the soul were God's creations and, as such, essentially good. Later he rejected the dualistic notion that the body is the source of temptation and sin which corrupts the purity of the mind by its appetites. For in the Sermon on the Mount Christ is "not discoursing about our limbs;—far from it,—for nowhere doth he say that our flesh is to be blamed for things, but everywhere it is the evil mind that is accused. For it is not the eye that sees, but the mind and the thought."[16] At a time when the teachers of the church, including Chrysostom, were cultivating the ascetic ideal and exalting virginity, they also continued to fight off the heretical doctrine that the body and its drives were creatures of the devil.

It was not only the human body, however, that called forth the aversion of the Gnostics and Manichaeans; it was the entire natural realm. They asserted that "the God who made the world, who 'makes his sun to rise on the evil and on the good, who sends the rain on the just and on the unjust,' is in some sense an evil being."[17] The dichotomy between soul and body had its counterpart and its basis in a dualism within the divine reality itself. The Creator of the natural world, and thus of the human body, was a different being from the heavenly Father; "some other one, who is not, nor made any of the things that are, they assign for a Father to Christ." This Father

[15] Chrysostom *Matt.* xv. 1.
[16] *Ibid.* xvii. 3.
[17] *Ibid.* xvi. 8.

so completely transcended the natural world of existence and of becoming that he could not even be said to "be," but could be properly described only in negative terms. When the doctrine of the Trinity identified God the Father with the Creator and asserted the unity of the Son and the Holy Spirit with him in one Godhead, it was defending monotheism simultaneously against Gnostic dualism and against Arian subordinationism. So far had the disparagement of the natural gone that even the use of illustrations drawn from the world of animals seemed improper: "It was not meet for one strengthening moral principle, to use natural advantages as enticements to that end."[18] And as Chrysostom defended the essential goodness of the body, so he affirmed the essential goodness of the entire creation. Even the wickedness of the devil was not "from nature," but had come by the devil's own choice; the devil, too, was part of creation.[19]

The heretical antipathy for creation and the body was part of a theological system that also rejected the Old Testament, and since the middle of the second century the church had been engaged in a defense of the Old Testament as Christian Scripture. Therefore the words of the Sermon on the Mount about the commandments given "by them of old time" did not mean an attack on the Old Testament and its law. On the contrary, by these words Christ "commends the old law, by making a comparison between it and the other. . . . He doth not, you see, find fault with the old law, but will have it made stricter."[20] The commandments of the Mosaic law and the commandments of the Sermon on the Mount differed in degree, not in kind, and belonged together in the history of God's revelation of his will to men. It was blasphemy to "say that the old covenant is of the devil."[21] Christ himself used the occasion of his announcement of the new and stricter law to make it clear that he had not come to destroy the law and the prophets of the Old Testament, but to fulfill them. Especially in St. Matthew's account of his teachings and actions was the theme of fulfillment dominant; from birth to death Christ

[18] *Ibid.* xxi. 4.
[19] *Ibid.* xix. 10.
[20] *Ibid.* xvi. 6.
[21] *Ibid.* xvi. 3.

labored at giving substance to this claim. And so "his sayings were no repeal of the former, but a drawing out, and filling up of them."[22] Chrysostom's commentaries on the Old Testament, notably his homilies on Genesis, illustrate how important this continuity between the old covenant and the new was for his understanding of the entire biblical message.[23] Both they and his homilies on the New Testament, including these on St. Matthew, also demonstrate the continuing threat of the Gnostic and Gnosticizing systems which exalted the novelty of the gospel by undermining its continuity with the old covenant, glorified grace by defacing nature, and sought to protect God from defilement by repudiating the biblical doctrine of creation. Both as a Christian and as a theologian, Chrysostom found such systems intolerable. His defense against them therefore became a leitmotiv of these homilies.

3. *Chrysostom as Antiochene Exegete*

Second only to Chrysostom's fame as a preacher is his renown as a biblical exegete. He is, in the phrase of G. L. Prestige, "the master and pattern of all biblical commentators belonging rather to the historical than to the dogmatic school of exposition."[1] Because he saw the task of preaching principally as one of interpreting the biblical text and applying it to the hearers, even so brief an introduction to Chrysostom as this must devote some consideration to this method of biblical exegesis as it pertains to these homilies on the Sermon on the Mount.

John Chrysostom is so completely the typical representative of the Antiochene school of exegesis that most of what we know about this school and its actual exegetical practice has come from him.[2] Chrysostom's friend, Theodore of Mopsuestia,

[22] *Ibid.* xvi. 4.

[23] Cf. Chrysostomus Baur, "Chrysostomus in Genesim," *Theologische Quartalschrift,* CVIII (1927), 221-32.

[1] G. L. Prestige, *Fathers and Heretics* (London: S. P. C. K., 1948), p. 20.

[2] I am indebted to the researches of my student and now colleague, Rowan A. Greer, "The Antiochene Exegesis of Hebrews" (Ph.D. dissertation, Yale University, 1965), for a clarification of the relation between Chrysostom and "the school of Antioch."

was the teacher of Nestorius, and the condemnation of Nestorianism led to the destruction of much of the scholarly literature of the Antiochene school, but Chrysostom's standing as a hero of the faith, revered by both East and West, helped to save his work from such a fate. Although he was evidently a more orthodox theologian than were some later exponents of Antiochene theology, that is, one whose principles of interpretation were more radical in their possible implications than in their dogmatic results, he does enable historians to trace the evolution of literal exegesis from its beginnings to its Nestorian foliation and to see its place within the context of the history of early Christian exegesis.[3] As von Campenhausen has observed, "The homilies of Chrysostom are probably the only ones from the whole of Greek antiquity which at least in part are still readable today as Christian sermons. They reflect something of the authentic life of the New Testament, just because they are so ethical, so simple, and so clear-headed"[4]—and, he could have added, because they are so sober and so restrained in their hermeneutical procedure.

That sobriety and restraint may be said to be the dominant characteristics of the hermeneutics of the Antiochene school. It seems that in its origins this school of Christian exegesis owed much to the Jewish tradition of biblical interpretation, i.e., not to the tradition represented by Philo, which harmonized the Old Testament with its developed philosophy by means of an allegorical method of explaining Scripture, but to the tradition of the literal interpretation of Scripture represented by the rabbis. Applying this method of interpretation to the Christian understanding of Scripture, the Christian exegetes of the Antiochene school drastically limited the application of allegorical techniques. A later explanation of the difference, even though it dates from the ninth century, states the problem with precision:

[3] Cf. Newman's comment: "There have been many literal expositors, but only one Chrysostom. It is St. Chrysostom who is the charm of the method, not the method that is the charm of St. Chrysostom." John Henry Newman, "The Last Years of St. Chrysostom," *Essays and Sketches*, ed. Charles Frederick Harrold III (New York: Thomas Nelson, 1948), p. 220.

[4] Hans von Campenhausen, *The Fathers of the Greek Church*, trans. Stanley Godman (New York: Pantheon, 1959), p. 144.

> People ask what the difference is between allegorical exegesis and historical exegesis. We reply that it is great and not small; just as the first leads to impiety, blasphemy, and falsehood, so the other is conformed to truth and faith. It was the impious Origen of Alexandria who invented this art of allegory. Just as poets and geometricians, when they wish to raise their disciples from material and visible things to things hidden and invisible, erring in regard to the eternity of incorporeal matter and to indivisible atoms, say: "Just as it is not these visible signs which are signs for reading, but their hidden meanings, so from created natures one must rise by the image of thought to their eternal nature"; just so, Origen taught. . . . The psalms and the prophets who spoke of the captivity and the return of the people, he explained as teaching the captivity of the soul far from truth and its return to faith. . . . They do not interpret paradise as it is, or Adam, or Eve, or any existing thing.[5]

It was against this form of exegetical alchemy, which sought to turn the lead of historical narrative into the gold of spiritual truth, that Antiochene hermeneutics protested.

In so doing, the school of Antioch was taking on a formidable opponent. The advocates of allegory could, of course, point to the use of this method within the New Testament itself, notably to the allegorical interpretation of the difference between Sarah and Hagar in Galatians 4:21-31.[6] In fact, however, this was one of the very few instances of the allegorical method in Scripture, and it was certainly more than counterbalanced by the meticulous attention to the minutiae of historical narrative evident not only in the Old Testament but also in the New. But by the time of its encounter with Antioch, allegory had more than Pauline precedent on its side. Against Marcion it had won the day as a vindication of the Christianization of the Old Testament; in the conflict with Gnosticism it had proved that the truly "spiritual" interpretation of the mystery of Christ did not reside only with Valentinus, Basilides, and their disciples, but was being set forth by the

[5] Ish'odad's *Introduction to the Psalms,* quoted in Robert M. Grant, *The Bible in the Church* (New York: The Macmillan Company, 1948), p. 75.

[6] Cf. Chrysostom *Matt.* xvi. 8.

orthodox exegesis of the church catholic.[7] And in the course of the controversy with Arianism allegory had marshaled the evidence of both Testaments in support of the consubstantiality of the Son with the Father, citing the Psalter, the eighth chapter of the Book of Proverbs, and the prologue to the Gospel of John as parts of the same Scripture, regardless of their chronological difference.[8] Cardinal Newman does not seem to have been exaggerating when he proposed that "it may almost be laid down as an historical fact, that the mystical interpretation and orthodoxy will stand or fall together."[9] Orthodoxy itself seemed to be in jeopardy when Antiochene exegesis sought to put a limitation on allegory.

Yet in some of its outstanding representatives Antiochene exegesis was impeccably orthodox. Thus, although the later identification of Theodore of Mopsuestia as a heretic raised some questions about the orthodoxy of his teacher, Diodore of Tarsus, Diodore's own intent was evidently to assert, against Arianism, the consubstantiality of Christ with the Father and, against Apollinarism, the consubstantiality of Christ with man. One of his disciples, Theodore, was indeed eventually labeled a heretic, but another of his disciples was John Chrysostom. Despite the close alliance to which Cardinal Newman points between "the mystical interpretation" of Scripture and "orthodoxy" in matters of the Trinitarian and christological dogmas, Chrysostom proved that it was possible to be altogether orthodox whenever one dealt with these dogmas—which, in his case, was not very often—and yet to follow the lead of Diodore in stressing the literal rather than the allegorical sense of Scripture.

Chrysostom's preference for the "literal" or historical sense over the allegorical is especially visible in his few surviving

[7] Adolf von Harnack, *Marcion: Das Evangelium vom fremden Gott* (new printing; Berlin: Akademie-Verlag, 1960), II, 259-60, collects the pertinent passages from Marcion's opponents. Henri de Lubac, *Histoire et esprit: L'intelligence de l'Écriture d'après Origène* (Paris: Aubier, 1950), pp. 166-78.

[8] Jaroslav Pelikan, *The Light of the World: A Basic Image in Early Christian Thought* (New York: Harper, 1962), pp. 55-57.

[9] John Henry Newman, *An Essay on the Development of Christian Doctrine* (Image Book Edition; New York: Doubleday, 1960), p. 327.

works on the Old Testament, just as, conversely, the Alexandrians applied a freer hand to the spiritualization of the historical materials of the Old Testament than to the application of the same method in their exegesis of the Gospels. Such difficulties in the New Testament as the miracle stories were a special problem, which could sometimes be solved by recourse to allegory,[10] but even the most extravagant of orthodox allegorists were restrained by the example of Gnostic demythologization from dissolving the gospel narratives into allegories of the soul's descent from God and its return to him through the strata of the cosmos. When they came to the narratives of, for example, the Book of Joshua, these restraints were off; and Origen made of the Book of Joshua a rich resource of doctrinal and ethical insight, proving from its own words, such as the phrase "to this day" in Joshua 6:25, that it had not been intended as a literal historical account but as a spiritual narrative.[11] Even in his *Homilies on Genesis*, however, Chrysostom showed himself an apt pupil of Diodore and an enemy of overly imaginative allegorization.

That inclination to be sober rather than imaginative in interpretation makes itself evident also in these homilies on the Sermon on the Mount, where there was, after all, little opportunity for the conflict between the two methods of scriptural exegesis to make itself felt. The conflict comes into view only at those points where Chrysostom himself attacks an excessively allegorical view or where we happen to have other commentaries on the same passage. Of the first sort is his explanation of the third of the beatitudes in Matthew 5:5: "Blessed are the meek, for they shall inherit the earth." Chrysostom raises the question, "What kind of earth?"[12] Without specifying his sources, he goes on to note that some exegetes had said that this was "a figurative earth." It is not

[10] Cf. Robert M. Grant, *Miracle and Natural Law in Graeco-Roman and Early Christian Thought* (Amsterdam: North Holland Publishing Company, 1952), esp. pp. 193-208.

[11] Origen *In Jesu Nave* vii. 5; cf. the comments on this passage by Annie Jaubert (ed.), *Origène, Homélies sur Josué* ("Sources chrétiennes," LXXI [Paris: Éditions du Cerf, 1960]), 206-7, n. 2.

[12] Chrysostom *Matt.* xv. 5.

clear whom he has in mind. This was indeed the interpretation of "inherit the earth" proposed just a few years later in Augustine's commentary on the Sermon on the Mount. But apparently both Augustine's acceptance of a spiritual interpretation of "earth" and Chrysostom's polemic against such an interpretation presuppose an exegetical tradition, now lost, which explained the words as a promise of "an undying inheritance, where the soul in a state of well-being rests as in its natural environment . . . the life and rest of the saints."[13] Not so, Chrysostom argued, "for nowhere in Scripture do we find any mention of an earth that is merely figurative." Hence the passage must mean that Christ sought to motivate his hearers both by the prospect of eternal glory and by the promise of temporal gain, a literal "earth" that they would possess by inheritance if they practiced true meekness.

Another passage in the Sermon on the Mount where earlier allegorists had applied their technique was Matthew 5:25. "Some say," Chrysostom informs us, "that [Christ] obscurely signifies the devil himself, under the name of the adversary; and bids us have nothing of his."[14] But there was no need for so far-fetched an explanation of the words, which could be taken simply and quite literally as referring to the judges, prisons, and way of this world. We are fortunate in this instance to have two earlier pieces of evidence about the provenance of the exegesis that identified the "adversary" of Matthew 5:25 with the devil. Irenaeus informs us that the followers of the Gnostic teacher Carpocrates "declare the 'adversary' is one of those angels who are in the world, whom they call the devil, maintaining that he was formed for this purpose, that he might lead those souls which have perished from the world to the Supreme Ruler."[15] According to Tertullian, too, Carpocrates taught the transmigration of souls and found in this passage a substantiation of this theory.[16] It was evidently some such allegory, perhaps even in an orthodox

[13] Augustine *The Lord's Sermon on the Mount* i. 2. 4 ("Ancient Christian Writers," V [Westminster, Md.: Newman Press, 1956]), 14.

[14] Chrysostom *Matt.* xvi. 13.

[15] Irenaeus *Against Heresies* i. 25. 4.

[16] Tertullian *On the Soul* 35.

form, that Chrysostom was attacking by urging in the same passage that Christ, "after he had abashed men by higher things, and things future . . . alarms them also by such as are in this life."

But the most striking illustration within these homilies of the antithesis between the two styles of exegesis comes in the interpretation of the fourth petition of the Lord's Prayer in Matthew 6:11. Here Chrysostom did not make his divergence from the exegetical tradition as explicit as he had in the explanation of the earlier passages; yet the divergence is even more far-reaching. Origen was speaking for a large body of exegetical tradition when he protested that the bread for which this petition prays could not be physical bread, as some interpreters of the passage proposed.[17] On the basis of the discourses of Jesus in John 6, Origen argued that Christ himself was the true bread and therefore that this petition was actually a prayer for the only bread that was in the fullest sense *epiousios,* that is, "of the divine substance."[18] Chrysostom's interpretation, on the other hand, was much more prosaic, but perhaps also more accurate. The command to pray this petition, like the whole of the Sermon on the Mount, was addressed "to men encompassed with flesh, and subject to the necessities of nature." Therefore the Lord's Prayer included not only requests for spiritual blessings, but also the prayer for what the body required, daily bread. Even here, however, the teachings of Christ were emphasizing the reality of the spiritual life, for all that we are permitted to request is the simple necessity of one day's bread at a time.[19]

Earlier we referred to the anti-Gnostic and anti-Manichaean accent in much of Chrysostom's polemic in these homilies. The discovery that in his identification of the "adversary" of Matthew 5:25 he was also voicing a polemic against an exegetical tradition of the Gnostic masters suggests a connection in Chrysostom's mind between the spiritualism of the Gnostic or Manichaean dualists and the spiritualism of allegorical exegesis. Against both of them his Antiochene realism emphasized the

[17] Origen *On Prayer* xxvii. 1.

[18] *Ibid.* xxvii. 7.

[19] Chrysostom *Matt.* xix. 8.

goodness and the importance of the literal, the historical, and the material, as part of God's good creation and as a means of his revelation. Readers who approach these homilies after having studied other exegetical traditions will find some interesting points of comparison. There are certain affinities between Antiochene exegesis and the methods of the Reformers, so that anyone who stands consciously in the exegetical tradition of the Reformation will recognize many of Chrysostom's methods. On the other hand, a student of patristic literature who is accustomed to the rich diet of Origenist allegory will find Chrysostom's exegesis rather bland by comparison. The elaborate system of symbols has been replaced by a rather matter-of-fact exposition of the text. Origen saw a succession of types and prototypes, in which the material world of experience mirrored the reality of the spiritual world in God. When Chrysostom resorted to the notion of prototypes, it was to develop the ethical point made in Proverbs 19:17, that God becomes the debtor to whom one lends when one gives to the poor and that God is therefore the debtor "in the original sense."[20] But all of this is rather tame after Origen's ingenious excavations into the text to find the gold of the spiritual sense. As we shall note in the fifth section of this Introduction, however, this method did enable Chrysostom to apply the Sermon on the Mount to the needs of his hearers with singular force and clarity. Apparently the Antiochene exegesis suited an Antiochene audience.

4. *Chrysostom as Rhetor*

It is impossible to read the homilies of Chrysostom without being constantly reminded that he was not only a Christian priest but also a Greek orator. Both the exegetical tradition of Antioch and the rhetorical tradition of Antioch helped to shape his composition. The outstanding representative of the latter during John's youth was Libanius (314-393).[1] As

[20] *Ibid.* xv. 13.

[1] The career and significance of Libanius are well summarized by Glanville Downey in a chapter on "The Old World of Libanius," *Antioch in the Age of Theodosius the Great* (Norman, Okla.: University of Oklahoma Press, 1962), pp. 85-102; see also the following chapter, pp. 103-132, on "John Chrysostom's New World."

Festugière has shown, Libanius was one of the most eloquent spokesmen of his day for the educational ideals of classical Greek paganism.[2] These he defended against the incursions of Roman paganism, by refusing to pay his worship to Roman gods or his respects to Roman literature, and against the rising tide of Christianity, by clinging to Greek astrology and to other practices of Greek religion.

Libanius was not only the most celebrated orator of his time, but also a gifted and influential teacher. He had the quite unparalleled distinction of having had as his pupils both the "apostate" emperor Julian and the Christian choryphaei John Chrysostom, Basil the Great, and Gregory of Nazianzus. A recent study of his work as a teacher has sought to describe the extent of his influence upon his disciples.[3] There has been some debate among scholars about the accuracy of the report of the church historian Socrates that John Chrysostom "studied rhetoric under Libanius the sophist and philosophy under Andragathius the philosopher,"[4] and some have attempted to prove that this was a later fiction.[5] Most historians and biographers, nevertheless, are still inclined to accept Socrates' account. As Baur has put it, "The first and greatest orator of Christian antiquity sat at the feet of the last great rhetorician of pagan antiquity."[6] Additional light both on Chrysostom's affinities for Libanius' style of rhetoric and on his independence of it has come from a close analysis of the rhetorical rhythms in several of Chrysostom's sermons.[7]

This is not to say, of course, that the sermons as we now have them represent a verbatim transcript of what Chrysostom actually said in the pulpit. Unfortunately, the evidence for an adjudication of this question is less substantial than the his-

[2] A. J. Festugière, *Antioche païenne et chrétienne* (Paris: Éditions E. de Boccard, 1959), pp. 91-139.

[3] P. Petit, *Les étudiants de Libanius* (Paris: Nouvelles éditions Latines, 1957), pp. 40-42.

[4] Socrates *Ecclesiastical History* vi. 3.

[5] Baur, *Chrysostom,* I, 22-23, summarizes the arguments.

[6] *Ibid.*, p. 21.

[7] Stanislaus Skimina, *De Ioannis Chrysostomi rhythmo oratorio* (Kraków: Archiwum filologiczne polskiej Akademji Umiej, 1927), esp. pp. 54-69, comparing Libanius, Chrysostom, and Gregory of Nyssa.

torian would wish. There are two radically different recensions of Chrysostom's *Homilies on Genesis,* which he delivered perhaps in 388.[8] One recension contains numerous allusions to current events and contemporary problems in the city of Antioch; the other is, in effect, a sermonic commentary on Genesis that could almost have been written and/or preached at any time in his career—or even in the career of some other Christian preacher in another city and another century. Perhaps the literary version of the homilies was a revision for publication based on stenographic notes taken down during the delivery of the sermons; but it is also possible, even likely, that the sermonic commentary was a literary composition in its own right. This may also be true of other series of homilies in the corpus of Chrysostom's works. As we noted early in this Introduction, it is this uneasy relation between the preached word and its written deposit that makes a history of preaching (in the sense of oral proclamation) a historiographic impossibility. Thus it seems that in their transmitted form the homilies of Chrysostom were delivered orally by hundreds and thousands of Greek preachers, but not by Chrysostom himself.

The fifth book of Chrysostom's treatise *On the Priesthood* is a succinct description of the qualities which a Christian preacher must have. Among these, two were of special importance to Chrysostom: an indifference to the plaudits of one's hearers, and an ability to speak skilfully. For

> if a preacher be indifferent to praise, and yet cannot produce the doctrine "which is grace seasoned with salt" [Col. 4:6], he becomes despised by the multitude, while he gains nothing from his own nobleness of mind; and if on the other hand he is successful as a preacher, and is overcome by the thought of applause, harm is equally done in turn, both to himself and the multitude, because in his desire for praise he is careful to speak rather with a view to please than to profit.[9]

[8] These have been investigated in a study which I have not had the opportunity to examine, W. A. Markowicz, "The Text Tradition of St. John Chrysostom's Homilies on Genesis" (Ph.D. Dissertation, University of Michigan, 1953).

[9] Chrysostom *On the Priesthood* v. 2.

Both of these qualities, as well as the correlative temptations, were familiar to Chrysostom, as his career demonstrates and his sermons and homilies attest. Yet his training as a rhetor betrayed its presence even when he was warning against the dangers of relying too much on rhetoric. The entire treatise *On the Priesthood* is both a gem of Christian literature and a masterpiece of the rhetorician's art.[10] There have not been enough investigations of the rhetorical method in other works, particularly in the exegetical series of homilies, to warrant any generalization beyond the hypothetical; but each time a scholar has applied painstaking analysis to one of Chrysostom's writings the virtuosity of his oratorical performance has been proved once more.[11] The rhetoric could be poison-mouthed as well as golden-mouthed; certainly the most shocking of Chrysostom's works, the *Homilies against the Jews,* delivered apparently from August, 387, to September, 389, document the way Christian rhetoric could serve as a vehicle for Christian anti-Semitism.[12]

Although there would seem to be a need also for a full-length analysis of the *Homilies on Saint Matthew*, the reader of the ten homilies assembled in the present volume should be alert to signs that techniques of classical oratory have been applied to the task of expounding the Scriptures. The complementary and yet often contradictory traits discussed abstractly in Book V of *On the Priesthood,* the preacher's resistance to the blandishments of the multitude and his cultivation of skill as a rhetor, are exhibited concretely in this sermonic commentary. If there existed stenographic notes of the sermons as they were delivered, we could perhaps identify many other points where the rhetorician and the pastor have

[10] W. A. Maat, *A Rhetorical Study of St. John Chrysostom's "De sacerdotio"* (Washington: Catholic University Press, 1944) is helpful for the study of other works as well.

[11] Two basic analyses are: T. E. Ameringer, *The Stylistic Influence of the Second Sophistic on the Panegyrical Sermons of St. John Chrysostom* (Washington: Catholic University Press, 1921); and Mary Albania Burns, *Saint John Chrysostom's Homilies on the Statues: A Study of their Rhetorical Qualities and Form* (Washington: Catholic University Press, 1930).

[12] A. Lukyn Williams, *Adversus Judaeos* (Cambridge: Cambridge University Press, 1935), pp. 132-39.

combined to produce the preacher. But even in their present state the homilies show many marks of the art that consists in concealing art, or at least in almost concealing it.

The last of the beatitudes in Matthew 5:11 provided an occasion for a disquisition on the necessity of cultivating an indifference to the flattery of one's hearers, as well as for a clarification of what this indifference did not imply. Chrysostom was not insensitive to the need for approval. He knew already in 390 what he was to learn many times again, that "it is not even possible that those who live in the practice of virtue should be well spoken of by all men."[13] He was obviously expressing his own feelings when he went on to say: "Most assuredly, men's evil reports have a sharper bite than their very deeds. For whereas, in our dangers, there are many things that lighten the toil, as to be cheered by all, to have many to applaud, to crown, to proclaim our praise; here in our reproach even this consolation is destroyed." The instructions in the Sermon on the Mount, as we shall note, did not pertain only to the disciples, but through them were addressed to all men.[14] Yet they did apply with special force both to the disciples and to their successors in the church, the bishops and clergy. This was particularly true of the admonition and encouragement of the final beatitude, which, while relevant to the life of all believers, spoke directly to the condition of the preacher. It was also with both preacher and hearers in mind that Chrysostom added the clarifying comment that two limitations were appended to this beatitude. Those who endured slander were blessed "when it is for [Christ's] sake, and when the things that are said are false."[15] One cannot help wondering whether words like these recurred to the mind of the patriarch of Constantinople when the "synod of the Oak" met in July, 403, to condemn him and urge his banishment.

In one of the passages of the present ten homilies which gives an indication that the text of the homilies probably rests upon a transcription of Chrysostom's actual preaching, the preacher had occasion to apply these warnings about applause to himself. As he was moving into the peroration of the

[13] Chrysostom *Matt.* xv. 9.
[14] *Ibid.* xv. 1.
[15] *Ibid.* xv. 7.

seventeenth homily, he seems to have been interrupted by applause. "Did ye give praise to what hath been said?" he asked. "Nay, I want not applause, nor tumults, nor noise. One thing only do I wish, that quietly and intelligently listening, you should do what is said. This is the applause, this the panegyric for me."[16] He attacked his hearers for treating the liturgy and the sermon as though they were a "dramatic spectacle" or a performance to be gawked at and cheered but not heeded. There are other passages in the corpus of Chrysostom's writings that refer to this custom, including one from the peroration of a homily on First Corinthians,[17] but one of the fullest discussions appears in the homilies on Acts.[18] Here he addressed himself specifically to those who had the gift of eloquence and the "grace of teaching," warning them that it was easy to teach by words but that the example of one's life was a better lesson. Some preachers went to great pains with their sermons. "And if they get applause from the multitude, it is to them as if they gained the very kingdom of heaven; but if silence follows the close of their speech, it is worse than hell itself, the dejection that falls upon their spirits from the silence!" Speaking now of his own feelings as a preacher, Chrysostom admitted that it was exhilarating to be applauded while he was in the pulpit; but the thrill was brief, for afterwards he reflected that many of those who had cheered would not take the message to heart. The only solution, he announced, was for all applause to be forbidden—and this announcement brought the house down with applause!

In the context of this lengthy discourse on applause in his *Homilies on the Acts of the Apostles,* Chrysostom also observed: "Christ spoke publicly on the mount: yet no one said aught, until he had finished his discourse."[19] Thus he sounded a theme that is relevant to an assessment of the rhetoric in the homilies collected in this volume. These were, after all, ser-

[16] *Ibid.* xvii. 6.

[17] Chrysostom *Homilies on First Corinthians* iv. 11 ("A Select Library of the Nicene and Post-Nicene Fathers of the Christian Church," XII [New York: The Christian Literature Company, 1889]), 22.

[18] *Homilies on the Acts of the Apostles* xxx, *ibid.,* XI, 192-94.

[19] *Ibid.,* p. 193.

mons based on the greatest of sermons, and John the rhetor was merely imitating the master of rhetors; as it was the aim of the Sermon on the Mount that its hearers should "become like God, in such wise as men might become so,"[20] thus it was also the function of the Christian preacher to be the mouthpiece through whom Christ preached. The structure and development of these homilies allowed Chrysostom the opportunity to watch Christ the rhetor in action and to take note of the oratorical skill with which Christ "varies his discourse"[21] or "made his argument more expressive, by trying its force in a parable."[22] Within the various units of the Sermon on the Mount and in the connections he found between them, Chrysostom discerned the aims of Christ's preaching and sought to conform his own preaching to them. Christ the skilled rhetorician knew how to adapt his words to his meaning and thus to produce the desired effect in his hearers.

Christ could, for example, produce a sense of urgency by a rapid progression from one stage of a process to the next. Matthew 5:25 was an illustration of this. "See here also how [Christ] hastens [the hearer]; for having said, 'Agree with thine adversary,' he added, 'quickly'; and he was not satisfied with this, but even of this quickness he hath required a further increase, saying, 'While thou art in the way with him'; pressing and hastening him hereby with great earnestness."[23] For nothing was a greater threat to the Christian life than procrastination and a lack of urgency about good works. Yet this technique of producing a sense of urgency was balanced by the technique of stressing positive rewards rather than negative punishments in inculcating good works. "This thing most especially we admire in his teaching [i.e., his method of teaching], that while in each instance he sets down with very great fullness the prizes of the conflicts . . ., if anywhere he must needs mention things grievous, he doth this in a subdued tone."[24] There was only one reference to hell amid all the warnings and teachings of the sermon, and his correction of his

[20] Chrysostom *Matt.* xviii. 4.
[21] *Ibid.* xxiv. 3.
[22] *Ibid.* xxiv. 4.
[23] *Ibid.* xvi. 13.
[24] *Ibid.* xviii. 9.

hearers was done "with reserve." In some instances Christ went so far as to avoid all reference to punishment, for merely naming the sin was enough to deter those among his hearers who had true understanding.

But it was especially in the transitions from one homily to the next that Chrysostom commented on the structure and development of Christ's rhetoric. As he began his exposition of the second of the contrasts between the old law and the new in Matthew 5:27-30, he pointed to the omission from these contrasts of the *Shema Yisrael* of Deuteronomy 6:4. The reason for this omission was that Christ "was for a while practicing his moral doctrine only" and holding back the dogmatic. In this way he would prepare his hearers to receive the dogmatic later on.[25] Again at the beginning of the eighteenth homily, Chrysostom noted that if Christ had introduced his most sublime commandments at the very beginning of his discourse, his hearers would have received neither the sublime commandments nor the lowly ones; "but now ordaining them severally in their due time, he hath by the two corrected the whole world," viz., both those who could not cope with more than the lowly commandments and those who were prepared to handle the sublime ones.[26] Still later, in the introduction to the twenty-first homily, Chrysostom called the attention of his readers to the progression in the Sermon on the Mount: "Seest thou how by degrees he withdraws us from the things that now are, and at greater length introduces what he hath to say!"[27] This gradual disclosure of the message, little by little, made it more acceptable to its hearers.[28] And again, in the introduction to the next homily, Chrysostom took note of the "amplifications and intensities [*tas hyperbolas kai tas epistaseis*] which Christ employed everywhere in his discourse."[29] Moreover, it was only after Christ had established his argument and supported it with proof that he proceeded to rebuke his hearers, and even then he developed his rebuke "by the contraries [*apo tōn enantiōn*]."

[25] *Ibid.* xvii. 1.
[26] *Ibid.* xviii. 1.
[27] *Ibid.* xxi. 1.
[28] *Ibid.* xxi. 3.
[29] *Ibid.* xxii. 1.

As the more or less technical phrases from Greek rhetoric just quoted suggest, the vocabulary of the rhetorical tradition has also affected Chrysostom's language in these homilies. Just how much it has done so would have to be left to that full-length analysis of the rhetoric in the *Homilies on Saint Matthew* whose desirability we mentioned earlier. At least two of the technical terms should probably be noted, if only because of the difficulties they have caused Chrysostom's editors and translators. We have already mentioned hyperbole, which Aristotle in his *Rhetoric* described as appropriate for use only by violent young men and by Attic orators.[30] In one passage Chrysostom wanted to make it clear that the vehement words of Christ "are not in any way hyperbolical,"[31] but in another passage he explained the enigma of other words of Christ by explaining that "he hath put the thing hyperbolically."[32] Similarly, the Hebrew "parallelism of members" suggested by such passages as Matthew 7:15-18[33] had to be defended against the charge that it had fallen into the sin of tautology, condemned by the Greek rhetoricians;[34] for the two statements of the point were not quite identical.

One other allusion to the classical tradition of rhetoric also deserves mention, even though, through Plutarch and others, it may have belonged to general folklore by this time. Having cited the aphorism that faltering in speech or lisping is not fitting for a philosopher,[35] Chrysostom went on to tell the story of how Demosthenes had cured himself of his speech problem.[36] Such illustrations as these came with special ease to one who had been trained in classical rhetoric, even when he was applying the rhetoric to Christian preaching.

In an earlier volume of the Preacher's Paperback Library, Archbishop Brilioth observed that "it is when Chrysostom attempts to free the sermon from the shackles of rhetoric that

[30] Aristotle *Rhetoric* 1413 a-b.

[31] Chrysostom *Matt.* xvi. 11.

[32] *Ibid.* xix. 2.

[33] Cf. C. F. Burney, *The Poetry of Our Lord* (Oxford: Oxford University Press, 1925), pp. 63-99; on this passage, cf. pp. 72, 104.

[34] Chrysostom *Matt.* xxiii. 8.

[35] *Ibid.* xvii. 5.

[36] *Ibid.* xvii. 6.

the power of these shackles becomes apparent. . . . The organic union of the exegetical, liturgical, and prophetic elements which would differentiate the sermon from the profane address Chrysostom introduced but did not actualize." He adds that "the highest point in the history of the Grecian sermon also became its conclusion."[37] Yet the fusion of preaching with oratory to form "sacred rhetoric" has continued to shape the literature about preaching, and perhaps to a lesser extent the literature of preaching, to the present day. Chrysostom as the heir of Demosthenes and of Isocrates, Augustine as the heir of Cicero and of Quintilian—both came into their pulpits less than a century after the peace of the church under Constantine. The bugbear of "the Hellenization of the gospel," whose traces have usually been sought in the influence of speculative metaphysics on the development of Christian doctrine, should perhaps be pursued instead in the history of Christian rhetoric, East and West. In any case, the cultural context within which preaching has developed has been the ecclesiastical establishment that began in the fourth century and did not end until modern times. The definition of the preaching office has itself been shaped by that establishment. We who are witnessing the progressive disestablishment of Christendom have good reason to inquire more carefully into the influence of sacred rhetoric on our understanding of the nature and function of Christian proclamation, and into the implications of the disestablishment for a new (or perhaps very old) definition of what Christian preaching is and does.

5. *Chrysostom as an Expositor of the Sermon on the Mount*

The history of the exposition of the Sermon on the Mount has not yet been written.[1] If one were to include in that history all the references to the Sermon on the Mount in the history of exegesis, and especially the expositions of the Lord's Prayer, it would be a massive historical enterprise. But within

[37] Yngve Brilioth, *A Brief History of Preaching,* trans. Karl E. Mattson (Philadelphia: Fortress Press, 1965), p. 39.

[1] Cf. Martin Dibelius, "Die Bergpredigt," *Botschaft und Geschichte,* I (Tübingen: J. C. B. Mohr, 1953), 77-174, esp. 147-74, on the history of interpretation.

the smaller circle of outright commentaries, Chrysostom's homilies deserve a place alongside those of Augustine and of Luther. Even a comparison of the three commentaries by Chrysostom, Augustine, and Luther would be a worthy and quite rewarding project.

In the preface to his sermonic commentary on the Sermon on the Mount of 1530-1532, Luther consciously set his own exposition apart from the exegetical tradition, on the grounds that the Sermon on the Mount had been taken over by monks, "who on the basis of this [fifth] chapter have laid claim to a more perfect station in life than other Christians."[2] Thus he identified the central question with which the history of the exposition of the Sermon on the Mount has continued to deal: Does the Sermon on the Mount claim to give instruction to Christian folk in their everyday life in the midst of this world, or is it intended as an idealized picture of discipleship, viable at most only for the full-time ascetics or for those who are living in the brief interval during which the messianic community awaits the return of the Son of man? In the twentieth century, as Reinhold Niebuhr has observed, "a certain type of Christian liberalism interprets the absolutism of the Sermon on the Mount as Oriental hyperbole, as a harmless extravagance,"[3] while the advocates of the thesis that Jesus taught a consistent eschatology have raised the question with a new poignancy.[4] But the history of exegesis makes the question both more profound and more subtle.

Chrysostom's basic answer to the question appears to be that the Sermon on the Mount was indeed intended for all Christians, including those who live in the midst of this world. As we noted in the first part of this introduction, the relation between Christians and "the world," and therefore the definition of "the world," were undergoing a transition during the years

[2] Martin Luther, "Preface to The Sermon on the Mount," trans. Jaroslav Pelikan, *Luther's Works,* XXI (Saint Louis: Concordia, 1956), 6.

[3] Reinhold Niebuhr, *An Interpretation of Christian Ethics* (New York: Meridian Books, 1958), p. 108.

[4] Cf. Albert Schweitzer, *Out of My Life and Thought: An Autobiography,* trans. C. T. Campion (New York: Henry Holt and Company, 1949), pp. 42-59.

of Chrysostom's life and ministry—a transition of which he was quite aware as he composed these homilies. The researches of Massaux have shown how the faith and life of the church catholic during the second century was able to resonate to the themes of the Sermon on the Mount, but also how the development of the church affected its understanding of the imperatives and promises of this message.[5] Nevertheless, even that church, which historians of the conflicts between heresy and orthodoxy have usually called "the great church," still saw itself as a little flock, one that was indeed great with the promise of the ultimate future but that meanwhile had to endure persecution from Caesar and from the other enemies of Christ. Chrysostom's church, however, had not only made its peace with Caesar, but had baptized him. For such a church to make sense of the Sermon on the Mount and to find means for obeying it amidst "the plots in king's courts and the troubles in the houses of the rich"[6] required some fundamental examination both of the text itself and of the translation of its imperatives into the concrete stuff of the Christian ethic.

Nowhere does the question of the address of the Sermon on the Mount become more problematical than at the very beginning, in the beatitudes. Not even the description of how a disciple of Jesus ought to treat his enemies (Matt. 5:38-48), unattainable as it seems for even the athletes of the Christian life, creates as many difficulties as the catalogue of virtues with which the Sermon on the Mount is introduced. Who is equal to the performance of such imperatives? Yet Chrysostom was utterly confident, almost cavalier, in his belief about the universal validity of these imperatives. He warned his readers not to suppose that when the text says that Christ taught "them," this referred only to the disciples. The Sermon on the Mount was formally addressed to the disciples, but it was intended for all "through them."[7] The multitude then was as the multitude always is, indifferent to the life of the Spirit. Therefore Christ spoke the sermon to the few, "in his con-

[5] E. Massaux, *Influence de l'Evangile de Saint Matthieu sur la littérature chrétienne avant Saint Irénée* (Louvain: Publications universitaires, 1950), pp. 7-17 and *passim.*

[6] Chrysostom *Matt.* xxiv. 3.

[7] *Ibid.* xv. 1.

versation with them providing that the rest also, who were yet very far from the level of his sayings, might find his lesson of self-denial no longer grievous unto them." What is more, it was not only "the multitude" of his contemporaries whom Christ had in mind as he spoke the beatitudes, "for though it was *spoken* unto them [the disciples], it was *written* for the sake also of all men afterwards."[8] This echo of I Corinthians 10:11 enabled Chrysostom to argue, in effect, that although Christ had said many things that were not recorded in the New Testament,[9] what had been set down was intended for everyone, not merely for the disciples.[10] Otherwise he would have said "Blessed are ye, if ye become poor" rather than "Blessed are the poor."

Specifically, within the class structure of Chrysostom's audience, this meant that the distinctions between social or economic classes could not be permitted to annul the imperatives of Christ's teaching. Although the beatitudes exalted those who were "poor in spirit," this was not a blanket endorsement of all that the poor did. For among the poor there were those who, lacking the pleasures of wealth, nevertheless managed to accumulate the evils of wealth.[11] They bickered over their meager goods as ravenously as did the rich and powerful over their wealth. Even brutes recognized a certain community of possessions and interests, but here, among human beings, "wrath and the love of money sweeps all away." To those who were poor in the goods of this world, however, the Sermon on the Mount addressed itself with the promise of a dignity that transcended human stratification, inviting them to rise above the bickering and the striving and to accept a new freedom and worth in Christ. "For though thou be poor, thou art free; though thou be a working man, thou art a Christian." In comparison with the difference between the God who forgave and the man who was forgiven, all human differences were so

[8] *Ibid.* xv. 2 (italics, of course, my own).

[9] Chrysostom *Homilies on the Gospel of Saint John* lxxxvii. 2 ("A Select Library of the Nicene and Post-Nicene Fathers of the Christian Church," [New York: The Christian Literature Company, 1886-1900]), XIV, 328.

[10] *Ibid.* lxxxviii. 2, p. 333.

[11] Chrysostom *Matt.* xv. 15.

trivial that we should "be humbled, and feel thankful to those who are in debt to us."[12] For they provided the occasion for both rich and poor to show the magnanimity which God had shown in the forgiveness of sins. And since he had shown this magnanimity not only to some but to all, it was presumably from all that it could be demanded.

Before the absolute character of the demands and promises in the Sermon on the Mount, there was a certain kind of equality, which rendered irrelevant the distinctions among men. So also in the admonition to pray "Our Father," the community created by a common Father made such distinctions meaningless. By this admonition "he at once takes away hatred, and quells pride, and casts out envy, and brings in the mother of all good things, even charity, and exterminates the inequality of human things, and shows how far the equality reaches between the king and the poor man, if at least in those things which are greatest and most indispensable, we are all of us fellows."[13] In this perspective the differences between rich and poor, master and servant, king and soldier, philosopher and barbarian were all outshone by the nobility with which God had endowed men when he permitted them to call him Father of all without distinction. Chrysostom evidently looked at the Sermon on the Mount in such a perspective, and therefore he found in it more reason to emphasize the intrinsic unity among all men than to differentiate between those who could obey all its commands and those who were able to conform only to a certain irreducible minimum of Christian behavior. His fundamental concern was to insist on the corporate nature of the message in the Sermon on the Mount. Although he did not draw the distinction noted by later interpreters between the second person singular in the law of Moses and the second person plural in the law of Christ, he did make an issue of the communal character of the message of Jesus as reflected in these chapters. "In every one of the clauses [of the Lord's Prayer] he commands us to make our prayers common, . . . everywhere commanding us to use this plural word ['us' and 'our']."[14]

[12] *Ibid.* xv. 16.
[13] *Ibid.* xix. 6.
[14] *Ibid.* xix. 11.

Nevertheless, there is some indication in these homilies of the later distinction between the evangelical counsels of perfection and the duties required of all Christians. As we noted in section four of this Introduction, Chrysostom repeatedly commented on the rhetorical skill with which Christ moved from the known to the unknown and from the attainable to the apparently unattainable. The assumption behind that progression was the inability of Christ's audience to comply with the denial of self and of the world that was implied in the call to discipleship. Chrysostom's audience was no better; we have already pointed out[15] that he was keenly aware of the low level of Christian perception among them. Therefore he followed the example of Christ's preaching and sought not to demand more of his audience than they were able to bear. Thus John the Baptist, anxious though he was to direct his hearers to the higher life, had called upon them to obey only his lesser commands, lest they become discouraged and give up all attempts at obedience. Similarly, this John made a practice of exercising his hearers "in the inferior duties . . . because as yet, we know, the burden of voluntary poverty is too great for you, and the heaven is not more distant from the earth, than such self-denial from you."[16] If the total renunciation of property was too much to ask for now, generous almsgiving was not. "Let us then," he concluded, "considering the measures of that discipline which is set before us, press on at least to the middle station."

But the middle station was not the final stop on the way, only the stage to which most of Chrysostom's hearers could be expected to attain. They were not to suppose from this that "his injunctions are impossible, for there are many who duly perform them, even as it is."[17] Such Christians proved that "the apostolic life" did lie within the range of human possibilities, incredible as that seemed to those who were the captives of their own appetites. So it was that "the drunkard would not easily believe, that there exists any man who does not taste even water, and yet this hath been achieved by many

[15] See above, pp. 7-9.

[16] Chrysostom *Matt.* xxi. 6.

[17] *Ibid.* xxi. 5.

solitaries in our time; nor he who connects himself with numberless women, that it is easy to live in virginity." Hermits and celibates thus stood as a judgment upon the easy compromises of Christians who lived "in the world." The law was indeed intended for all, but according to their ability to obey it. And "the societies of the monks, who have taken up their dwelling on the mountains" were the ones "who have taken the most pains to keep" the law.[18] Later in the *Homilies on Saint Matthew* Chrysostom developed more fully his admiration for the monastic ideal[19] and his belief that "even one dwelling in a city may imitate the self-denial of the monks" both in devotion and in the manner of his life.[20]

Seen in the context of the exegetical tradition, therefore, Chrysostom's exposition of the Sermon on the Mount seems to occupy a middle ground between the thorough-going monastic exegesis, which interpreted the imperatives of the Sermon as counsels of perfection, and Luther's radical exegesis, which demanded that the imperatives be applied to every Christian, albeit under the sign of justification by grace through faith. Chrysostom was a realistic churchman who knew his audience and a careful exegete who knew his text. In his commentary on the Sermon on the Mount both the churchman and the exegete spoke. The ambiguities of that speaking may well endear him to those preachers of a later day who, as churchmen and exegetes simultaneously, face no less formidable a set of ambiguities.

6. *A Note on the Present Edition*

As we have indicated in various ways, the homilies on the Sermon on the Mount presented in this edition are part of a larger work, the *Homilies on the Gospel of Saint Matthew.* They "represent the oldest complete commentary on the first Gospel that has survived from the patristic period."[1] The manuscript tradition of these homilies, indeed of all of Chrysostom, is enormous; the number of manuscripts of

[18] *Ibid.* xx. 1.
[19] *Ibid.* lv. 6; cf. Festugière, *op. cit.*, pp. 329-46.
[20] Chrysostom *Matt.* lv. 8.
[1] Johannes Quasten, *Patrology,* III (Utrecht: Spectrum, 1960), 437.

Chrysostom runs into the thousands, totaling more than the combined manuscripts of literally dozens of other Greek and Latin fathers.[2] Many of the manuscripts of Chrysostom, including some that contain these homilies, have never been edited; the oldest has never been used in any edition.[3] It is to be hoped that they will be edited in our time, for only with the appearance of a critical edition based on all the extant textual evidence in all languages will it be possible to produce a definitive English translation.

For this volume, meanwhile, we have relied on the best existing Greek edition and on the standard English translation. The Greek text was published in three volumes in 1839 by Frederick Field; his edition was taken over into Migne's *Patrologia Graeca,* with which we have worked in the study of the text.[4] Sir George Prevost translated the Field edition into English,[5] and M. B. Riddle revised that translation for Philip Schaff's edition of the Nicene and Post-Nicene Fathers.[6] Riddle's comment in the preface to his revision, that "the archaic style of the English translation . . . even when obscure and involved . . . seemed to be a fitting dress for the original,"[7] was reinforced by a study of the Greek text and by the counsel of several specialists, who urged that, in the absence of the critical edition of Chrysostom for which scholarship is still waiting, the rather Victorian English of Prevost's translation and the archaisms of the Authorized Version are still the most appropriate vehicle for the *Homilies.*

Readers of this volume who compare its quotations from the Bible with their own editions of Holy Scripture, whether English or Greek, will find a great number of discrepancies

[2] Chrysostomus Baur, *S. Jean Chrysostome et ses oeuvres dans l'histoire littéraire* (Louvain: Bureaux du Recueil, 1907), p. 30, refers to 174 manuscripts of the *Homilies.*

[3] Cf. Quasten, *op. cit.,* p. 438.

[4] *Patrologiae cursus completus, Series graeca,* Vols. LVII-LVIII (Paris, 1862).

[5] "A Library of the Fathers of the Holy Catholic Church," Vols. XI, XV, XXXIV (Oxford: John Henry Parker, 1843-1851), with pages numbered consecutively throughout.

[6] "A Select Library of the Nicene and Post-Nicene Fathers of the Christian Church," Vol. X (New York: The Christian Literature Company, 1888).

[7] *Ibid.,* p. iii.

between Chrysostom's text and those on which we rely today. In part this is due to the preacher's habit of citing from memory, of weaving together passages from various biblical sources in a single and conflated quotation, of expanding and improvising as the rhetoric bore him along. Chrysostom's quotations from the Old Testament were, of course, based on the Septuagint and often reflect the differences of both canon and text between the Greek and the Hebrew versions of the Old Testament. A study has been made of the text of the Gospel of Mark that seems to underlie Chrysostom's quotations, but its results are inconclusive, partly because of the question of rhetorical technique.[8] No similar study of Chrysostom's Matthew seems to exist, but it would not be surprising if this too were, as Geerlings and New say of Mark, "first of all [a text] peculiar to himself and full of unattested variants. Secondly, it is the particular mixture of Neutral, Western, Caesarean, and other readings."

The homilies on the fifth, sixth, and seventh chapters of Saint Matthew begin with Homily XV and end with Homily XXIV. In the exposition of the Sermon on the Mount, as in the commentary as a whole, Chrysostom had in mind the practical needs of the Christian life of his hearers. Therefore in "the ninety sermons on the Gospel of St. Matthew, Chrysostom spoke forty times on almsgiving alone; he spoke some thirteen times on poverty, more than thirty times on avarice, and about twenty times against wrongly acquired and wrongly used wealth; all in all, ninety or a hundred sermons on the social themes of poverty and wealth."[9] As we have suggested earlier, this very preoccupation, which the preacher himself found rather embarrassing, ought to commend his preaching to the present generation, which is discovering that the summons of Jesus Christ to discipleship does not depend upon an ecclesiastical establishment but can be heard today out of the pages of the Gospels. It can also be heard out of the pages of Chrysostom's homilies on the Sermon on the Mount.

[8] Jacob Geerlings and Silva New, "Chrysostom's Text of the Gospel of Mark," *Harvard Theological Review,* XXIV (1931), 122-42.

[9] Chrysostomus Baur, *John Chrysostom and His Time,* trans. M. Gonzaga (2 vols.; Westminster, Md.; Newman Press, 1959-60), I, 217.

Saint John Chrysostom:

Homilies on the Sermon on the Mount

Homily XV

"And Jesus seeing the multitudes went up into the mountain, and when he was set, his disciples came unto him. And he opened his mouth, and taught them." —*Matt. 5:1, 2*

SEE HOW UNAMBITIOUS HE was, and void of boasting: in that he did not lead people about with him, but whereas, when healing was required, he had himself gone about everywhere, visiting both towns and country places; now when the multitude is become very great, he sits in one spot: and that not in the midst of any city or forum, but on a mountain and in a wilderness; instructing us to do nothing for display, and to separate ourselves from the tumults of ordinary life, and this most especially, when we are to study wisdom, and to discourse of things needful to be done.

But when he had gone up into the mount, and "was set down, his disciples came unto him." Seest thou their growth in virtue? and how in a moment they became better men? Since the multitude were but gazers on the miracles, but these from that hour desired also to hear some great and high thing. And indeed this it was set him on his teaching, and made him begin this discourse.

For it was not men's bodies only that he was healing, but he was also amending their souls; and again from the care of these he would pass to attendance on the other. Thus he at once varied the succor that he gave, and likewise mingled with the instruction afforded by his words, the manifestation of his glory from his works; and besides, he stopped the shameless mouths of the heretics[1] signifying by this his care of both

[1] A reference to the Gnostic and especially to the Manichaean heretics, whom Chrysostom attacks throughout the commentary; cf. Introduction, pp. 10-12.

parts of our being, that he himself is the Maker of the whole creation. Therefore also on each nature he bestowed abundant providence, now amending the one, now the other.

And in this way he was then employed. For it is said, that "he opened his mouth, and taught them." And wherefore is the clause added, "he opened his mouth"? To inform thee that in his very silence he gave instruction, and not when he spoke only: but at one time by "opening his mouth," at another uttering his voice by the works which he did.

But when thou hearest that he taught *them*, do not think of him as discoursing with his disciples only, but rather with all through them.

For since the multitude was such as a multitude ever is, and consisted moreover of such as creep on the ground, he withdraws the choir of his disciples, and makes his discourse unto them: in his conversation with them providing that the rest also, who were yet very far from the level of his sayings, might find his lesson of self-denial no longer grievous unto them. Of which indeed both Luke gave intimation, when he said, that He directed his words unto them [Luke 6:20, 27]: and Matthew too, clearly declaring the same, wrote, "his disciples came unto him, and he taught them." For thus the others also were sure to be more eagerly attentive to him, than they would have been, had he addressed himself unto all.

2. Whence then doth he begin? and what kind of foundations of his new polity doth he lay for us?

Let us hearken with strict attention unto what is said. For though it was spoken unto them, it was written for the sake also of all men afterwards.[2] And accordingly on this account, though he had his disciples in his mind in his public preaching, yet unto them he limits not his sayings, but applies all his words of blessing without restriction. Thus he said not, "Blessed are ye, if ye become poor," but "Blessed are the poor." And I may add that even if he had spoken of them, the advice

[2] On the address of the Sermon on the Mount, see Introduction, pp. 29-34.

would still be common to all. For so, when he saith, "Lo! I am with you always, even unto the end of the world" [Matt. 28:20], he is discoursing not with them only, but also, through them, with all the world. And in pronouncing them blessed, who are persecuted, and chased, and suffer all intolerable things; not for them only, but also for all who arrive at the same excellency, he weaves his crown.

However, that this may be yet plainer, and to inform thee that thou hast great interest in his sayings, and so indeed hath all mankind, if any choose to give heed; hear how he begins these wondrous words.

"Blessed are the poor in spirit; for theirs is the kingdom of Heaven" [Matt. 5:3].

What is meant by "the poor in spirit"? The humble and contrite in mind. For by "spirit" he hath here designated the soul, and the faculty of choice. That is, since many are humble not willingly, but compelled by stress of circumstances; letting these pass (for this were no matter of praise), he blesses them first, who by choice humble and contract themselves.

But why said he not, "the humble," but rather "the poor"? Because this is more than that. For he means here them who are awestruck, and tremble at the commandments of God. Whom also by his prophet Isaiah God earnestly accepting said, "To whom will I look, but to him who is meek and quiet, and trembleth at my words?" [Isa. 66:2]. For indeed there are many kinds of humility: one is humble in his own measure, another with all excess of lowliness. It is this last lowliness of mind which that blessed prophet commends, picturing to us the temper that is not merely subdued, but utterly broken, when he saith, "The sacrifice for God is a contrite spirit, a contrite and an humble heart God will not despise" [Ps. 51:17]. And the Three Children also offer this unto God as a great sacrifice, saying, "Nevertheless, in a contrite soul, and in a spirit of lowliness, may we be accepted" [Dan. 3:39; or Song of Three Children, v. 16]. This Christ also now blesses.

3. For whereas the greatest of evils, and those which make

havoc of the whole world, had their entering in from pride:—for both the devil, not being such before, did thus become a devil; as indeed Paul plainly declared, saying, "Lest being lifted up with pride, he fall into the condemnation of the devil" [I Tim. 3:6]—and the first man, too, puffed up by the devil with these hopes, was made an example of, and became mortal (for expecting to become a god, he lost even what he had; and God also upbraiding him with this, and mocking his folly, said, "Behold, Adam is become as one of us" [Gen. 3:22]); and each one of those that came after did hereby wreck himself in impiety, fancying some equality with God:—since, I say, this was the stronghold of our evils, and the root and fountain of all wickedness, he, preparing a remedy suitable to the disease, laid this law first as a strong and safe foundation. For this being fixed as a base, the builder in security lays on it all the rest. But if this be taken away, though a man reach to the heavens in his course of life, it is all easily undermined, and issues in a grievous end. Though fasting, prayer, almsgiving, temperance, any other good thing whatever, be gathered together in thee; without humility all fall away and perish.

It was this very thing that took place in the instance of the Pharisee. For even after he had arrived at the very summit, he "went down" [Luke 18:14] with the loss of all, because he had not the mother of virtues: for as pride is the fountain of all wickedness, so is humility the principle of all self-command. Wherefore also he begins with this, pulling up boasting by the very root out of the soul of his hearers.

"And what," one may ask, "is this to his disciples, who were on every account humble? For in truth they had nothing to be proud of, being fishermen, poor, ignoble, and illiterate." Even though these things concerned not his disciples, yet surely they concerned such as were then present, and such as were hereafter to receive the disciples, lest they should on this account despise them. But it were truer to say that they did also concern his disciples. For even if not then, yet by and by they were sure to require this help, after their signs and wonders, and their honor from the world, and their confidence towards God. For neither wealth, nor power, nor royalty itself, had so much power to exalt men, as the things which they possessed in all fullness. And besides, it was natural that even before the signs they might be lifted up, at that very time when they saw the multitude, and all that audience surrounding their Master; they might feel some human weakness. Wherefore he at once represses their pride.

And he doth not introduce what he saith by way of advice or of commandments, but by way of blessing, so making his word less burthensome, and opening to all the course of his discipline. For he said not, "This or that person," but "they who do so, are all of them *blessed.*" So that though thou be a slave, a beggar, in poverty, a stranger, unlearned, there is nothing to hinder thee from being blessed, if thou emulate this virtue.

4. Now having begun, as you see, where most need was, he proceeds to another commandment, one which seems to be opposed to the judgment of the whole world. For whereas all think that they who rejoice are enviable, those in dejection, poverty, and mourning, wretched, he calls these blessed rather than those; saying thus,

"Blessed are they that mourn" [Matt. 5:4].

Yet surely all men call them miserable. For therefore he wrought the miracles beforehand, that in such enactments as these he might be entitled to credit.

And here too again he designated not simply all that mourn, but all that do so for sins: since surely that other kind of mourning is forbidden, and that earnestly, which relates to anything of this life. This Paul also clearly declared, when he said, "The sorrow of the world worketh death, but godly sorrow worketh repentance unto salvation, not to be repented of" [II Cor. 7:10].

These then he too himself calls blessed, whose sorrow is of that kind; yet not simply them that sorrow did he designate, but them that sorrow intensely. Therefore he did not say, "they that sorrow," but "they that mourn." For this commandment again is fitted to teach us entire self-control. For if those who grieve for children, or wife, or any other relation gone from them, have no fondness for gain or pleasure during that period of their sorrow; if they aim not at glory, are not provoked by insults, nor led captive by envy, nor beset by any other passion, their grief alone wholly possessing them; much more will they who mourn for their own sins, as they ought to mourn, show forth a self-denial greater than this.

Next, what is the reward for these? "For they shall be comforted," saith he.

Where shall they be comforted! tell me. Both here and there. For since the thing enjoined was exceeding burthensome and galling, he promised to give that, which most of all made it light. Wherefore, if thou wilt be comforted, mourn: and think not this a dark saying. For when God doth comfort, though sorrows come upon thee by thousands like snow-flakes, thou wilt be above them all. Since in truth, as the returns which God gives are always far greater than our labors; so he hath wrought in this case, declaring them that mourn to be blessed, not after the value of what they do, but after his own love towards man. For they that mourn, mourn for misdoings, and to such it is enough to enjoy forgiveness, and obtain wherewith to answer for themselves. But forasmuch as he is full of love towards man, he doth not limit his recompense either to the removal of our punishments, or to the deliverance from our sins, but he makes them even blessed, and imparts to them abundant consolation.

But he bids us mourn, not only for our own, but also for other men's misdoings. And of this temper were the souls of the saints: such was that of Moses, of Paul, of David; yea, all these many times mourned for evils not their own.

5. "Blessed are the meek, for they shall inherit the earth." Tell me, what kind of earth? Some say a figurative earth,[3] but

[3] A reference to the "spiritual" or allegorical explanation which appears in Augustine but belongs to an earlier tradition of exegesis; cf. Introduction, p. 17.

it is not this, for nowhere in Scripture do we find any mention of an earth that is merely figurative. But what can the saying mean? He holds out a sensible prize; even as Paul also doth, in that when he had said, "Honor thy father and thy mother" [Eph. 6:2], he added, "For so shalt thou live long upon the earth." And He himself unto the thief again, "Today shalt thou be with me in Paradise" [Luke 23:43].

Thus he doth not incite us by means of the future blessings only, but of the present also, for the sake of the grosser sort of his hearers, and such as before the future seek those others.

Thus, for example, further on also he said, "Agree with thine adversary" [Matt. 5:25]. Then he appoints the reward of such self-command, and saith, "Lest at any time the adversary deliver thee to the judge, and the judge to the officer" [Matt. 5:25]. Seest thou whereby he alarmed us? By the things of sense, by what happens before our eyes. And again, "Whosoever shall say to his brother, Raca, shall be in danger of the council" [Matt. 5:22].

And Paul too sets forth sensible rewards at great length, and uses things present in his exhortations; as when he is discoursing about virginity. For having said nothing about the heavens there, for the time he urges it by things present, saying, "Because of the present distress," and, "But I spare you," and, "I would have you without carefulness" [1 Cor. 7:26, 28, 32].

Thus accordingly Christ also with the things spiritual hath mingled the sensible. For whereas the meek man is thought to lose all his own, he promises the contrary, saying, "Nay, but this is he who possesses his goods in safety, namely, he who is not rash, nor boastful: while that sort of man shall often lose his patrimony, and his very life."

And besides, since in the Old Testament the prophet used to say continually, "The meek shall inherit the earth" [Ps. 37:11], He thus weaves into his discourse the words to which they were accustomed, so as not everywhere to speak a strange language.

And this he saith, not as limiting the rewards to things

present, but as joining with these the other sort of gifts also. For neither in speaking of any spiritual thing doth he exclude such as are in the present life; nor again in promising such as are in our life, doth he limit his promise to that kind. For he saith, "Seek ye the kingdom of God, and all these things shall be added unto you" [Matt. 6:33]. And again: "Whosoever hath left houses or brethren, shall receive an hundred fold in this world, and in the future shall inherit everlasting life" [Matt. 19:29].

6. "Blessed are they which do hunger and thirst after righteousness" [Matt. 5:6].

What sort of righteousness? He means either the whole of virtue, or that particular virtue which is opposed to covetousness.[4] For since he is about to give commandment concerning mercy, to show how we must show mercy, as, for instance, not of rapine or covetousness, he blesses them that lay hold of righteousness.

And see with what exceeding force he puts it. For he said not, "Blessed are they which keep fast by righteousness," but, "Blessed are they which do hunger and thirst after righteousness": that not merely anyhow, but with all desire we may pursue it. For since this is the most peculiar property of covetousness, and we are not so enamored of meat and drink, as of gaining, and compassing ourselves with more and more, he bade us to transfer this desire to a new object, freedom from covetousness.

Then he appoints the prize, again from things sensible; saying, "for they shall be filled." Thus, because it is thought that the rich are commonly made such by covetousness, "Nay," saith he, "it is just contrary: for it is righteousness that doeth this. Wherefore, so long as thou doest righteously, fear not poverty, nor tremble at hunger. For the extortioners, they are the very persons who lose all, even as he certainly who is in love with righteousness, possesses himself the goods of all men in safety."

[4] Aristotle speaks of "the justice [or righteousness] which is a part of virtue," *Nicomachean Ethics* 1130 a.

But if they who covet not other men's goods enjoy so great abundance, much more they who give up their own.

"Blessed are the merciful" [Matt. 5:7].

Here he seems to me to speak not of those only who show mercy in giving of money, but those likewise who are merciful in their actions. For the way of showing mercy is manifold, and this commandment is broad.

What then is the reward thereof?

"For they shall obtain mercy."

And it seems indeed to be a sort of equal recompense, but it is a far greater thing than the act of goodness. For whereas they themselves show mercy as men, they obtain mercy from the God of all; and it is not the same thing, man's mercy, and God's; but as wide as is the interval between wickedness and goodness, so far is the one of these removed from the other.

"Blessed are the pure in heart, for they shall see God" [Matt. 5:8].

Behold again the reward is spiritual. Now he here calls "pure," either those who have attained unto all virtue, and are not conscious to themselves of any evil; or those who live in temperance. For there is nothing which we need so much in order to see God, as this last virtue. Wherefore Paul also said, "Follow peace with all men, and holiness, without which no man shall see the Lord" [Heb. 12:14]. He is here speaking of such sight as it is possible for man to have.

For because there are many who show mercy, and who commit no rapine, nor are covetous, who yet are guilty of fornication and uncleanness; to signify that the former alone suffices not, he hath added this, much in the same sense as Paul, writing to the Corinthians, bore witness of the Macedonians, that they were rich not only in almsgiving, but also in all other virtue. For having spoken of the noble spirit they had shown in regard of their goods, he saith, "They gave also their own selves to the Lord, and to us" [II Cor. 8:5].

7. "Blessed are the peacemakers" [Matt. 5:9].

Here he not only takes away altogether our own strife and

hatred amongst ourselves, but he requires besides this something more, namely, that we should set at one again others, who are at strife.

And again, the reward which he annexes is spiritual. Of what kind then is it?

"For they shall be called the children of God."

Yea, for this became the work of the Only Begotten, to unite the divided, and to reconcile the alienated.

Then, lest thou shouldest imagine peace in all cases a blessing, he hath added,

"Blessed are they which are persecuted for righteousness' sake" [Matt. 5:10].

That is, for virtue's sake, for succor given to others, and for godliness: it being ever his wont to call by the name of "righteousness" the whole practical wisdom of the soul.

"Blessed are ye, when men shall revile you and persecute you, and say all manner of evil against you falsely, for my sake. Rejoice, and be exceeding glad" [Matt. 5:11, 12].

As if he said, "Though they should call you sorcerers, deceivers, pestilent persons, or whatever else, blessed are ye": so he speaks. What could be newer than these injunctions? wherein the very things which all others avoid, these he declares to be desirable; I mean, being poor, mourning, persecution, evil report. But yet he both affirmed this, and convinced not two, nor ten, nor twenty, nor an hundred, nor a thousand men, but the whole world. And hearing things so grievous and galling, so contrary to the accustomed ways of men, the multitudes "were astonished." So great was the power of him who spake.

However, lest thou shouldest think that the mere fact of being evil spoken of makes men blessed, he hath set two limitations; when it is for his sake, and when the things that are said are false: for without these, he who is evil spoken of, so far from being blessed, is miserable.

Then see the prize again: "Because your reward is great in heaven." But thou, though thou hear not of a kingdom given in each one of the blessings, be not discouraged. For although he give different names to the rewards, yet he brings all into his kingdom. Thus, both when he saith, "they that mourn shall be comforted"; and, "they that show mercy shall obtain mercy"; and, "the pure in heart shall see God"; and, the peace-makers "shall be called the children of God"; nothing else but the kingdom doth he shadow out by all these sayings. For such as enjoy these, shall surely attain unto that. Think not therefore that this reward is for the poor in spirit only, but for those also who hunger after righteousness, for the meek, and for all the rest without exception.

Since on this account he hath set his blessing on them all, that thou mightest not look for anything sensible: for that man cannot be blessed, who is crowned with such things as come to an end with this present life, and hurry by quicker than a shadow.

8. But when he had said, "your reward is great," he added also another consolation, saying, "For so persecuted they the prophets which were before you."

Thus, since that first, the promise of the kingdom, was yet to come, and all in expectation, he affords them comfort from this world; from their fellowship with those who before them had been ill-treated.

For "think not," saith he, "that for something inconsistent in your sayings and enactments ye suffer these things: or, as being teachers of evil doctrines, ye are to be persecuted by them; the plots and dangers proceed not of any wickedness in your sayings, but of the malice of those who hear you. Wherefore neither are they any blame to you who suffer wrong, but to them who do the wrong. And to the truth of these things all preceding time bears witness. For against the prophets they did not even bring any charge of transgressing the law, and of sentiments of impiety, that they stoned some, chased away others, encompassed others with innumerable afflictions. Wherefore let not this trouble you, for of the very same mind they do all that is done now." Seest thou how he raised up their spirits, by placing them near to the company of Moses and Elias?

Thus also Paul writing to the Thessalonians, saith, "For ye became followers of the churches of God, which are in Judea; for ye also have suffered the same things of your own fellow-countrymen, even as they have of the Jews: who both killed the Lord Jesus, and their own prophets, and have driven us out; and they please not God, and are contrary to all men" [I Thess. 2:14, 15]. Which same point here also Christ hath established.

And whereas in the other beatitudes, he said, "Blessed are the poor," and "the merciful"; here he hath not put it generally, but addresses his speech unto themselves, saying, "Blessed are ye, when they shall revile you, and persecute you, and say every evil word": signifying that this is an especial privilege of theirs; and that beyond all others, teachers have this for their own.

At the same time he here also covertly signifies his own dignity, and his equality in honor with him who begat him. For, "as they on the Father's account," saith he, "so shall ye also for me suffer these things." But when he saith, "the prophets which were before you," he implies that they were also by this time become prophets.

Next, declaring that this above all profits them, and makes them glorious, he did not say, "they will calumniate and persecute you, but I will prevent it." For not in their escaping evil report, but in their noble endurance thereof, and in refuting them by their actions, he will have their safety stand: this being a much greater thing than the other; even as to be struck and not hurt, is much greater than escaping the blow.

9. Now in this place he saith, "Your reward is great in heaven." But Luke [Luke 6:23, 26] reports him to have spoken this, both earnestly, and with more entire consolation; for he not only, as you know, pronounces them blessed, who are evil spoken of for God's sake, but declares them likewise wretched, who are well spoken of by all men. For, "Woe unto

you," saith he, "when all men shall speak well of you." And yet the apostles were well spoken of, but not by all men. Wherefore he said not, "Woe unto you, when men shall speak well of you," but, "when all men" shall do so: for it is not even possible that those who live in the practice of virtue should be well spoken of by all men.

And again he saith, "When they shall cast out your name as evil, rejoice ye, and leap for joy" [Luke 6:22, 23]. For not only of the dangers they underwent, but of the calumny also, he appoints the recompense to be great. Wherefore he said not, "When they shall persecute, and kill you," but, "When they shall revile you, and say all manner of evil." For most assuredly, men's evil reports have a sharper bite than their very deeds. For whereas, in our dangers, there are many things that lighten the toil, as to be cheered by all, to have many to applaud, to crown, to proclaim our praise; here in our reproach even this consolation is destroyed. Because we seem not to have achieved anything great; and this galls the combatant more than all his dangers: at least many have gone on even to hang themselves, not bearing evil report. And why marvellest thou at the others? since that traitor, that shameless and accursed one, he who had ceased to blush for anything whatever, was wrought upon by this chiefly to hurry to the halter. And Job again, all adamant as he was, and firmer than a rock; when he had been robbed of all his possessions, and was suffering those incurable ills, and had become on a sudden childless, and when he saw his body pouring out worms like a fountain, and his wife attacking him, he repelled it all with ease; but when he saw his friends reproaching and trampling upon him, and entertaining an evil opinion of him, and saying that he suffered those things for some sins, and was paying the penalty of wickedness: then was there trouble, then commotion, even in that great and noble-hearted man.

And David also, letting pass all that he had suffered, sought of God a retribution for the calumny alone. For, "Let him curse," saith he, "for the Lord hath bidden him; that the Lord may see my humiliation, and requite me for this cursing of his own on this day" [II Sam. 16:11, 12].

And Paul too proclaims the triumph not of those only who incur danger, or are deprived of their goods, but of these also, thus saying, "Call to remembrance the former days, in which after ye were illuminated ye endured a great fight of afflictions; partly whilst ye were made a gazing stock by reproaches, and afflictions" [Heb. 10:32, 33]. On this account then Christ hath appointed the reward also to be great.

After this, lest anyone should say, "Here thou givest no redress, nor stoppest men's mouths; and dost thou assign a reward there?" He hath put before us the prophets, to show that neither in their case did God give redress. And if, where the rewards were at hand, he cheered them with things to come; much more now, when this hope is become clearer, and self-denial is increased.

And observe too, after how many commandments he hath put this: for surely he did it not without reason, but to show that it is not possible for one unprovided, and unarmed with all those other virtues, to go forth unto these conflicts. Therefore, you see, in each instance, by the former precept making way for the following one, he hath woven a sort of golden chain for us. Thus, first, he that is "humble," will surely also "mourn" for his own sins: he that so "mourns," will be both "meek," and "righteous," and "merciful"; he that is "merciful," and "righteous," and "contrite," will of course be also "pure in heart": and such a one will be "a peacemaker" too: and he that hath attained unto all these, will be moreover arrayed against dangers, and will not be troubled when evil is spoken of him, and he is enduring grievous trials innumerable.

10. Now then, after giving them due exhortation, he refreshes them again with praises. As thus: the injunctions being high, and far surpassing those in the Old Testament: lest they should be disturbed, and confounded, and say, "How shall we be able to achieve these things?" hear what he saith:

"Ye are the salt of the earth" [Matt. 5:13].

Implying, that of absolute necessity he enjoins all this. For "not for your own life apart," saith he, "but for the whole world, shall your account be. For not to two cities, nor to ten or twenty, nor to a single nation am I sending you, as I sent the prophets; but to earth, and sea, and the whole world; and that in evil case." For by saying, "Ye are the salt of the earth," he signified all human nature to have "lost its savor," and to be decayed by our sins. For which cause, you see, he requires of them such virtues, as are most necessary and useful for the superintendence of the common sort. For first, the meek, and yielding, and merciful, and righteous, shuts not up his good deeds unto himself only, but also provides that these good fountains should run over for the benefit of others. And he again who is pure in heart, and a peacemaker, and is persecuted for the truth's sake; he again orders his way of life for the common good. "Think not then," he saith, "that ye are drawn on to ordinary conflicts, or that for some small matters you are to give account." "Ye are the salt of the earth."

What then? did they restore the decayed? By no means; for neither is it possible to do any good to that which is already spoilt, by sprinkling it with salt. This therefore they did not. But rather, what things had been before restored, and committed to their charge, and freed from that ill savor, these they then salted, maintaining and preserving them in that freshness, which they had received of the Lord. For that men should be set free from the rottenness of their sins was the good work of Christ; but their not returning to it again any more was the object of these men's diligence and travail.

Seest thou how by degrees he indicates their superiority to the very prophets? in that he saith they are teachers, not of Palestine, but of the whole world; and not simply teachers, but awful ones too. For this is the marvellous thing, that not by flattering, nor soothing, but by sharply bracing them, as salt, even so they became dear to all men.

"Now marvel not," saith he, "if leaving all others, I discourse to you, and draw you on to so great dangers. For consider over how many cities, tribes, and nations, I am to send you to preside. Wherefore I would have you not only be prudent yourselves, but that you should also make others the same. And such persons have great need to be intelligent, in whom the salvation of the rest is at stake: they ought so much to abound in virtue, as to impart of the profit to others also. For if ye do not become such as this, ye will not suffice even for your own selves.

"Be not then impatient, as though my sayings were too burdensome. For while it is possible for others who have lost their savor to return by your means, you, if you should come to this, will with yourselves destroy others also. So that in proportion as the matters are great, which ye have put into your hands, you need so much the greater diligence." Therefore he saith,

"But if the salt have lost its savor, wherewith shall it be salted? it is thenceforth good for nothing, but to be cast out, and to be trodden under foot of men" [Matt. 5:13].

For other men, though they fall never so often, may possibly obtain indulgence: but the teacher, should this happen to him, is deprived of all excuse, and will suffer the most extreme vengeance. Thus, lest at the words, "When they shall revile you, and persecute you, and say all manner of evil against you," they should be too timid to go forth: he tells them, "unless ye are prepared to combat with all this, ye have been chosen in vain." For it is not evil report that ye should fear, but lest ye should prove partners in dissimulation [cf. Gal. 2:13]. For then, "Ye will lose your savor, and be trodden under foot": but if ye continue sharply to brace them up, and then are evil spoken of, rejoice; for this is the very use of salt, to sting the corrupt, and make them smart. And so their censure follows of course, in no way harming you, but rather testifying your firmness. But if through fear of it you give up the earnestness that becomes you, ye will have to suffer much more grievously, being both evil spoken of, and despised by all. For this is the meaning of "trodden under foot."

11. After this he leads on to another, a higher image. "Ye are the light of the world" [Matt. 5:14].

"Of the world" again; not of one nation, nor of twenty states, but of the whole inhabited earth. And "a light" to the mind, far better than this sunbeam: like as they were also a spiritual *salt*. And before they are *salt*, and now *light*; to teach thee how great is the gain of these strict precepts, and the profit of that grave discipline: how it binds, and permits not to become dissolute; and causes clear sight, leading men on to virtue.

"A city that is set on a hill cannot be hid, neither do men light a candle, and put it under the bushel" [Matt. 5:14, 15].

Again, by these words he trains them to strictness of life, teaching them to be earnest in their endeavors, as set before the eyes of all men, and contending in the midst of the amphitheatre of the world. For, "look not to this," he saith, "that we are now sitting here, that we are in a small portion of one corner. For ye shall be as conspicuous to all as a city set on the ridge of a hill, as a candle in a house on the candlestick, giving light."

Where now are they who persevere in disbelieving the power of Christ? Let them hear these things, and let them adore his might, amazed at the power of the prophecy. For consider how great things he promised to them, who were not known even in their own country: that earth and sea should know them, and that they should by their fame reach to the limits of the inhabited world; or rather, not by their fame, but by the working of the good they wrought. For it was not fame that bearing them everywhere made them conspicuous, but also the actual demonstration by their works. Since, as though they had wings, more vehemently than the sunbeam did they overrun the whole earth, sowing the light of godliness.

But here he seems to me to be also training them to boldness of speech. For to say, "A city set on a hill cannot be hid," is to speak as declaring his own powers. For as that city can by no means be hidden, so it was impossible that what they preached should sink into silence and obscurity. Thus, since he had spoken of persecutions and calumnies, of plots and wars, for fear they might think that these would have power to stop their mouths; to encourage them, he saith, that so far from being hid, it should overshine the whole world; and that on this very account they should be illustrious and renowned.

By this then he declares his own power. In what follows, he requires that boldness of speech which was due on their part; thus saying,

"Neither do men light a candle and put it under the bushel, but on the candlestick, and it giveth light unto all that are in the house. Let your light so shine before men, that they may see your good works, and glorify your Father which is in heaven" [Matt. 5:15, 16].

"For I," saith he, "it is true, have kindled the light, but its continuing to burn, let that come of your diligence: not for your own sakes alone, but also for their sake, who are to profit by these rays, and to be guided unto the truth. Since the calumnies surely shall not be able to obscure your brightness, if you be still living a strict life, and as becomes those who are to convert the whole world. Show forth therefore a life worthy of his grace; that even as it is everywhere preached, so this light may everywhere accompany the same.

Next he sets before them another sort of gain, besides the salvation of mankind, enough to make them strive earnestly, and to lead them unto all diligence. As thus, "Ye shall not only," saith he, "amend the world, if ye live aright, but ye will also give occasion that God shall be glorified; even as if ye do the contrary, ye will both destroy men, and make God's name to be blasphemed."

And how, it may be asked, shall God be glorified through us, if at least men are to speak evil of us? Nay, not all men, and even they themselves who in envy do this, will in their conscience admire and approve you; even as the outward flatterers of such as live in wickedness do in mind accuse them.

What then? Dost thou command us to live for display and

vainglory? Far from it; I say not this; for I did not say, "Give ye diligence to bring forward your own good deeds," neither did I say, "Show them"; but "Let your light shine." That is, "Let your virtue be great, and the fire abundant, and the light unspeakable." For when virtue is so great, it cannot lie hid, though its pursuer shade it over ten thousand fold. Present unto them an irreprehensible life, and let them have no true occasion of evil speaking; and then, though there be thousands of evil-speakers, no man shall be able to cast any shade upon you. And well did he say, "your light," for nothing makes a man so illustrious, how manifold soever his will to be concealed, as the manifestation of virtue. For as if he were clad with the very sunbeam, so he shines, yet brighter than it; not spending his rays on earth, but surmounting also heaven itself.

Hence also he comforts them more abundantly. For, "What though the slander pain you," saith he; "yet shall ye have many to honor God on your account. And in both ways your recompense is gathering, as well because God is glorified through you, as because ye are defamed for God's sake. Thus, lest we should on purpose seek to be reproached, on hearing that there is a reward for it: first, he hath not expressed that sentiment simply, but with two limitations, namely, when what is said is false, and when it is for God's sake:—and next he signifies how not that only, but also good report, hath its great profit, the glory of it passing on to God. And he holds out to them those gracious hopes. "For," saith he, "the calumny of the wicked avails not so much as to put all others in the dark, in respect of seeing your light. For then only when you have "lost your savor" shall they tread you under foot; but not when you are falsely accused, doing right. Yet, rather then shall there be many admiring, not you only, but for your sake your Father also." And he said not "God," but "your Father"; already sowing beforehand the seeds of that noble birth, which was about to be bestowed upon them. Moreover, indicating his parity in honor, as he said above, "Grieve not when ye are evil spoken of, for it is enough for you that for my sake you are thus spoken of"; so here he mentions the Father: everywhere manifesting his equality.

12. Since then we know the gain that arises from this earnestness, and the danger of indolence (for if our Lord be blasphemed because of us, that were far worse than our perdition), let us "give none offense, neither to the Jews, nor to the Gentiles, nor to the Church of God" [I Cor. 10:32]. And while the life which we present before them is brighter than the sun, yet if any one will speak evil of us, let us not grieve at being defamed, but only if we be defamed with justice.

For, on the one hand, if we live in wickedness, though there be none to speak ill of us, we shall be the most wretched of all men: on the other hand, if we apply ourselves to virtue, though the whole world speak evil of us, at that very time we shall be more enviable than any. And we shall draw on to follow us all who choose to be saved, for not the calumny of the wicked, but our good life, will draw their attention. For indeed no trumpet is so clear as the proof that is given by our actions: neither is the light itself so transparent as a pure life, though our calumniators be beyond number.

I say, if all the above-mentioned qualities be ours; if we be meek and lowly and merciful; if we be pure, and peacemakers; if hearing reproach, we revile not again, but rather rejoice; then shall we attract all that observe us no less than the miracles do. And all will be kindly disposed towards us, though one be a wild beast, a demon, or what you will.

Or if there should even be some who speak evil of thee, be not thou at all troubled thereat, nor because they revile thee in public, regarding it; but search into their conscience, and thou shalt see them applauding and admiring thee, and numbering up ten thousand praises.

See, for instance, how Nebuchadnezzar praises the children in the furnace; yet surely he was an adversary and an enemy. But upon seeing them stand nobly, he proclaims their triumph, and crowns them: and that for nought else, but because they disobeyed him, and hearkened unto the law of God. For the devil, when he sees himself effecting nothing, from that time departs, fearing lest he should be the cause of our winning more crowns. And when he is gone, even one who is abominable and depraved will recognize virtue, that mist being withdrawn. Or if men still argue perversely, thou shalt have from God the greater praise and admiration.

Grieve not now, I pray thee, neither despond; since the very apostles were to some a "savor of death" [II Cor. 2:16]; to others, a "savor of life." And if there be nothing to lay hold of in thyself, thou art rid of all their charges; or rather, thou art become the more blessed. Shine out therefore in thy life, and take no account of them who speak evil of thee. For it cannot, it cannot be, that one careful of virtue, should not have many enemies. However, this is nothing to the virtuous man. For by such means his brightness will increase the more abundantly.

Let us then, bearing these things in mind, look to one object only; how to order our own life with strictness. For thus we shall also guide to the life that is there, such as are now sitting in darkness. For such is the virtue of that light, as not only to shine here, but also to conduct its followers thither. For when men see us despising all things present, and preparing ourselves for that which is to come, our actions will persuade them sooner than any discourse. For who is there so senseless, that at sight of one, who within a day or two was living in luxury and wealth, now stripping himself of all, and putting on wings, and arrayed to meet both hunger and poverty, and all hardship, and dangers, and blood, and slaughter, and everything that is counted dreadful; will not from this sight derive a clear demonstration of the things which are to come?

But if we entangle ourselves in things present, and plunge ourselves in them more and more, how will it be possible for them to be persuaded that we are hastening to another sojourn?

And what excuse after this shall we have, if the fear of God avail not so much with us, as human glory availed with the

Greek philosophers? For some of them did really both lay aside wealth, and despised death, that they might make a show before men; wherefore also their hopes became vain. What plea then shall deliver us, when with so great things set before us, and with so high a rule of self-denial laid open to us, we are not able even to do as they did, but ruin both ourselves and others besides? For neither is the harm so great when a heathen commits transgression, as when a Christian doeth the same. Of course not; for their character is already lost, but ours, by reason of the grace of God, is even among the ungodly venerable and glorious. Therefore when they would most revile us, and aggravate their evil speech, they add some such taunt as, "Thou Christian": a taunt which they would not utter, did they not secretly entertain a great opinion of our doctrine.

Hast thou not heard how many, and how great precepts Christ enjoined? Now when wilt thou be able to fulfill one of those commandments, while thou leavest all, and goest about gathering interest, tacking together usuries, setting on foot transactions of business, buying herds of slaves, procuring silver vessels, purchasing houses, fields, goods without end? And I would this were all. But when to these unseasonable pursuits, thou addest even injustice, removing landmarks, taking away houses by violence, aggravating poverty, increasing hunger, when wilt thou be able to set thy foot on these thresholds?

13. But sometimes thou showest mercy to the poor. I know it as well as thou. But even in this again great is the mischief. For thou doest this either in pride or in vainglory, so as not to profit even by thy good deeds. What can be more wretched than this, to be making thy shipwreck in the very harbor? To prevent this, when thou hast done any good action, seek not thanks from me, that thou mayest have God thy debtor. For, "Lend," saith he, "unto them from whom ye do not expect to receive" [cf. Luke 6:34].

Thou hast thy Debtor; why leave him, and require it of me,

a poor and wretched mortal? What? is that Debtor displeased, when the debt is required of him? What? is he poor? Is he unwilling to pay? Seest thou not his unspeakable treasures? Seest thou not his indescribable munificence? Lay hold then on him, and make thy demand; for he is pleased when one thus demands the debt of him. Because, if he see another required to pay for what he himself owes, he will feel as though he were insulted, and repay thee no more; nay, he justly finds fault, saying, "Why, of what ingratitude hast thou convicted me? what poverty dost thou know to be in me, that thou hastenest by me, and resortest unto others? Hast thou lent to One, and dost thou demand the debt of another?"

For although man received it, it was God that commanded thee to bestow; and his will is to be himself, and in the original sense,[5] debtor, and surety, affording thee ten thousand occasions to demand the debt of him from every quarter. Do not thou then let go so great facility and abundance, and seek to receive of me who have nothing. Why, to what end dost thou display to me thy mercy shown to the poor? What! was it I that said to thee, Give? was it from me that thou didst hear this; that thou shouldest demand it back of me? He himself hath said, "He that hath pity upon the poor lendeth to God" [Prov. 19:17]. Thou hast lent to God: put it to his account.

"But he doth not repay the whole now." Well, this too he doth for thy good. For such a debtor is he: not as many, who are anxious simply to repay that which is lent; whereas he manages and doeth all things, with a view of investing likewise in security that which hath been given unto him. Therefore some, you see, he repays here: some he assigns in the other place.

14. Knowing therefore as we do these things, let us make our mercifulness abundant, let us give proof of much love to man, both by the use of our money, and by our actions. And if we see any one ill-treated and beaten in the market-place, whether we can pay down money, let us do it: or whether by

[5] The Greek word is *prōtotypos*; see Introduction, p. 19.

words we may separate them, let us not be backward. For even a word has its reward, and still more have sighs. And this the blessed Job said: "But I wept for every helpless one, and I sighed when I saw a man in distress" [Job 30:25]. But if there be a reward for tears and sighs; when words also, and an anxious endeavor, and many things besides are added, consider how great the recompense becomes. Yea, for we too were enemies to God, and the Only-begotten reconciled us, casting himself between, and for us receiving stripes, and for us enduring death.

Let us then likewise do our diligence to deliver from countless evils such as are incurring them; and not as we now do, when we see any beating and tearing one another: we are apt to stand by, finding pleasure in the disgrace of others, and forming a devilish amphitheatre around: than which what can be more cruel? Thou seest men reviled, tearing each other to pieces, rending their clothes, smiting each other's faces, and dost thou endure to stand by quietly?

What! is it a bear that is fighting? a wild beast? a serpent? It is a man, one who hath in every respect fellowship with thee: a brother, a member [Eph. 4:25]. Look not on, but separate them. Take no pleasure, but amend the evil. Stir not up others to the shameful sight, but rather drive off and separate those who are assembled. It is for shameless persons, and born slaves, to take pleasure in such calamities; for those that are mere refuse, for asses without reason.

Thou seest a man behaving himself unseemly, and dost thou not account the unseemliness thine own? Dost thou not interpose, and scatter the devil's troop, and put an end to men's miseries?

"That I may receive blows myself," saith one; "is this also thy bidding?" Thou wilt not have to suffer even this; but if thou shouldest, the thing would be to thee a sort of martyrdom; for thou didst suffer on God's behalf. And if thou art slow to receive blows, consider that thy Lord was not slow to endure the cross for thee.

Since they for their part are drunken and in darkness, wrath being their tyrant and commander; and they need some one who is sound to help them, both the wrong-doer, and he who is injured; the one that he may be delivered from suffering evil, the other that he may cease to do it. Draw nigh, therefore, and stretch forth the hand, thou that art sober to him that is drunken. For there is a drunkenness of wrath too, and that more grievous than the drunkenness of wine.

Seest thou not the seamen, how, when they see any meeting with shipwreck, they spread their sails, and set out with all haste, to rescue those of the same craft out of the waves? Now, if partakers in an art show so much care one for another, how much more ought they who are partakers of the same nature to do all these things! Because in truth here too is a shipwreck, a more grievous one than that; for either a man under provocation blasphemes, and so throws all away: or he forswears himself under the sway of his wrath, and that way falls into hell: or he strikes a blow and commits murder, and thus again suffers the very same shipwreck. Go thou then, and put a stop to the evil; pull out them that are drowning, though thou descend into the very depth of the surge; and having broken up the theatre of the devil, take each one of them apart, and admonish him to quell the flame, and to lull the waves.

But if the burning pile wax greater, and the furnace more grievous, be not thou terrified; for thou hast many to help thee, and stretch forth the hand, if thou furnish but a beginning; and above all thou surely hast with thee the God of peace. And if thou wilt first turn aside the flames, many others also will follow, and of what they do well, thou wilt thyself receive the reward.

Hear what precept Christ gave to the Jews, creeping as they did upon the earth: "If thou see," saith he, "thine enemy's beast of burden falling down, do not hasten by, but raise it" [Exod. 23:5; Deut. 22:4]. And thou must see that to separate and reconcile men that are fighting is a much lighter thing than to lift up the fallen beast. And if we ought to help in raising our enemies' ass, much more our friends' souls: and most when the fall is more grievous; for not into mire do these fall, but into the fire of hell, not bearing the burden of their wrath. And thou, when thou seest thy brother lying under the load, and the devil standing by, and kindling the pile, thou runnest by, cruelly and unmercifully; a kind of thing not safe to do, even where brutes are concerned.

And whereas the Samaritan, seeing a wounded man, unknown, and not at all appertaining to him, both staid, and set him on a beast, and brought him home to the inn, and hired a physician, and gave some money, and promised more: thou, seeing one fallen not among thieves, but amongst a band of demons, and beset by anger; and this not in a wilderness, but in the midst of the forum; not having to lay out money, nor to hire a beast, nor to bring him on a long way, but only to say some words:—art thou slow to do it? and holdest back, and hurriest by cruelly and unmercifully? And how thinkest thou, calling upon God, ever to find him propitious?

15. But let me speak also to you, who publicly disgrace yourselves: to him who is acting despitefully, and doing wrong. Art thou inflicting blows? tell me; and kicking, and biting? art thou become a wild boar, and a wild ass? and art thou not ashamed? dost thou not blush at thus being changed into a wild beast, and betraying thine own nobleness? For though thou be poor, thou art free; though thou be a working man, thou art a Christian.

Nay, for this very reason, that thou art poor, thou shouldest be quiet. For fightings belong to the rich, not to the poor; to the rich, who have many causes to force them to war. But thou, not having the pleasure of wealth, goest about gathering to thyself the evils of wealth, enmities, and strifes, and fightings; and takest thy brother by the throat, and goest about to strangle him, and throwest him down publicly in the sight of all men: and dost thou not think that thou art thyself rather disgraced, imitating the violent passions of the brutes; nay rather, becoming even worse than they? For they have all things in common; they herd one with another, and go about together: but we have nothing in common, but all in confusion: fightings, strifes, revilings, and enmities, and insults. And we neither reverence the heaven, unto which we are called all of us in common; nor the earth, which he hath left free to us all in common; nor our very nature, but wrath and the love of money sweeps all away.

Hast thou not seen him who owed the ten thousand talents, and then, after he was forgiven that debt, took his fellow-servant by the throat for an hundred pence, what great evils he underwent, and how he was delivered over to an endless punishment? Hast thou not trembled at the example? Hast thou no fear, lest thou too incur the same? For we likewise owe to our Lord many and great debts: nevertheless, he forbears, and suffers long, and neither urges us, as we do our fellow-servants, nor chokes and takes us by the throat; yet surely had he been minded to exact of us but the least part thereof, we had long ago perished.

16. Let us then, beloved, bearing these things in mind, be humbled, and feel thankful to those who are in debt to us. For they become to us, if we command ourselves, an occasion of obtaining most abundant pardon; and giving a little, we shall receive much. Why then exact with violence, it being meet, though the other were minded to pay, for thee of thine accord to excuse him, that thou mayest receive the whole of God? But now thou doest all things, and art violent, and contentious, to have none of thy debts forgiven thee; and whilst thou art thinking to do despite unto thy neighbor, thou art thrusting the sword into thyself, so increasing thy punishment in hell: whereas if thou wilt show a little self-command here, thou makest thine own accounts easy. For indeed God therefore wills us to take the lead in that kind of bounty, that he may take occasion to repay us with increase.

As many therefore as stand indebted to thee, either for money, or for trespasses, let them all go free, and require of God the recompense of such *thy* magnanimity. For so long as they continue indebted to thee, thou canst not have God thy debtor. But if thou let them go free, thou wilt be able to detain thy God, and to require of him the recompense of so great self-restraint in bountiful measure. For suppose a man had come up and seeing thee arresting thy debtor, had called upon thee to let him go free, and transfer to himself thy account with the other: he would not choose to be unfair after such remission, seeing he had passed the whole demand to himself: how then shall God fail to repay us manifold, yea, ten thousand fold, when for his commandment's sake, if any be indebted to us, we urge no complaint against them, great or small, but let them go exempt from all liability? Let us not then think of the temporary pleasure that springs up in us by exacting of our debtors, but of the loss, rather, how great! which we shall thereby sustain hereafter, grievously injuring ourselves in the things which are eternal. Rising accordingly above all, let us forgive those who must give account to us, both their debts and their offenses; that we may make our own accounts prove indulgent, and that what we could not reach by all virtue besides, this we may obtain by not bearing malice against our neighbors; and thus enjoy the eternal blessings, by the grace and love towards man of our Lord Jesus Christ, to whom be glory and might now and always, even forever and ever. Amen.

Homily XVI

"Think not that I am come to destroy the Law or the Prophets." —*Matt. 5:17*

WHY, WHO SUSPECTED THIS? or who accused him, that he should make a defense against this charge? Since surely from what had gone before no such suspicion was generated. For to command men to be meek, and gentle, and merciful, and pure in heart, and to strive for righteousness, indicated no such design, but rather altogether the contrary.

Wherefore then can he have said this? Not at random, nor vainly: but inasmuch as he was proceeding to ordain commandments greater than those of old, saying, "It was said to them of old time, Thou shalt not kill [Matt. 5:21]; but I say unto you, Be not even angry"; and to mark out a way for a kind of divine and heavenly conversation; in order that the strangeness thereof might not disturb the souls of the hearers, nor dispose them quite to mutiny against what he said, he used this means of setting them right beforehand.

For although they fulfilled not the law, yet nevertheless they were possessed with much conscientious regard to it; and whilst they were annulling it every day by their deeds, the letters thereof they would have remain unmoved, and that no one should add anything more to them. Or rather, they bore with their rulers adding thereto, not however for the better, but for the worse. For so they used to set aside the honor due to our parents by additions of their own, and very many others also of the matters enjoined them, they would free themselves of by these unseasonable additions.

Therefore, since Christ in the first place was not of the sacerdotal tribe[1] and next, the things which he was about to introduce were a sort of addition, not however lessening, but enhancing virtue; he knowing beforehand that both these circumstances would trouble them, before he wrote in their mind those wondrous laws, casts out that which was sure to be harboring there. And what was it that was harboring there, and making an obstacle?

2. They thought that he, thus speaking, did so with a view to the abrogation of the ancient institutions. This suspicion therefore he heals; nor here only doth he so, but elsewhere also again. Thus, since they accounted him no less than an adversary of God, from this sort of reason, namely, his not keeping the sabbath; he, to heal such their suspicion, there also again sets forth his pleas, of which some indeed were proper to himself; as when he saith, "My Father worketh, and I work" [John 5:17]; but some had in them much condescension, as when he brings forward the sheep lost on the sabbath day [Matt. 12:11], and points out that the law is disturbed for its preservation, and makes mention again of circumcision, as having this same effect [John 7:23].

Wherefore we see also that he often speaks words somewhat beneath him, to remove the semblance of his being an adversary of God.

For this cause he who had raised thousands of the dead with a word only, when he was calling Lazarus, added also a prayer; and then, lest this should make him appear less than him that begat him, he, to correct this suspicion, added, "I said these things, because of the people which standeth by, that they may believe that thou hast sent me" [John 11:42]. And neither doth he work all things as one who acted by his own power, that he might thoroughly correct their weakness; nor doth he all things with prayer, lest he should leave matter of evil suspicion to them that should follow, as though he were without strength or power: but he mingles the latter with the former,

[1] I.e., he belonged to the tribe of Judah rather than to that of Levi.

and those again with these. Neither doth he this indiscriminately, but with his own proper wisdom. For while he doeth the greater works authoritatively, in the less he looks up unto Heaven. Thus, when absolving sins, and revealing his secrets, and opening Paradise, and driving away devils, and cleansing lepers, and bridling death, and raising the dead by thousands, he did all by way of command: but when, what was much less than these, he was causing many loaves to spring forth out of few, then he looked up to heaven: signifying that not through weakness he doth this. For he who could do the greater with authority, how in the lesser could he need prayer? But as I was saying, he doeth this to silence their shamelessness. The same reckoning, then, I bid thee make of his words also, when thou hearest him speak lowly things. For many in truth are the causes both for words and for actions of that cast: as, for instance, that he might not be supposed alien from God; his instructing and waiting on all men; his teaching humility; his being encompassed with flesh; the Jews' inability to hear all at once; his teaching us to utter no high word of ourselves. For this cause many times, having in his own person said much that is lowly of himself, the great things he leaves to be said by others. Thus he himself indeed, reasoning with the Jews, said, "Before Abraham was, I AM" [John 8:58]: but his disciple not thus, but, "In the beginning was the Word, and the Word was with God, and the Word was God" [John 1:1].

Again, that he himself made heaven, and earth, and sea, and all things visible and invisible, in his own person he nowhere expressly said: but his disciple, speaking plainly out, and suppressing nothing, affirms this once, twice, yea often: writing that "all things were made by him"; and, "without him was not one thing made"; and, "he was in the world, and the world was made by him" [John 1:3, 10].

And why marvel, if others have said greater things of him than he of himself; since (what is more) in many cases, what he showed forth by his deeds, by his words he uttered not openly? Thus that it was himself who made mankind he showed clearly even by that blind man; but when he was speaking of our formation at the beginning, he said not, "I made," but "he who made them, made them male and female" [Matt. 19:4]. Again, that he created the world and all things therein, he demonstrated by the fishes, by the wine, by the loaves, by the calm in the sea, by the sunbeam which he averted on the cross; and by very many things besides: but in words he hath nowhere said this plainly, though his disciples are continually declaring it, both John, and Paul, and Peter.

For if they who night and day hear him discourse, and see him work marvels; to whom he explained many things in private, and gave so great power as even to raise the dead; whom he made so perfect, as to forsake all things for him: if even they, after so great virtue and self-denial, had not strength to bear it all, before the supply of the Spirit; how could the people of the Jews, being both void of understanding, and far behind such excellency, and only by hazard present when he did or said anything, how could they have been persuaded but that he was alien from the God of all, unless he had practiced such great condescension throughout?

For on this account we see that even when he was abrogating the sabbath, he did not as of set purpose bring in such *his* legislation, but he puts together many and various pleas of defense. Now if, when he was about to cause one commandment to cease, he used so much reserve in his language, that he might not startle the hearers; much more, when adding to the law, entire as it was, another entire code of laws, did he require much management and attention, not to alarm those who were then hearing him.

For this same cause, neither do we find him teaching everywhere clearly concerning his own Godhead. For if his adding to the law was sure to perplex them so greatly, much more his declaring himself God.

3. Wherefore many things are uttered by him, far below his proper dignity, and here when he is about to proceed upon his addition to the law, he hath used abundance for correction

beforehand. For neither was it once only that he said, "I do not abrogate the law," but he both repeated it again, and added another and a greater thing; in that, to the words, "Think not that I am come to destroy," he subjoined, "I am not come to destroy, but to fulfill."

Now this not only obstructs the obstinacy of the Jews, but stops also the mouths of those heretics,[2] who say that the old covenant is of the devil. For if Christ came to destroy his tyranny, how is this covenant not only not destroyed, but even fulfilled by Him? For he said not only, "I do not destroy it"; though this had been enough; but "I even fulfill it": which are the words of one so far from opposing himself, as to be even establishing it.

And how, one may ask, did he not destroy it? in what way did he rather fulfill either the law or the prophets? The prophets he fulfilled, inasmuch as he confirmed by his actions all that had been said concerning him; wherefore also the evangelist used to say in each case, "That it might be fulfilled which was spoken by the prophet." Both when he was born [Matt. 1:22, 23], and when the children sung that wondrous hymn to him, and when he sat on the ass [Matt. 21:5-16], and in very many more instances he worked this same fulfillment: all which things must have been unfulfilled, if he had not come.

But the law he fulfilled, not in one way only, but in a second and third also. In one way, by transgressing none of the precepts of the law. For that he did fulfill it all, hear what he saith to John, "For thus it becometh us to fulfill all righteousness" [Matt. 3:15]. And to the Jews also he said, "Which of you convinceth me of sin" [John 8:46]. And to his disciples again, "The prince of this world cometh, and findeth nothing in me" [John 14:30]. And the prophet too from the first had said that "He did no sin" [Isa. 53:9].

This then was one sense in which he fulfilled it. Another,

[2] This is another reference to the Gnostics and Manichaeans and to their rejection of the Old Testament.

that he did the same through us also; for this is the marvel, that he not only himself fulfilled it, but he granted this to us likewise. Which thing Paul also declaring said, "Christ is the end of the law for righteousness to every one that believeth" [Rom. 10:4]. And he said also, that "He judged sin in the flesh, that the righteousness of the law might be fulfilled in us who walk not after the flesh" [Rom. 8:3, 4]. And again, "Do we then make void the law through faith? God forbid! yea, we establish the law" [Rom. 3:31]. For since the law was laboring at this, to make man righteous, but had not power, he came and brought in the way of righteousness by faith, and so established that which the law desired: and what the law could not by letters, this he accomplished by faith. On this account he saith, "I am not come to destroy the law."

4. But if any one will inquire accurately, he will find also another, a third sense, in which this hath been done. Of what sort is it then? In the sense of that future code of laws, which he was about to deliver to them.

For his sayings were no repeal of the former, but a drawing out, and filling up of them. Thus, "not to kill," is not annulled by the saying, "Be not angry," but rather is filled up and put in greater security: and so of all the others.

Wherefore, you see, as he had before unsuspectedly cast the seeds of this teaching; so at the time when from his comparison of the old and new commandments, he would be more distinctly suspected of placing them in opposition, he used his corrective beforehand. For in a covert way he had indeed already scattered those seeds, by what he had said. Thus, "Blessed are the poor," is the same as that we are not to be angry; and, "Blessed are the pure in heart," as not to "look upon a woman for lust"; and the "not laying up treasures on earth," harmonizes with, "Blessed are the merciful"; and "to mourn" also, "to be persecuted" and "reviled," coincide with "entering in at the strait gate"; and, "to hunger and thirst after righteousness," is nothing else than that which he saith afterwards, "Whatsoever ye would that men should do to you, do ye also to them." And having declared "the peacemaker blessed," he again almost said the same, when he gave command "to leave the gift," and hasten to reconciliation with him that was grieved, and about "agreeing with our adversary."

But there he set down the rewards of them that do right, here rather the punishments of them who neglect practice. Wherefore as in that place he said, "The meek shall inherit earth"; so here, "He who calleth his brother fool, shall be in danger of hell-fire"; and there, "The pure in heart shall see God"; here, he is a complete adulterer who looks unchastely. And having there called "the peacemakers, sons of God"; here he alarms us from another quarter, saying, "Lest at any time the adversary deliver thee to the judge." Thus also, whereas in the former part he blesses them that mourn, and them that are persecuted; in the following, establishing the very same point, he threatens destruction to them that go not that way; for, "They that walk 'in the broad way,' saith he, 'make their end there.' " And, "Ye cannot serve God and mammon," seems to me the same with, "Blessed are the merciful," and, "those that hunger after righteousness."

But as I said, since he is going to say these things more clearly, and not only more clearly, but also to add again more than had been already said (for he no longer merely seeks a merciful man, but bids us give up even our coat; not simply a meek person, but to turn also the other cheek to him that would smite us): therefore he first takes away the apparent contradiction.

On this account, then, as I have already stated, he said this not once only, but once and again; in that to the words, "Think not that I am come to destroy," he added, "I am not come to destroy, but to fulfill."

"For verily I say unto you, Till heaven and earth pass, one jot or one tittle shall in no wise pass from the law, till all come to pass" [Matt. 5:18].

Now what he saith is like this: it cannot be that it should remain unaccomplished, but the very least thing therein must needs be fulfilled. Which thing he himself performed, in that he completed it with all exactness.

And here he signifies to us obscurely that the fashion of the whole world is also being changed. Nor did he set it down without purpose, but in order to arouse the hearer, and indicate, that he was with just cause introducing another discipline; if at least the very works of the creation are all to be transformed, and mankind is to be called to another country, and to a higher way of practicing how to live.

5. "Whosoever therefore shall break one of these least commandments, and shall teach men so, he shall be called least in the kingdom of heaven" [Matt. 5:19].

Thus, having rid himself of the evil suspicion, and having stopped the mouths of them who would fain gainsay, then at length he proceeds to alarm, and sets down a heavy denunciation in support of the enactments he was entering on.

For as to his having said this in behalf not of the ancient laws, but of those which he was proceeding to enact, listen to what follows, "For I say unto you," saith he, "Except your righteousness shall exceed the righteousness of the Scribes and Pharisees, ye shall in no case enter into the kingdom of heaven" [Matt. 5:20].

For if he were threatening with regard to the ancient laws, how said he, "except it shall exceed?" since they who did just the same as those ancients, could not exceed them on the score of righteousness.

But of what kind was the required excess? Not to be angry, not even to look upon a woman unchastely.

For what cause then doth he call these commandments "least," though they were so great and high? Because he himself was about to introduce the enactment of them; for as he humbled himself, and speaks of himself frequently with measure, so likewise of his own enactments, hereby again teaching us to be modest in everything. And besides, since there seemed to be some suspicion of novelty, he ordered his discourse for a while with reserve.

But when thou hearest, "least in the kingdom of heaven," surmise thou nothing but hell and torments. For he was used to mean by "the kingdom," not merely the enjoyment thereof, but also the time of the resurrection, and that awful coming. And how could it be reasonable, that while he who called his brother fool, and transgressed but one commandment, falls into hell; the breaker of them all, and instigator of others to the same, should be within the kingdom? This therefore is not what he means, but that such a one will be at that time *least,* that is, cast out, last. And he that is last will surely then fall into hell. For, being God, he foreknew the laxity of the many, he foreknew that some would think these sayings were merely hyperbolical, and would argue about the laws, and say, What, if any one call another a fool, is he punished? If one merely look on a woman, doth he become an adulterer? For this very cause he, destroying such insolence beforehand, hath set down the strongest denunciation against either sort, as well them who transgress, as them who lead on others so to do.

Knowing then his threat as we do, let us neither ourselves transgress, nor discourage such as are disposed to keep these things.

"But whosoever shall do and teach," saith he, "shall be called great."

For not to ourselves alone, should we be profitable, but to others also; since neither is the reward as great for him who guides himself aright, as for one who with himself adds also another. For as teaching without doing condemns the teacher (for "thou which teachest another," it is said, "teachest thou not thyself?" [Rom. 2:21]), so doing but not guiding others lessens our reward. One ought therefore to be chief in either work, and having first set one's self right, thus to proceed also to the care of the rest. For on this account he himself hath set the doing before the teaching; to intimate that so most of all may one be able to teach, but in no other way. For one will be told, "Physician, heal thyself" [Luke 4:23]. Since he who cannot teach himself, yet attempts to set others right, will have many to ridicule him. Or rather such a one will have no power to teach at all, his actions uttering their voice against him. But if he be complete in both respects, "he shall be called great in the kingdom of heaven."

6. "For I say unto you, Except your righteousness shall exceed the righteousness of the Scribes and Pharisees, ye shall in no case enter into the kingdom of heaven" [Matt. 5:20].

Here by righteousness he means the whole of virtue;[3] even as also discoursing of Job, he said, "He was a blameless man, righteous" [Job 1:1]. According to the same signification of the word, Paul also called that man "righteous" for whom, as he said, no law is even set. "For," saith he, "a law is not made for a righteous man" [I Tim. 1:9]. And in many other places too one might find this name standing for virtue in general.

But observe, I pray thee, the increase of grace; in that he will have his newly-come disciples better than the teachers in the old covenant. For by "Scribes and Pharisees" here, he meant not merely the lawless, but the well-doers. For, were they not doing well, he would not have said they have a righteousness; neither would he have compared the unreal to the real.

And observe also here, how he commends the old law, by making a comparison between it and the other; which kind of thing implies it to be of the same tribe and kindred. For *more* and *less*, is in the same kind. He doth not, you see, find fault with the old law, but will have it made stricter. Whereas, had it been evil, he would not have required more of it; he would not have made it more perfect, but would have cast it out.

And how one may say, if it be such, doth it not bring us into the kingdom? It doth not now bring in them who live after the coming of Christ, favored as they are with more strength, and bound to strive for greater things: since as to its own foster-children, them it doth bring in one and all. Yea, for "many shall come," saith he, "from east and west, and shall

[3] Cf. p. 46, n. 4.

lie down in the bosoms of Abraham, Isaac, and Jacob" [Matt. 8:11]. And Lazarus also receiving the great prize, is shown dwelling in Abraham's bosom. And all, as many as have shone forth with excellency in the old dispensation, shone by it, every one of them. And Christ himself, had it been in anything evil or alien from him, would not have fulfilled it all when he came. For if only to attract the Jews he was doing this, and not in order to prove it akin to the new law, and concurrent therewith; wherefore did he not also fulfill the laws and customs of the Gentiles, that he might attract the Gentiles also?

So that from all considerations it is clear, that not from any badness in itself doth it fail to bring us in, but because it is now the season of higher precepts.

And if it be more imperfect than the new, neither doth this imply it to be evil: since upon this principle the new law itself will be in the very same case. Because in truth our knowledge of this, when compared with that which is to come, is a sort of partial and imperfect thing, and is done away on the coming of that other. "For when," saith he, "that which is perfect is come, then that which is in part shall be done away" [I Cor. 13:10]: even as it befell the old law through the new. Yet we are not to blame the new law for this, though that also gives place on our attaining unto the kingdom: for "then," saith he, "that which is in part shall be done away": but for all this we call it great.

Since then both the rewards thereof are greater, and the power given by the Spirit more abundant, in reason it requires our graces to be greater also. For it is no longer "a land that floweth with milk and honey," nor a comfortable old age, nor many children, nor corn and wine, and flocks and herds: but heaven, and the good things in the heavens, and adoption and brotherhood with the Only-Begotten, and to partake of the inheritance and to be glorified and to reign with him, and those unnumbered rewards. And as to our having received more abundant help, hear thou Paul, when he saith, "There is therefore no condemnation now to them which are in Christ Jesus, who walk not after the flesh, but after the Spirit: for the law of the Spirit of life hath made me free from the law of sin and death" [Rom. 8:1, 2].

7. And now after threatening the transgressors, and setting great rewards for them that do right, and signifying that he justly requires of us something beyond the former measures; he from this point begins to legislate, not simply, but by way of comparison with the ancient ordinances, desiring to intimate these two things: first, that not as contending with the former, but rather in great harmony with them, he is making these enactments; next, that it was meet and very seasonable for him to add thereto these second precepts.

And that this may be made yet clearer, let us hearken to the words of the Legislator.

What then doth he himself say?

"Ye have heard that it was said to them of old time, Thou shalt not kill" [Matt. 5:21].

And yet it was himself who gave those laws also, but so far he states them impersonally. For if on the one hand he had said, "Ye have heard that I said to them of old," the saying would have been hard to receive, and would have stood in the way of all the hearers. If again, on the other hand, after having said, "Ye have heard that it was said to them of old by my Father," he had added, "But I say," he would have seemed to be taking yet more on himself.

Wherefore he hath simply stated it, making out thereby one point only; the proof that in fitting season he had come saying these things. For by the words, "It was said to them of old," he pointed out the length of the time, since they received this commandment. And this he did to shame the hearer, shrinking from the advance to the higher class of his commandments; as though a teacher should say to a child that was indolent, "Knowest thou not how long a time thou hast consumed in learning syllables?" This then he also covertly intimates by the expression, "them of old time," and thus for the future summons them on to the higher order of his instructions: as if he had said, "Ye are learning these lessons long enough, and you must henceforth press on to such as are higher than these."

And it is well that he doth not disturb the order of the commandments, but begins first with that which comes earlier, with which the law also began. Yea, for this too suits with one showing the harmony between them.

"But I say unto you, that whosoever is angry with his brother without a cause, shall be in danger of the judgment" [Matt. 5:22].

Seest thou authority in perfection? Seest thou a bearing suited to a legislator? Why, which among prophets ever spake on this wise? which among righteous men? which among patriarchs? None; but, "Thus saith the Lord." But the Son not so. Because they were publishing their Master's commands, he his Father's. And when I say, "his Father's," I mean his own. "For mine," saith he, "are thine, and thine are mine" [John 17:10]. And they had their fellow-servants to legislate for, he his own servants.

Let us now ask those who reject the law, "Is, 'Be not angry' contrary to 'Do no murder'? or is not the one commandment the completion and the development of the other?" Clearly the one is the fulfilling of the other, and that is greater on this very account. Since he who is not stirred up to anger, will much more refrain from murder; and he who bridles wrath will much more keep his hands to himself. For wrath is the root of murder. And you see that he who cuts up the root will much more remove the branches; or rather, will not permit them so much as to shoot out at all. Not therefore to abolish the law did he make these enactments, but for the more complete observation of it. For with what design did the law enjoin these things? Was it not, that no one might slay his neighbor? It follows, that he who was opposing the law would have to enjoin murder. For to murder, were the contrary to doing no murder. But if he doth not suffer one even to be angry, the mind of the law is established by him more completely. For he that studies to avoid murder will not refrain from it equally with him that hath put away even anger; this latter being further removed from the crime.

8. But that we may convict them in another way also, let us bring forward all their allegations. What then do they affirm? They assert that the God who made the world, who "makes his sun to rise on the evil and on the good, who sends the rain on the just and on the unjust," is in some sense an evil being.[4] But the more moderate (forsooth) among them, though declining this, yet while they affirm him to be just, they deprive him of being good. And some other one, who is not, nor made any of the things that are, they assign for a Father to Christ. And they say that he, who is not good, abides in his own, and preserves what are his own; but that He, that is good, seeks what are another's, and desires of a sudden to become a Saviour to them whose Creator he was not.[5] Seest thou the children of the devil, how they speak out of the fountain of their father, alienating the work of creation from God: while John cries out, "He came unto his own," and, "The world was made by him" [John 1:11, 10].

In the next place, they criticise the law in the old covenant, which bids put out "an eye for an eye," and "a tooth for a tooth";[6] and straightway they insult and say, "Why, how can he be good who speaks so?"

What then do we say in answer to this? That it is the highest kind of philanthropy. For he made this law, not that we might strike out one another's eyes, but that fear of suffering by others might restrain us from doing any such thing to them. As therefore he threatened the Ninevites with overthrow, not that he might destroy them (for had that been his will, he

[4] According to Pseudo-Tertullian *Against All Heresies* 6, this was the doctrine of Cerdo, a Syrian Gnostic.

[5] According to Irenaeus *Against Heresies* v. 2 and other accounts, Marcion taught that the God of the Old Testament was just, but not good; Harnack and other scholars conclude that Marcion did not call Him evil.

[6] The Manichaeans claimed that there was a contradiction between these words of Jesus in Matt. 5:39 and the Mosaic law in Exod. 21:24; cf. Augustine *Reply to Faustus the Manichaean* xix. 25.

ought to have been silent), but that he might by fear make them better, and so quiet his wrath: so also hath he appointed a punishment for those who wantonly assail the eyes of others, that if good principle dispose them not to refrain from such cruelty, fear may restrain them from injuring their neighbors' sight.

And if this be cruelty, it is cruelty also for the murderer to be restrained, and the adulterer checked. But these are the sayings of senseless men, and of those that are made to the extreme of madness. For I, so far from saying that this comes of cruelty, should say, that the contrary to this would be unlawful, according to men's reckoning. And whereas, thou sayest, "Because he commanded to pluck out 'an eye for an eye,' therefore he is cruel"; I say, that if he had not given this commandment, then he would have seemed, in the judgment of most men, to be that which thou sayest he is.

For let us suppose that this law had been altogether done away, and that no one feared the punishment ensuing thereupon, but that license had been given to all the wicked to follow their own disposition in all security, to adulterers, and to murderers, to perjured persons, and to parricides; would not all things have been turned upside down? would not cities, market-places, and houses, sea and land, and the whole world, have been filled with unnumbered pollutions and murders? Every one sees it. For if, when there are laws, and fear, and threatening, our evil dispositions are hardly checked; were even this security taken away, what is there to prevent men's choosing vice? and what degree of mischief would not then come revelling upon the whole of human life?

The rather, since cruelty lies not only in allowing the bad to do what they will, but in another thing too quite as much; to overlook, and leave uncared for, him who hath done no wrong, but who is without cause or reason suffering ill. For tell me; were any one to gather together wicked men from all quarters, and arm them with swords, and bid them go about the whole city, and massacre all that came in their way, could there be anything more like a wild beast than he? And what if some-other should bind, and confine with the utmost strictness those whom that man had armed, and should snatch from those lawless hands them, who were on the point of being butchered; could anything be greater humanity than this?

Now then, I bid thee transfer these examples to the law likewise; for he that commands to pluck out "an eye for an eye," hath laid the fear as a kind of strong chain upon the souls of the bad, and so resembles him, who detains those assassins in prison; whereas he who appoints no punishment for them, doth all but arm them by such security, and acts the part of that other, who was putting the swords in their hands, and letting them loose over the whole city.

Seest thou not, how the commandments, so far from coming of cruelty, come rather of abounding mercy? And if on account of these thou callest the Lawgiver grievous, and hard to bear with; tell me which sort of command is the more toilsome and grievous, "Do no murder," or, "Be not even angry"? Which is more in extreme, he who exacts a penalty for murder, or for mere anger? He who subjects the adulterer to vengeance after the fact, or he who enjoins a penalty even for the very desire, and that penalty everlasting? See ye not how their reasoning comes round to the very contrary? how the God of the old covenant, whom they call cruel, will be found mild and meek: and he of the new, whom they acknowledged to be good, will be hard and grievous, according to their madness? Whereas we say, that there is but one and the same Legislator of either covenant, who dispensed all meetly, and adapted to the difference of the times the difference between the two systems of law. Therefore neither are the first commandments cruel, nor the second hard and grievous, but all of one and the same providential care.

For that he himself gave the old covenant also, hear the affirmation of the prophet, or rather (so we must speak), of him who is both the one and the other: "I will make a covenant with you, not according to the covenant which I made with your fathers" [Jer. 31:31, 32].

But if he receive not this, who is diseased with the Manichaean doctrines,[7] let him hear Paul saying the very same in another place, "For Abraham had two sons, one by the bondmaid, and another by the freewoman; and these are two covenants" [Gal. 4:22, 24]. As therefore in that case the wives are different, the husband the same; so here too the covenants are two, the Lawgiver one.

And to prove to thee that it was of one and the same mildness; in the one he saith, "An eye for an eye," but in this other,

"If one smite thee on thy right cheek, turn to him the other also" [Matt. 5:39].

For as in that case he checks him that doth the wrong with the fear of this suffering, even so also in this. "How so," it may be said, "when he bids turn to him the other cheek also?" Nay, what of that? Since not to take away his fear did he enjoin this, but as charging yourself to allow him to take his fill entirely. Neither did he say, that the other continues unpunished, but, "do not thou punish"; at once both enhancing the fear of him that smiteth, if he persist, and comforting him who is smitten.

9. But these things we have said, as one might say them incidentally, concerning all the commandments. Now we must go on to that which is before us, and keep to the thread of what had been affirmed. "He that is angry with his brother without a cause shall be in danger of the judgment": so he speaks. Thus he hath not altogether taken the thing away: first, because it is not possible, being a man, to be freed from passions: we may indeed get the dominion over them, but to be altogether without them is out of the question.

Next, because this passion is even useful, if we know how to use it at the suitable time. See, for instance, what great good was wrought by that anger of Paul, which he felt against the Corinthians, on that well-known occasion; and how, as it de-

[7] I.e., one who will not acknowledge Jer. 31:31-32 as Scripture because it is in the Old Testament should hear Gal. 4:22.

livered them from a grievous pest, so by the same means again he recovered the people of the Galatians likewise, which had fallen aside; and others too beside these.

What then is the proper time for anger? When we are not avenging ourselves, but checking others in their lawless freaks, or forcing them to attend in their negligence.

And what is the unsuitable time? When we do so as avenging ourselves: which Paul also forbidding, said "Avenge not yourselves, dearly beloved, but rather give place unto wrath" [Rom. 12:19]. When we are contending for riches: yea, for this hath he also taken away, where he saith, "Why do ye not rather take wrong? why do ye not rather suffer yourselves to be defrauded?" [I Cor. 6:7]. For as this last sort is superfluous, so is the first necessary and profitable. But most men do the contrary; becoming like wild beasts when they are injured themselves, but remiss and cowardly when they see despite done to another: both which are just opposite to the laws of the Gospel.

Being angry then is not a transgression, but being so unseasonably. For this cause the prophet also said, "Be ye angry, and sin not" [Ps. 4:4; cf. Eph. 4:26].

10. "And whosoever shall say to his brother, 'Raca,' shall be in danger of the council."

By the council in this place he means the tribunal of the Hebrews: and he hath mentioned this now, on purpose that he might not seem everywhere to play the stranger and innovator.

But this word, "Raca," is not an expression of a great insolence, but rather of some contempt and slight on the part of the speaker. For as we, giving orders either to our servants, or to any very inferior person, say, "Away with thee; you here, tell such an one": so they who make use of the Syrians' language say, "Raca," putting that word instead of "thou."[8] But

[8] On the basis of this passage and others like it, biographers of Chrysostom have concluded that, though a native of Antioch, he spoke only Greek.

God, the lover of man, roots up even the least faults, commanding us to behave to one another in seemly manner, and with due respect; and this with a view of destroying hereby also the greater.

"But whosoever shall say, Thou fool, shall be in danger of hell fire."

To many this commandment hath appeared grievous and galling, if for a mere word we are really to pay so great a penalty. And some even say that it was spoken rather hyperbolically. But I fear lest, when we have deceived ourselves with words here, we may in deeds there suffer that extreme punishment.

For wherefore, tell me, doth the commandment seem overburdensome? Knowest thou not that most punishments and most sins have their beginning from words? Yea, for by words are blasphemies, and denials are by words, and revilings, and reproaches, and perjuries, and bearing false witness. Regard not then its being a mere word, but whether it have not much danger, this do thou inquire. Art thou ignorant that in the season of enmity, when wrath is inflamed, and the soul kindled, even the least thing appears great, and what is not very reproachful is counted intolerable? And often these little things have given birth even to murder, and overthrown whole cities. For just as where friendship is, even grievous things are light, so where enmity lies beneath, very trifles appear intolerable. And however simply a word be spoken, it is surmised to have been spoken with an evil meaning. And as in fire: if there be but a small spark, though thousands of planks lie by, it doth not easily lay hold of them; but if the flame have waxed strong and high, it readily seizes not planks only, but stones, and all materials that fall in its way; and by what things it is usually quenched, by the same it is kindled the more (for some say that at such a time not only wood and tow, and the other combustibles, but even water darted forth upon it doth but fan its power the more); so is it also with anger; whatever anyone may say, becomes food in a moment for this evil conflagration. All which kind of evils Christ checking beforehand, had condemned first him that is angry without a cause to the judgment (this being the very reason why he said, "He that is angry shall be in danger of the judgment"); then him that saith "Raca," to the council. But as yet these are no great things; for the punishments are here. Therefore for him who calleth "fool" he hath added the fire of hell, now for the first time mentioning the name of hell. For having before discoursed much of the kingdom, not until then did he mention this; implying, that the former comes of his own love and indulgence towards man, this latter of our negligence.

11. And see how he proceeds by little and little in his punishments, all but excusing himself unto thee, and signifying that his desire indeed is to threaten nothing of the kind, but that we drag him on to such denunciations. For observe: "I bade thee," saith he, "not be angry for nought, because thou art in danger of the judgment. Thou hast despised the former commandment: see what anger hath produced; it hath led thee on straightway to insult, for thou hast called thy brother 'Raca.' Again, I set another punishment, 'the council.' If thou overlook even this, and proceed to that which is more grievous, I visit thee no longer with these finite punishments, but with the undying penalty of hell, lest after this thou shouldest break forth even to murder." For there is nothing, nothing in the world more intolerable than insolence; it is what hath very great power to sting a man's soul. But when the word too which is spoken is in itself more wounding than the insolence, the blaze becomes twice as great. Think it not then a light thing to call another "fool." For when of that which separates us from the brutes, and by which especially we are human beings, namely, the mind and the understanding—when of this thou hast robbed thy brother, thou hast deprived him of all his nobleness.

Let us not then regard the words merely, but realizing the things themselves, and his feeling, let us consider how great a wound is made by this word, and unto how much evil it proceeds. For this cause Paul likewise cast out of the kingdom not only "the adulterous" and "the effeminate," but "the revilers" [I Cor. 6:9, 10] also. And with great reason: for the insolent man mars all the beauty of charity, and casts upon his neighbor unnumbered ills, and works up lasting enmities, and tears asunder the members of Christ, and is daily driving away that peace which God so desires: giving much vantage ground unto the devil by his injurious ways, and making him the stronger. Therefore Christ himself, cutting out the sinews of the devil's power, brought in this law.

For indeed he makes much account of love: this being above all things the mother of every good, and the badge of his disciples, and the bond which holds together our whole condition. With reason therefore doth he remove with great earnestness the roots and the sources of that hatred which utterly spoils it.

Think not therefore that these sayings are in any wise hyperbolical,[9] but consider the good done by them, and admire the mildness of these laws. For there is nothing for which God takes so much pains, as this; that we should be united and knit together one with another. Therefore both in his own person, and by his disciples, as well those in the Old, as in the New Testament, he makes so much account of this commandment; and is a severe avenger and punisher of those who despise the duty. For in truth nothing so effectually gives entrance and root to all wickedness, as the taking away of love. Wherefore he also said, "When iniquity abounds, the love of the many shall wax cold" [Matt. 24:12]. Thus Cain became his brother's murderer; thus Esau; thus Joseph's brethren; thus our unnumbered crimes have come revelling in, this bond being dissevered. You see why he himself also roots out whatever things injure this, on every side, with great exactness.

12. Neither doth he stop at those precepts only which have been mentioned, but adds also others more than those: whereby he signifies how much account he makes thereof. Namely, having threatened by "the council," by "the judg-

[9] See our Introduction, p. 27.

ment," and by "hell," he added other sayings again in harmony with the former, saying thus:

"If thou bring thy gift to the altar, and there rememberest that thy brother hath ought against thee; leave there thy gift before the altar, and go away; first be reconciled to thy brother, and then come and offer thy gift" [Matt. 5:23, 24].

O goodness! O exceeding love to man! He makes no account of the honor due unto himself, for the sake of our love towards our neighbor; implying that not at all from any enmity, nor out of any desire to punish, had he uttered those former threatenings, but out of very tender affection. For what can be milder than these sayings? "Let my service," saith he, "be interrupted, that thy love may continue; since this also is a sacrifice, thy being reconciled to thy brother." Yea, for this cause he said not, "after the offering," or "before the offering"; but, while the very gift lies there, and when the sacrifice is already beginning, he sends thee to be reconciled to thy brother; and neither after removing that which lies before us, nor before presenting the gift, but while it lies in the midst, he bids thee hasten thither.

With what motive then doth he command so to do, and wherefore? These two ends, as it appears to me, he is hereby shadowing out and providing for. First, as I have said, his will is to point out that he highly values charity, and considers it to be the greatest sacrifice: and that without it he doth not receive even that other; next, he is imposing such a necessity of reconciliation, as admits of no excuse. For whoso hath been charged not to offer before he be reconciled, will hasten, if not for love of his neighbor, yet, that this may not lie unconsecrated, to run unto him who hath been grieved, and do away the enmity. For this cause he hath also expressed it all most significantly, to alarm and thoroughly to awaken him. Thus, when he had said, "Leave thy gift," he stayed not at this, but added, "before the altar" (by the very place again causing him to shudder); "and go away." And he said not merely, "Go away," but he added, "first, and then come and offer thy gift."

By all these things making it manifest, that this table receives not them that are at enmity with each other.

Let the initiated hear this, as many as draw nigh in enmity: and let the uninitiated hear too: yea, for the saying hath some relation to them also.[10] For they too offer a gift and a sacrifice: prayer, I mean, and almsgiving. For as to this also being a sacrifice, hear what the prophet saith: "A sacrifice of praise will glorify me" [Ps. 50:23]; and again, "Sacrifice to God a sacrifice of praise" [Ps. 50:14]; and, "The lifting up of mine hands is an evening sacrifice" [Ps. 141:2]. So that if it be but a prayer, which thou art offering in such a frame of mind, it were better to leave thy prayer, and become reconciled to thy brother, and then to offer thy prayer.

For to this end were all things done: to this end even God became man, and took order for all those works, that he might set us at one.

And whereas in this place he is sending the wrong doer to the sufferer, in his prayer he leads the sufferer to the wrong doer, and reconciles them. For as there he saith, "Forgive men their debts"; so here, "If he hath ought against thee, go thy way unto him."

Or rather, even here too he seems to me to be sending the injured person: and for some such reason he said not, "Reconcile thyself to thy brother," but, "Be thou reconciled." And while the saying seems to pertain to the aggressor, the whole of it really pertains to him that is aggrieved. Thus, "If thou art reconciled to him," saith Christ, "through thy love to him thou wilt have me also propitious, and wilt be able to offer thy sacrifice with great confidence. But if thou art still irritated, consider that even I readily command that which is mine to be lightly esteemed, that ye may become friends; and let these thoughts be soothing to thine anger."

And he said not, "When thou hast suffered any of the

[10] Chrysostom is referring to the distinction between those who were permitted to attend the "mass of the faithful" and those who were dismissed from the service at the end of the "mass of the catechumens"; cf. Introduction, p. 8.

greater wrongs, then be reconciled"; but, "Though it be some trifle that he hath against thee." And he added not, "Whether justly or unjustly"; but merely, "If he hath ought against thee." For though it be justly, not even in that case oughtest thou to protract the enmity; since Christ also was justly angered with us, yet nevertheless he gave himself for us to be slain, "not imputing those trespasses" [II Cor. 5.19].

For this cause Paul also, when urging us in another way to reconciliation, said, "Let not the sun go down upon your wrath" [Eph. 4:26]. For much as Christ by this argument of the sacrifice, so there Paul by that of the day, is urging us on to the self-same point. Because in truth he fears the night, lest it overtake him that is smitten alone, and make the wound greater. For whereas in the day there are many to distract, and draw him off; in the night, when he is alone, and is thinking it over by himself, the waves swell, and the storm becomes greater. Therefore Paul, you see, to prevent this, would fain commit him to the night already reconciled, that the devil may after that have no opportunity, from his solitude, to rekindle the furnace of his wrath, and make it fiercer. Thus also Christ permits not, though it be ever so little delay, lest, the sacrifice being accomplished, such an one become more remiss, procrastinating from day to day: for he knows that the case requires very speedy treatment. And as a skillful physician exhibits not only the preventives of our diseases, but their correctives also, even so doth he likewise. Thus, to forbid our calling "fool," is a preventive of enmity; but to command reconciliation is a means of removing the diseases that ensue on the enmity.

And mark how both commands are set forth with earnestness. For as in the former case he threatened hell, so here he receives not the gift before the reconciliation, indicating great displeasure, and by all these methods destroying both the root and the produce.

And first of all he saith, "Be not angry"; and after that, "revile not." For indeed both these are augmented, the one by the other: from enmity is reviling, from reviling enmity. On this account then he heals now the root, and now the fruit; hindering indeed the evil from ever springing up in the first instance: but if perchance it may have sprouted up and borne its most evil fruit, then by all means he burns it down the more.

13. Therefore, you see, having mentioned, first the judgment, then the council, then hell, and having spoken of his own sacrifice, he adds other topics again, thus speaking:

"Agree with thine adversary quickly, whilst thou art in the way with him" [Matt. 5:25].

That is, that thou mayest not say, "What then, if I am injured"; "what if I am plundered, and dragged too before the tribunal?" even this occasion and excuse he hath taken away: for he commands us not even so to be at enmity. Then, since this injunction was great, he draws his advice from the things present, which are wont to restrain the grosser sort more than the future. "Why, what sayest thou?" saith he. "That thine adversary is stronger, and doeth thee wrong? Of course then he will wrong thee more, if thou do not make it up, but art forced to go into court. For in the former case, by giving up some money, thou wilt keep thy person free; but when thou art come under the sentence of the judge, thou wilt both be bound, and pay the utmost penalty. But if thou avoid the contest there, thou wilt reap two good results: first, not having to suffer anything painful; and secondly, that the good done will be thereafter thine own doing, and no longer the effect of compulsion on his part. But if thou wilt not be ruled by these sayings, thou wrongest not him, so much as thyself."

And see here also how he hastens him; for having said, "Agree with thine adversary," he added, "quickly"; and he was not satisfied with this, but even of this quickness he hath required a further increase, saying, "Whilst thou art in the way with him"; pressing and hastening him hereby with great earnestness. For nothing doth so much turn our life upside down, as delay and procrastination in the performance of our good works. Nay, this hath often caused us to lose all. Therefore, as Paul for his part saith, "Before the sun set, do away the enmity"; and as he himself had said above, "Before the offering is completed, be reconciled"; so he saith in this place also, "Quickly, whilst thou art in the way with him," before thou art come to the doors of the court; before thou standest at the bar, and art come to be thenceforth under the sway of him that judgeth. Since, before entering in, thou hast all in thine own control; but if thou set thy foot on that threshold, thou wilt not by ever so earnest efforts be able to arrange thy matters at thy will, having come under the constraint of another.

But what is it "to agree"? He means either, "consent rather to suffer wrong" or, "so plead the cause, as if thou wert in the place of the other"; that thou mayest not corrupt justice by self-love, but rather, deliberating on another's cause as thine own, mayest so proceed to deliver thy vote in this matter. And if this be a great thing, marvel not; since with this view did he set forth all those his blessings, that having beforehand smoothed and prepared the hearer's soul, he might render it apter to receive all his enactments.

Now some say that he obscurely signifies the devil himself, under the name of the adversary;[11] and bids us have nothing of his, (for this, they say, is to "agree" with him): no compromise being possible after our departure hence, nor anything awaiting us, but that punishment, from which no prayers can deliver. But to me he seems to be speaking of the judges in this world, and of the way to the court of justice, and of this prison.

For after he had abashed men by higher things, and things future, he alarms them also by such as are in this life. Which thing Paul also doth, using both the future and the present to sway his hearer: as when, deterring from wickedness, he points out to him that is inclined to evil, the ruler armed: thus saying, "But if thou do that which is evil, be afraid; for he beareth not the sword in vain; for he is a minister of God" [Rom.

[11] On this interpretation of "adversary," see Introduction, pp. 17-18.

13:4]. And again, enjoining us to be subject unto him, he sets forth not the fear of God only, but the threatening also of the other party, and his watchful care. "For ye must needs be subject, not only for wrath, but also for conscience sake" [Rom. 13:5]. Because the more irrational, as I have already said, are wont to be sooner corrected by these things, things which appear and are at hand. Wherefore Christ also made mention, not of hell only, but also of a court of justice, and of being dragged thither, and of the prison, and of all the suffering there; by all these means destroying the roots of murder. For he who neither reviles, nor goes to law, nor prolongs enmity, how will he ever commit murder? So that from hence also it is evident, that in the advantage of our neighbor stands our own advantage. For he that agrees with his adversary, will benefit himself much more; becoming free, by his own act, from courts of law, and prisons, and the wretchedness that is there.

14. Let us then be obedient to his sayings; let us not oppose ourselves, nor be contentious; for first of all, even antecedently to their rewards, these injunctions have their pleasure and profit in themselves. And if to the more part they seem to be burdensome, and the trouble which they cause, great; have it in thy mind that thou art doing it for Christ's sake, and the pain will be pleasant. For if we maintain this way of reckoning at all times, we shall experience nothing burdensome, but great will be the pleasure we reap from every quarter; for our toil will no longer seem toil, but by how much it is enhanced, so much the sweeter and pleasanter doth it grow.

When therefore the custom of evil things, and the desire of wealth, keep on bewitching thee; do thou war against them with that mode of thinking which tells us, "Great is the reward we shall receive, for despising the pleasure which is but for a season"; and say to thy soul; "Art thou quite dejected because I defraud thee of pleasure? Nay, be of good cheer, for I am introducing thee into heaven. Thou doest it not for man's sake, but for God's. Be patient therefore a little while, and thou shalt see how great is the gain. Endure for the present life, and thou shalt receive an unspeakable confidence." For if we would thus discourse with our own soul, and not only consider that which is burdensome in virtue, but take account also of the crown that comes thereof, we shall quickly withdraw it from all wickedness.

For if the devil, holding out pleasure for a season, but pain forever, is yet strong, and prevails; seeing our case is just the reverse in these matters, the labor temporary, the pleasure and profit immortal, what plea shall we have, if we follow not virtue after so great encouragement? Why, the object of our labors is enough to set against all, and our clear persuasion that for God's sake we are enduring all this. For if one having the king his debtor, thinks he hath sufficient security for all his life; consider how great will he be, who hath made the gracious and everlasting God a debtor to himself, for good deeds both small and great. Do not then allege to me labors and sweats; for not by the hope only of the things to come, but in another way also, God hath made virtue easy, assisting us everywhere, and putting his hand to our work. And if thou wilt only contribute a little zeal, everything else follows. For to this end he will have thee too to labor a little, even that the victory may be thine also. And just as a king would have his own son present indeed in the array; he would have him shoot with the bow, and show himself, that the trophy may be reckoned his, while he achieves it all himself: even so doth God in our war against the devil: he requires of thee one thing alone, that thou show forth a sincere hatred against that foe. And if thou contribute this to him, he by himself brings all the war to an end. Though thou burn with anger, with desire of riches, with any tyrannical passion whatever; if he see thee only stripping thyself and prepared against it, he comes quickly to thee, and makes all things easy, and sets thee above the flame, as he did those children of old in the Babylonian furnace: for they too carried in with them nought but their good will.

In order then that we also may extinguish all the furnace

of disordered pleasure here, and so escape the hell that is there, let these each day be our counsels, our cares, and our practice, drawing towards us the favor of God, both by our full purpose concerning good works, and by our frequent prayers. For thus even those things which appear insupportable now, will be most easy, and light, and lovely. Because, so long as we are in our passions, we think virtue rugged and morose and arduous, vice desirable and most pleasing; but if we would stand off from these but a little, then both vice will appear abominable and unsightly, and virtue easy, mild, and much to be desired. And this you may learn plainly from those who have done well. Hear, for instance, how of those passions Paul is ashamed, even after his deliverance from them, saying, "For what fruit had ye then in those things, whereof ye are now ashamed?" [Rom. 6:21]. But virtue, even after his labor, he affirms to be light, calling [II Cor. 4:17, 12:10; Rom. 5:3; Gal. 6:17; Col. 1:24] the laboriousness of our affliction momentary and "light," and rejoicing in his sufferings, and glorying in his tribulations, and taking a pride in the marks wherewith he had been branded for Christ's sake.

In order then that we too may establish ourselves in this habit, let us order ourselves each day by what hath been said, and "forgetting those things which are behind, and reaching forth unto those things which are before, let us press on towards the prize of the high calling" [Phil. 3:13, 14]: unto which God grant that we may all attain, by the grace and love towards man of our Lord Jesus Christ, to whom be glory and power for ever and ever. Amen.

Homily XVII

"Ye have heard that it was said to them of old time, thou shalt not commit adultery; but I say unto you, that every one who looketh upon a woman to lust after her, hath committed adultery with her already in his heart." —*Matt. 5:27, 28*

HAVING NOW FINISHED THE former commandment, and having extended it unto the height of self-denial, he, advancing in course and order, proceeds accordingly unto the second, herein too obeying the law.

"And yet," it may be said, "this is not the second, but the third; for neither is the first, 'Thou shalt not kill,' but 'The Lord thy God is one Lord'" [Deut. 6:4; cf. Mark 12:29].

Wherefore it is worth inquiring too, why he did not begin with that. Why was it then? Because, had he begun from thence, he must have enlarged it also, and have brought in himself together with his Father. But it was not as yet time to teach any such thing about himself.

And besides, he was for a while practicing his moral doctrine only, being minded from this first, and from his miracles, to convince the hearers that he was the Son of God. Now, if he had said at once, before he had spoken or done anything, "Ye have heard that it was said to them of old time, 'I am the Lord thy God, and there is none other but me,' but I say unto you, Worship me even as him"; this would have made all regard him as a madman. For if, even after his teaching, and his so great miracles, while not even yet was he saying this openly, they called him possessed with a devil [John 8:48]; had he before all these attempted to say any such thing, what would they not have said? what would they not have thought?

But by keeping back at the proper season his teaching on

these subjects, he was causing that the doctrine should be acceptable to the many. Wherefore now he passed it by quickly, but when he had everywhere established it by his miracles, and by his most excellent teaching, he afterwards unveiled it in words also.[1]

For the present, however, by the manifestation of his miracles, and by the very manner of his teaching, he unfolds it on occasion, gradually and quietly. For his enacting such laws, and such corrections of laws, with authority, would lead on the attentive and understanding hearer, by little and little, unto the word of his doctrine. For it is said, "they were astonished at him, because he taught not as their Scribes" [Matt. 7:28, 29].

2. For beginning from those passions, which most belong to our whole race, anger, I mean, and desire (for it is these chiefly that bear absolute sway within us, and are more natural than the rest); he with great authority, even such as became a legislator, both corrected them, and reduced them to order with all strictness. For he said not that the adulterer merely is punished; but what he had done with respect to the murderer, this he doth here also, punishing even the unchaste look: to teach thee wherein lies what he had more than the scribes. Accordingly, he saith, "He that looketh upon a woman to lust after her hath already committed adultery with her": that is, he who makes it his business to be curious about bright forms, and to hunt for elegant features, and to feast his soul with the sight, and to fasten his eyes on fair countenances.

For he came to set free from all evil deeds not the body only, but the soul too before the body. Thus, because in the heart we receive the grace of the Spirit, he cleanses it out first.

"And how," one may say, "is it possible to be freed from desire?" I answer, first, if we were willing, even this might be deadened, and remain inactive.

In the next place, he doth not here take away desire absol-

[1] On the element of "reserve" in the Sermon on the Mount, cf. Introduction, p. 26.

utely, but that desire which springs up in men from sight. For he that is curious to behold fair countenances, is himself chiefly the enkindler of the furnace of that passion, and makes his own soul a captive, and soon proceeds also to the act.

Thus we see why he said not, "whosoever shall lust to commit adultery," but, "whosoever shall look to lust." And in the case of anger he laid down a certain distinction, saying, "without a cause," and "for nought"; but here not so; rather once for all he took away the desire. Yet surely both are naturally implanted, and both are set in us for our profit; both anger, and desire: the one that we may chastise the evil, and correct those who walk disorderly; the other that we may have children, and that our race may be recruited by such successions.

Why then did he not make a distinction here also? Nay, very great is the distinction which, if thou attend, thou wilt see here also included. For he said not simply, "whosoever shall desire," since it is possible for one to desire even when sitting in the mountains; but, "Whosoever shall look to lust"; that is to say, he who gathers in lust unto himself; he who, when nothing compels him, brings in the wild beast upon his thoughts when they are calm. For this comes no longer of nature, but of self-indulgence. This even the ancient Scripture corrects from the first, saying, "Contemplate not beauty which is another's" [Ecclus. 9:8]. And then, lest any one should say, "what then, if I contemplate, and be not taken captive," he punishes the look, lest confiding in this security thou shouldest some time fall into sin. "What then," one may say, "if I should look, and desire indeed, but do no evil?" Even so thou art set among the adulterers. For the Lawgiver hath pronounced it, and thou must not ask any more questions. For thus looking once, twice, or thrice, thou wilt perhaps have power to refrain; but if thou art continually doing this, and kindling the furnace, thou wilt assuredly be taken; for thy station is not beyond that nature which is common to men. As we then, if we see a child holding a knife, though we do not see him hurt, beat him, and forbid his ever holding it; so

God likewise takes away the unchaste look even before the act, lest at any time thou shouldest fall in act also. For he who hath once kindled the flame, even when the woman whom he hath beheld is absent, is forming by himself continually images of shameful things, and from them often goes on even to the deed. For this cause Christ takes away even that embrace which is in the heart only.

What now can they say, who have those virgin inmates?[2] Why, by the tenor of this law they must be guilty of ten thousand adulteries, daily beholding them with desire. For this cause the blessed Job [Job 31:1] also laid down this law from the beginning, blocking out from himself on all sides this kind of gazing.

For in truth greater is the struggle on beholding, and not possessing the object of fondness: nor is the pleasure so great which we reap from the sight, as the mischief we undergo from increasing this desire; thus making our opponent strong, and giving more scope to the devil, and no longer able to repulse him, now that we have brought him into our inmost parts, and have thrown our mind open unto him. Therefore he saith, "commit no adultery with thine eyes, and thou wilt commit none with thy mind."

For one may indeed behold in another way, sure as are the looks of the chaste; wherefore he did not altogether prohibit our seeing, but that seeing which is accompanied with desire. And if he had not meant this, he would have said simply, "He who looketh on a woman." But now he said not thus, but, "He who looketh to lust," "he who looketh to please his sight."

For not at all to this end did God make thee eyes, that thou shouldest thereby introduce adultery, but that, beholding his creatures, thou shouldest admire the Artificer.

[2] This refers to the *virgines subintroductae* (Greek *syneisaktoi*), unmarried women who lived in spiritual marriage with men, especially with celibate clergy. This dubious practice, widely followed, also in Antioch, and sometimes subject to abuse, was condemned by many church fathers and by several councils, including the Council of Nicaea, whose third canon "stringently" forbade the custom.

Just then as one may feel wrath at random, so may one cast looks at random; that is, when thou doest it for lust. Rather, if thou desirest to look and find pleasure, look at thine own wife, and love her continually; no law forbids that. But if thou art to be curious about the beauties that belong to another, thou art injuring both thy wife by letting thine eyes wander elsewhere, and her on whom thou hast looked, by touching her unlawfully. Since, although thou hast not touched her with the hand, yet hast thou caressed her with thine eyes; for which cause this also is accounted adultery, and before that great penalty draws after it no slight one of its own. For then all within him is filled with disquiet and turmoil, and great is the tempest, and most grievous the pain, and no captive nor person in chains can be worse off than a man in this state of mind. And oftentimes she who hath shot the dart is flown away, while the wound even so remains. Or rather, it is not she who hath shot the dart, but thou gavest thyself the fatal wound, by thine unchaste look. And this I say to free modest women from the charge: since assuredly, should one deck herself out, and invite towards herself the eyes of such as fall in her way; even though she smite not him that meets with her, she incurs the utmost penalty: for she mixed the poison, she prepared the hemlock, even though she did not offer the cup. Or rather, she did also offer the cup, though no one were found to drink it.

3. "Why then doth he not discourse with them also?" it may be said. Because the laws which he appoints are in every case common, although he seem to address himself unto men only. For in discoursing with the head, he makes his admonition common to the whole body also. For woman and man he knows as one living creature, and nowhere distinguishes their kind.

But if thou desirest to hear also his rebuke for them in particular, listen to Isaiah [Isa. 3:16], in many words inveighing against them, and deriding their habit, their aspect, their gait, their trailing garments, their tripping feet, their drooping necks. Hear with him the blessed Paul [I Tim. 2:9; Titus 2:3-5] also, setting many laws for them; and both about garments, and ornaments of gold, and plaiting of hair, and luxurious [I Tim. 5:6] living, and all other such things, vehemently rebuking this sex. And Christ too, by what follows next, obscurely intimated this very same; for when he saith, "pluck out and cut off the eye that offendeth thee," he speaks as indicating his anger against them.

3. Wherefore also he subjoins,

"If thy right eye offend thee, pluck it out, and cast it from thee" [Matt. 5:29].

Thus, lest thou shouldest say, "But what if she be akin to me? what if in any other way she belong to me?" therefore he hath given these injunctions; not discoursing about our limbs; —far from it,—for nowhere doth he say that our flesh is to be blamed for things, but everywhere it is the evil mind that is accused. For it is not the eye that sees, but the mind and the thought.[3] Often, for instance, we being wholly turned elsewhere, our eye sees not those who are present. So that the matter does not entirely depend upon its working. Again, had he been speaking of members of the body, he would not have said it of one eye, nor of the right eye only, but of both. For he who is offended by his right eye, most evidently will incur the same evil by his left also. Why then did he mention the right eye, and add the hand? To show thee that not of limbs is he speaking, but of them who are near unto us. Thus, "If," saith he, "thou so lovest any one, as though he were in stead of a right eye; if thou thinkest him so profitable to thee as to esteem him in the place of a hand, and he hurts thy soul; even these do thou cut off." And see the emphasis; for he saith not, "Withdraw from him," but to show the fullness of the separation, "pluck it out," saith he, "and cast it from thee."

Then, forasmuch as his injunction was sharp, he shows also the gain on either hand, both from the benefits and from the evils, continuing in the metaphor.

[3] This is, at least by implication, an attack on the Gnostic and Manichaean heretics; see our Introduction, p. 10.

"For it is profitable for thee," saith he, "that one of thy members should perish, and not that thy whole body should be cast into hell" [Matt. 5:29, 30].

For while he neither saves himself, nor fails to destroy thee too, what kindness is it for both to sink, whereas if they were separated, one at least might have been preserved?

But why did Paul then, it may be said, choose to become accursed? [Rom. 9:3]. Not on condition of gaining nothing, but with a view to the salvation of others. But in this case the mischief pertains to both. And therefore he said not, "pluck out" only, but also "cast from thee": to receive him again no more, if he continue as he is. For so shalt thou both deliver him from a heavier charge, and free thyself from ruin.

But that thou mayest see yet more clearly the profit of this law; let us, if you please, try what hath been said, in the case of the body itself, by way of supposition. I mean, if choice were given, and thou must either, keeping thine eye, be cast into a pit and perish, or plucking it out, preserve the rest of thy body; wouldest thou not of course accept the latter? It is plain to everyone. For this were not to act as one hating the eye, but as one loving the rest of the body. This same reckoning do thou make with regard to men also and women: that if he who harms thee by his friendship should continue incurable, his being thus cut off will both free thee from all mischief, and he also will himself be delivered from the heavier charges, not having to answer for thy destruction along with his own evil deeds.

Seest thou how full the law is of gentleness and tender care, and that which seems to men in general to be severity, how much love towards man it discloses?

Let them hearken to these things, who hasten to the theatres, and make themselves adulterers every day. For if the law commands to cut off him, whose connexion with us tends to our hurt; what plea can they have, who, by their haunting those places, attract towards them daily those even that have not yet become known to them, and procure to themselves occasions of ruin without number?

For henceforth, he not only forbids us to look unchastely, but having signified the mischief thence ensuing, he even straitens the law as he goes on, commanding to cut off, and dissever, and cast somewhere far away. And all this he ordains, who hath uttered words beyond number about love, that in either way thou mightest learn his providence, and how from every source he seeks thy profit.

4. "Now it hath been said, Whosoever shall put away his wife, let him give her a writing of divorcement [Mark 10:4]. But I say unto you, Whosoever shall put away his wife, saving for the cause of fornication, causeth her to commit adultery; and whosoever marrieth her that is put away, committeth adultery" [Matt. 5:31, 32].

He goes not on to what lies before him, until he have well cleared out the former topics. For, lo, he shows us yet another kind of adultery. And what is this? There was an ancient law made [Deut. 24:1-4], that he who hated his wife, for whatever kind of cause, should not be forbidden to cast her out, and to bring home another instead of her. The law however did not command him simply to do this, but after giving the woman a writing of divorcement, that it might not be in her power to return to him again; that so at least the figure of the marriage might remain.

For if he had not enjoined this, but it were lawful first to cast her out, and take another, then afterwards to take back the former, the confusion was sure to be great, all men continually taking each other's wives; and the matter thenceforth would have been direct adultery. With a view to this, he devised, as no small mitigation, the writing of divorcement.

But these things were done by reason of another, a far greater wickedness; I mean, had he made it necessary to keep in the house her even that was hated, the husband, hating, would have killed her. For such was the race of the Jews. For they who did not spare children, who slew prophets, and "shed blood as water" [Ps. 79:3], much more would they have showed no mercy to women. For this cause he allowed the less, to remove the greater evil. For that this was not a primary law, hear him saying, "Moses wrote these things according to the hardness of your hearts" [Matt. 19:8], that ye might not slay them in the house, but rather put them out. But forasmuch as he had taken away all wrath, having forbidden not murder only, but even the mere feeling of anger, he with ease introduces this law likewise. With this view also he is ever bringing to mind the former words, to signify that his sayings are not contrary to them, but in agreement: that he is enforcing, not overthrowing them; perfecting, not doing them away.

And observe him everywhere addressing his discourse to the man. Thus, "he that putteth away his wife," saith he, "causeth her to commit adultery, and he that marrieth a woman put away, committeth adultery." That is, the former, though he take not another wife, by that act alone hath made himself liable to blame, having made the first an adulteress; the latter again is become an adulterer by taking her who is another's. For tell me not this, "the other hath cast her out"; nay, for when cast out she continues to be the wife of him that expelled her. Then lest he should render the wife more self-willed, by throwing it all upon him who cast her out, he hath shut against her also the doors of him who was afterwards receiving her; in that he saith, "He who marrieth her that is put away committeth adultery"; and so makes the woman chaste even though unwilling, and blocks up altogether her access to all, and suffers her not to give an occasion for jealousy. For she who hath been made aware that she positively must either keep the husband, who was originally allotted to her, or being cast out of that house, not have any other refuge;—she even against her will was compelled to make the best of her consort.

And if he discourse not at all unto her concerning these things, marvel not; for the woman is rather a weak creature. For this cause letting her go, in his threatening against the men he fully corrects her remissness. Just as if any one who had a prodigal child, leaving him, should rebuke those who make him such, and forbid them to have intercourse, or to approach him. And if that be galling, call to mind, I pray thee, his former sayings, on what terms he had blessed his hearers; and thou wilt see that it is very possible and easy. For he that is meek, and a peacemaker, and poor in spirit, and merciful, how shall he cast out his wife? He that is used to reconcile others, how shall he be at variance with her that is his own?

And not thus only, but in another way also he hath lightened the enactment: forasmuch as even for him he leaves one manner of dismissal, when he saith, "Except for the cause of fornication"; since the matter had else come round again to the same issue. For if he had commanded to keep her in the house, though defiling herself with many, he would have made the matter end again in adultery.

Seest thou how these sayings agree with what had gone before? For he who looks not with unchaste eyes upon another woman, will not commit whoredom; and not committing whoredom, he will give no occasion to the husband to cast out his wife.

Therefore, you see, after this he presses the point without reserve, and builds up this fear as a bulwark, urging on the husband the great danger, if he do cast her out, in that he makes himself accountable for her adultery. Thus, lest thou being told, "pluck out the eye," shouldest suppose this to be said even of a wife: he added in good time this corrective, in one way only by giving leave to cast her out, but no otherwise.

5. "Again, ye have heard that it was said to them of old time, Thou shalt not forswear thyself, but shalt perform unto the Lord thine oaths. But I say unto you, swear not at all" [Matt. 5:33, 34].

Why did he go straightway not to theft, but to false witness, passing over that commandment? Because he that steals, doth upon occasion swear also; but he that knows not either swearing or speaking falsehood, much less will he choose to steal. So that by this he hath overthrown the other sin likewise: since falsehood comes of stealing.

But what means, "Thou shalt perform unto the Lord thine

oaths?" [Num. 30:2; Deut. 23:23]. It is this, "thou shalt be true in swearing." "But I say unto you, swear not at all."

Next, to lead them farther away from swearing by God, he saith, "Neither by heaven, for it is God's throne, nor by the earth, for it is the footstool of his feet; nor by Jerusalem, for it is the city of the great King" [Isa. 66:1; Ps. 48:2]: still speaking out of the prophetical writings, and signifying himself not to be opposed to the ancients. This was because they had a custom of swearing by these objects, and he intimates this custom near the end of his Gospel [Matt. 23:16].

But mark, I pray thee, on what ground he magnifies the elements; not from their own nature, but from God's relation to them, such as it had been in condescension declared. For because the tyranny of idolatry was great, that the elements might not be thought worthy of honor for their own sake, he hath assigned this cause, which we have mentioned, which again would pass on to the glory of God. For he neither said, "because heaven is beautiful and great," nor, "because earth is profitable"; but "because the one is God's throne, the other his footstool"; on every side urging them on towards their Lord.

"Neither by thy head," saith he, "because thou canst not make one hair white or black" [Matt. 5:36].

Here again, not as wondering at man, hath he withdrawn him from swearing by his head (for so man himself would be worshipped), but as referring the glory to God, and signifying that thou are not master even of thyself, and of course therefore not of the oaths made by thy head. For if no one would give up his own child to another, much more will not God give up his own work to thee. For though it be thy head, yet is it the property of another; and so far from being master thereof, thou shalt not be able to do with it, no not the least thing of all. For he said not, "Thou canst not make one hair grow"; but, "not so much as change its quality."

"But what," it may be said, "if any one should require an oath, and apply constraint?" Let the fear of God be more powerful than the constraint: since, if thou art to bring forward such excuses, thou wilt keep none of the things which are enjoined.

Yea, for first with respect to thy wife thou wilt say, "what if she be contentious and extravagant"; and then as to the right eye, "what if I love it, and am quite on fire?" and of the unchaste look, "what then, if I cannot help seeing?" and of our anger against a brother, "what if I be hasty, and not able to govern my tongue?" and in general, all his sayings thou mayest on this wise trample under foot. Yet surely with regard to human laws thou darest not in any case use this allegation, nor say, "what then if this or that be the case," but, willing or unwilling, thou receivest what is written.

And besides, thou wilt never have compulsion to undergo at all. For he that hath hearkened unto those former blessings, and hath framed himself to be such as Christ enjoined, will have no such constraint to endure from any, being held in reverence and veneration by all.

"But let your yea, be yea; and your nay, nay: for that which exceedeth these cometh of the evil one" [Matt. 5:37].

What is it then that "exceeds yea" and "nay"? It is the oath, not the perjury. For this latter is quite acknowledged, and no man needs to learn that it is of the evil one; and it is not an excess, but an opposite: whereas an excess means something more, and added over and above: which kind of thing swearing is.

"What then," saith one, "was it of the evil one? and if it was of the evil one, how was it a law?" Well, this same thing thou wilt say concerning the wife also; how is that now accounted adultery, which was before permitted?

What now may one reply to this? That the precepts then uttered had reference to the weakness of them who were receiving the laws; since also to be worshipped with the vapor of sacrifice is very unworthy of God, just as to lisp is unworthy of a philosopher.[4] That kind of thing accordingly was now

[4] Cf. Aristotle *Metaphysics* 985 a.

laid down to be adultery, and swearing to be of the evil one, now that the principles of virtue have advanced. But if these things had been, from the first, laws of the devil, they would not have attained to so great goodness. Yea, for had those not been forerunners in the first place, these which we now have would not have been so easily received. Do not thou then require their excellency now, when their use is past: but then, when the time was calling for them. Or rather, if thou wilt, even now: yea, for now also is their virtue shown: and most of all for the very cause, by reason of which we find fault with them. For their appearing such now, is the greatest commendation of them. For had they not brought us up well, and made us meet for the reception of the greater precepts, they would not have appeared such.

Therefore as the breast, when it hath fulfilled all its part, and is dismissing the child to the more manly diet, after that appears useless; and the parents who before thought it necessary for the babe, now abuse it with ten thousand mockeries (and many even not content with words of abuse, anoint it also with bitter drugs; that when their words have not power to remove the child's unseasonable propensity towards it, the real things may quench their longing): so also Christ saith, that they are of the evil one, not to indicate that the old law is of the devil, but in order that with most exceeding earnestness he might lead them away from their ancient poverty. And to them he saith these things; but with regard to the Jews, who were insensible and persevered in the same ways, he hath anointed their city all round with the terror of captivity, as with some bitter drug, and made it inaccessible. But since not even this had power to restrain them, but they desired to see it again, running to it, just as a child to the breast, he hid it from them altogether; both pulling it down, and leading away the more part of them far from it: as it is with our cattle; many, by shutting out the calves, in time induce them to forego their old familiar use of the milk.

But if the old law had belonged to the devil, it would not

have led people away from idolatry, but rather would have drawn them on and cast them into it; for this did the devil desire. But now we see the opposite effect produced by the old law. And indeed this very thing, the oath, was ordained of old for this cause, that they might not swear by the idols. For "ye shall swear," saith he, "by the true God" [Jer. 4:2]. They were then no small advantages which the law effected, but rather very great. For that they came unto the "strong meat," was the work of its care.

"What then," it may be said, "is not swearing of the evil one?" Yes, indeed it is altogether of the evil one; that is, now, after so high a rule of self-restraint; but then not so.

"But how," one may say, "should the same thing become at one time good, at another time not good?" Nay, I say the very contrary: how could it help becoming good and not good, while all things are crying aloud, that they are so: the arts, the fruits of the earth, and all things else?

See it, for example, taking place first in our own kind. Thus, to be carried, in the earliest age of life, is good, but afterwards pernicious; to eat food that hath been softened in the mouth, in the first scene of our life, is good, but afterwards it is full of disgust; to be fed upon milk and to fly to the breast, is at first profitable and healthful, but tends afterwards to decay and harm. Seest thou how the same actions, by reason of the times, appear good, and again not so? Yea, and to wear the robe of a child is well as long as you are a boy, but contrariwise, when you are become a man, it is disgraceful. Wouldest thou learn of the contrary case too, how to the child again the things of the man are unsuited? Give the boy a man's robe, and great will be the laughter; and greater the danger, he being often upset in walking after that fashion. Allow him to handle public affairs, and to traffic, and sow, and reap, and great again will be the laughter.

And why do I mention these things? when killing, which among all is acknowledged to be an invention of the evil one, killing, I say, having found its proper occasion, caused Phinehas, who committed it, to be honored with the priesthood [Num. 25:7, 8]. For that killing is a work of him whom I just now mentioned, hear what Christ saith; "Ye will do the works of your father; he was a manslayer from the beginning" [John 8:44]. But Phinehas became a manslayer, and "it was counted unto him" (so He speaks) "for righteousness" [Ps. 106:31]: and Abraham again on becoming not a manslayer only, but (which was far worse) the slayer of his child, won more and more approbation. And Peter too wrought a two-fold slaughter, nevertheless what he did was of the Spirit [Acts 5:1-10].

Let us not then examine simply the acts, but the season too, and the causes, and the mind, and the difference of persons, and whatsoever else may accompany them, these let us search out with all exactness: for there is no arriving at the truth otherwise.

And let us be diligent, if we would attain unto the kingdom, to show forth something more than the old commandments; since we cannot otherwise lay hold of the things of heaven. For if we arrive but at the same measure, that of the ancients, we shall stand without that threshold; for "except your righteousness shall exceed the righteousness of the Scribes and Pharisees, ye cannot enter into the kingdom of heaven" [Matt. 5:20].

6. Yet, although so heavy a threat is set down, there are some who so far from overpassing this righteousness, even come short of it; so far from shunning oaths, they even swear falsely; so far from avoiding an unchaste gaze, they even fall into the very act of wickedness. And all the rest of the things which are forbidden, they dare to do, as though past feeling: waiting for one thing only, the day of punishment, and the time when they are to pay the most extreme penalty for their misdoings. And this is the portion of those only who have ended their lives in wickedness. For these have reason to despair, and thenceforth to expect nothing else but punish-

ment; whereas they who are yet here, may have power both to renew the fight and to conquer and be crowned with ease.

Despond not therefore, O man, neither put away thy noble earnestness; for in truth the things are not grievous, which are enjoined. What trouble is it, I pray thee, to shun an oath? What, does it cost any money? Is it sweat and hardship? It is enough to have willed only, and the whole is done.

But if you allege to me thine habit; for this very reason most of all do I say, that thy doing right is easy. For if thou bring thyself to another habit, thou hadst effected all.

Consider, for example, how among the Greeks, in many instances, persons lisping have entirely cured by much practice their halting tongue; while others, who were used to shrug up their shoulders in an unseemly way, and to be continually moving them, by putting a sword over them, have broken themselves of it.

For since you are not persuaded out of the Scriptures, I am compelled to shame you by them that are without. This God also did unto the Jews, when he said, "Go ye forth unto the Isles of Chittim, and send unto Kedar, and know if nations will change their gods; which yet are no gods" [Jer. 2:10, 11]. And to the brutes likewise he sends us oftentimes, saying on this wise, "Go to the ant, thou sluggard, and emulate her ways": and "go forth to the bee" [Prov. 6:6-8].

This therefore I also now say unto you; consider the philosophers of the Greeks; and then ye will know of how great punishment we are worthy, who disobey the laws of God: in that they for seemliness before men have taken exceeding pains, and you bestow not the same diligence, no, not for the things of heaven.

But if thou shouldest reply, "Habit has a wonderful power to beguile even those who are very much in earnest": this I likewise acknowledge; however, there is another thing which I say with it; that as it is powerful to beguile, so also is it easy to be corrected. For if thou wilt set over thyself at home many to watch thee, such as thy servant, thy wife, thy friend, thou wilt easily break off from the bad habits, being hard pressed and closely restrained by all. If thou succeed in doing this for ten days only, thou wilt after that no longer need any further time, but all will be secured to thee, rooted anew in the firmness of the most excellent habit.

When therefore thou art beginning to correct this, though thou shouldest transgress thy law a first, a second, a third, a twentieth time, do not despair, but rise up again, and resume the same diligence, and thou wilt surely prevail.

For perjury surely is no trifling mischief. If to swear is of the evil one, how great the penalty which false swearing will bring! Did ye give praise to what hath been said?[5] Nay, I want not applause, nor tumults, nor noise. One thing only do I wish, that quietly and intelligently listening, you should do what is said. This is the applause, this the panegyric for me. But if thou praisest what I say, but doest not what thou applaudest, greater is the punishment, more aggravated the accusation: and to us it is shame and ridicule. For the things here present are no dramatic spectacle; neither do ye now sit gazing on actors, that ye may merely applaud. This place is a spiritual school. Wherefore also there is but one thing aimed at, duly to perform the things that have been spoken, and to show forth our obedience by our works. For then only shall we have obtained all. Since as things are, to say the truth, we have fairly given up in despair. For I have not ceased giving these admonitions either to those whom I meet in private, or in discourse with you all in common. Yet I see no advantage at all gained, but you are still clinging to the former rude beginnings, which thing is enough to fill the teacher with weariness.

See, for example, Paul himself, hardly bearing it, because his scholars were delaying a long time in their earlier lessons: "For when for the time," saith he, "ye ought to be teachers, ye have need to be taught again which be the first principles of the oracles of God" [Heb. 5:12].

Wherefore we too mourn and lament. And if I see you per-

[5] Cf. Introduction, pp. 23-24.

sisting, I will forbid you for the future to set foot on this sacred threshold, and partake of the immortal mysteries; as we do fornicators and adulterers, and persons charged with murder. Yea, for it is better to offer our accustomed prayers, with two or three, who keep the laws of God, than to sweep together a multitude of transgressors and corrupters of others.

Let me have no rich man, no potentate, puffing at me here, and drawing up his eyebrows; all these things are to me a fable, a shade, a dream. For no one of those who are now rich, will stand up for me there, when I am called to account and accused, as not having thoroughly vindicated the laws of God, with all due earnestness. For this, this ruined even that admirable old man [I Sam. 3:13], though in his own life giving no handle for blame; yet for all that, because he overlooked the treading under foot of God's laws, he was chastised with his children, and paid that grievous penalty. And if, where the absolute authority of nature was so great, he who failed to treat his own children with due firmness endured so grievous a punishment; what indulgence shall we have, freed as we are from that dominion, and yet ruining all by flattery?

In order therefore that ye may not destroy both us and your own selves with us, be persuaded, I entreat you; set very many to watch over you, and call you to account, and so free yourselves from the habit of oaths; that going on orderly from thence, ye may both with all facility succeed in attaining unto all other virtue, and may enjoy the good things to come; which God grant that we may all win, by the grace and love towards man of our Lord Jesus Christ, to whom be glory and might now and always, even for ever and ever. Amen.

Homily XVIII

"Ye have heard that it hath been said, an eye for an eye and a tooth for a tooth. But I say unto you, that ye resist not the evil: but whosoever shall smite thee on the right cheek, turn to him the other also. And if any man will sue thee at the law, and take away thy coat, let him have thy cloak also." —*Matt. 5:38-40*

SEEST THOU THAT IT WAS NOT of an eye that he was speaking before, when he made the law to pluck out the offending eye, but of him who by his friendship is harming us, and casting us into the gulf of destruction? For he who in this place uses so great strength of expression, and who, not even when another is plucking out your eye, permits you to strike out his; how should he have made it a law to strike out one's own?

But if any one accuses the ancient law[1] because it commands such retaliation, he seems to me very unskillful in the wisdom that becomes a legislator, and ignorant of the virtue of opportunities, and the gain of condescension. For if he considered who were the hearers of these sayings, and how they were disposed, and when they received this code of laws, he will thoroughly admit the wisdom of the Lawgiver, and will see that it is one and the same, who made both those laws and these, and who wrote each of them exceeding profitably, and in its due season. Yes, for if at the beginning he had introduced these high and most weighty commandments, men would not have received either these, or the others; but now ordaining them severally in their due time, he hath by the two corrected the whole world.

[1] Cf. Introduction, pp. 11-12.

And besides, he commanded this, not that we might strike out one another's eyes, but that we might keep our hands to ourselves. For the threat of suffering hath effectually restrained our inclination to be doing.

And thus in fact he is silently dropping seed of much self-restraint, at least in that he commands to retaliate with just the same acts. Yet surely he that began such transgression were worthy of a greater punishment, and this the abstract nature of justice demands. But forasmuch as he was minded to mingle mercy also with justice, he condemns him whose offenses were very great to a punishment less than his desert: teaching us even while we suffer to show forth great consideration.

Having therefore mentioned the ancient law, and recognized it all, he signifies again, that it is not our brother who hath done these deeds, but the evil one. For this cause he hath also subjoined, "But I say unto you, that ye resist not the evil one." He did not say, "resist not your brother," but "the evil one," signifying that on his motion men dare so to act; and in this way relaxing and secretly removing most of our anger against the aggressor, by transferring the blame to another.

"What then?" it is said, "ought we not to resist the evil one?" Indeed we ought, but not in this way, but as he hath commanded, by giving one's self up to suffer wrongfully; for thus shalt thou prevail over him. For one fire is not quenched by another, but fire by water. And to show thee that even under the old law he that suffered rather prevails, that he it is who wins the crown; examine just what is done, and thou wilt see that his advantage is great. For as he that hath begun with unjust acts, will have himself destroyed the eyes of both, his neighbor's and his own (wherefore also he is justly hated of all, and ten thousand accusations are aimed at him): so he that hath been injured, even after his equal retaliation, will have done nothing horrible. Wherefore also he hath many to sympathize with him, as being clear from that offense even after he hath retaliated. And though the calamity be equal to both parties, yet the sentence passed on it is not equal, either with God, or with men. It should seem then, that neither is the calamity equal in the end.

Now whereas at the beginning he said, "he that is angry with his brother without a cause," and "he that calleth him fool shall be in danger of hell fire," here he requires yet more entire self-restraint, commanding him that suffers ill not merely to be quiet, but even to be more exceedingly earnest in his turn, by offering the other cheek.

And this he saith, not as legislating about such a blow as this only, but as teaching also what forbearance we should practise in all our other trials. For just as when he saith, "whoso calleth his brother fool, is in danger of hell," he speaks not of this word only, but also of all reviling; even so here also he is making a law, not so much for our bearing it manfully, when smitten, as that we should be undisturbed, whatever we suffer. Because of this he both there singled out the extremest insult, and here hath set down that which seems to be of all blows most opprobrious, the blow on the cheek, so full of all insolence. And he commands this as having regard both of him that strikes and of him that is stricken. Since both he that is insulted will not think that he suffers any harm, being thus framed to self-restraint (nay, he will not even have any sense of the insult, as striving rather for a prize than as receiving a blow); and he that is offering the affront will be made ashamed, and not add a second blow, though he be fiercer than any wild beast, yea, rather will condemn himself heartily for the former. For nothing so restrains the wrong doers, as when the injured bear what is done with gentleness. And it not only restrains them from rushing onward, but works upon them also to repent for what has gone before, and in wonder at such forbearance to draw back. And it makes them more our own, and causes them to be slaves, not merely friends, instead of haters and enemies; even as avenging one's self does just the contrary: for it both disgraces each of the two, and makes them worse, and their anger it heightens into a greater flame; yea, often no less than death itself is the end of it, going on from bad to worse. Wherefore he not only forbade thee to be angry when smitten, but even enjoined thee to satiate the other's desire, that so neither may the former blow appear to have befallen thee against thy will. For thus, lost as he may be to shame, thou wilt be able to smite him with a mortal blow, rather than if thou hadst smitten him with thine hand; or if his shamelessness be still greater, thou wilt make him gentle in proportion.

2. "And if any man will sue thee at the law, and take away thy coat, let him have thy cloak also" [Matt. 5:40].

For not in the matter of blows only, but of our goods also, he would have such forbearance exhibited. Wherefore he again employs the same strong figure. That is, as in the other case he commands to overcome in suffering, so here again, by allowing ourselves to be deprived of more than the wrong doer expected. However, he did not put it so merely, but with something to enhance it: not saying, "give thy cloak to him that asketh," but "to him that would sue thee at the law," that is, "if he drag thee into court, and give thee trouble."

And just as, after he had bidden not to call another fool, nor to be angry without cause, he went on and required more, in that he commanded to offer the right cheek also; even so here, having said, "Agree with thine adversary," he again amplifies the precept. For now he orders us not only to give what the other would have, but even to show forth a greater liberality.

"What then!" one may say, "am I to go about naked?" We should not be naked, if we obeyed these sayings with exactness; rather more abundantly than any should we be clothed. For first, no one would attack men of this disposition; and next, if there chanced to be anyone so savage and ungentle, as to proceed even so far, yet many more would be found to clothe him, who acted with such self-denial, not with garments only, but even with their own flesh, if it were possible.

Further: even though one were of necessity to go about

naked on account of this sort of self-denial, neither so were it any disgrace. Since Adam too was "naked" [Gen. 2:25] in Paradise, "and was not ashamed"; and Isaiah was "naked, and barefoot," and more glorious than all the Jews [Isa. 20:2, 3]; and Joseph [Gen. 39:12] also, when he stripped himself, did then more than ever shine forth. For to be thus naked is no evil, but to be so clad, as we now are, with costly garments, this is both disgraceful and ridiculous. For this cause, you see, those had praise of God, but these he blames, both by prophets and by apostles.

Let us not therefore suppose his injunctions impossible. Nay, for besides their expediency, they are very easy, if we are sober-minded; and the profit of them is so great as to be an exceeding help, not to ourselves only, but to those also who are using us despitefully. And in this chiefly stands their excellence, that while they induce us to suffer wrong, they by the same means teach them also that do the wrong to control themselves. For while he on his part thinks it a great thing to take what belongs to others, but thou signifiest to him, that to thee it is easy to give even what he doth not ask: while thou bringest in liberality for a counterpoise to his meanness, and a wise moderation to his covetousness: consider what a lesson he will get, being taught not by sayings, but by actual deeds, to scorn vice and to seek after virtue.

For God will have us profitable not to ourselves alone, but to all our neighbors as well. Now if thou givest, and abstainest from suing, thou hast sought thine own advantage only; but if thou give him some other thing, thou hast made him too better, and so sent him away. Of this nature is salt, which is what he would have them to be; seeing it both recruits itself, and keeps all other bodies with which it may associate: of this nature is light; for it shows objects both to a man's self and to all others. Forasmuch then as he hath set thee in the rank of these things, help thou likewise him who is sitting in darkness, and teach him that neither before did he take anything by force: persuade him that he hath done no despite.

Yea, for thus thou thyself also wilt be had in more respect and reverence, if thou signify that thou gavest freely and wert not robbed. Make therefore his sin, through thy moderation, an instance of thine own bounty.

3. And if thou think this a great thing, wait, and thou wilt see clearly, that neither yet hast thou attained to perfection. For not even here doth he stop with thee, who is laying down the laws of patient endurance, but he proceeds even further, thus saying,

"If any one shall compel thee to go one mile, go with him twain" [Matt. 5:41].

Seest thou the height of self-denial? in this at least, that after giving thy coat, and thy cloak, not even if thine enemy should wish to use thy naked body for hardships and labors, not even so (saith he), must thou forbid him. For he would have us possess all things in common, both our bodies and our goods, as with them that are in need, so with them that insult us: for the latter comes of manliness, the former of mercifulness.

Because of this, he said, "If any one shall compel thee to go one mile, go with him twain": again leading thee higher up, and commanding thee to show forth the same kind of ambition.

For if the things of which he spake at the beginning, being far less than these, have so great blessings pronounced on them; consider what sort of portion awaits them, who duly perform these, and what they become even before their rewards, in a human and passible body winning entire freedom from passion. Since when neither insult, nor blows, nor the spoiling of their property, galls them; while they give way to no such thing, but rather add in large measure to their endurance; reflect what kind of training their soul is undergoing.

On this account then, as in regard of blows, as in regard of our goods, so in this case also, he hath bidden us act. "For why," saith he, "do I mention insult, and property? Though he should want to make use of thy very own limbs for toil and weary work, and this unjustly, do thou again conquer and overpass his unjust desire."

For "to compel" is this, to drag unjustly and without any reason, and by way of despite. Nevertheless, for this also be thou ready in thy station, so as to suffer more than the other would fain do to thee.

"Give to him that asketh thee, and from him that would borrow of thee, turn not thou away" [Matt. 5:42].

These last are less than what went before; but marvel not, for this he is ever wont to do, mingling the small with the great. And if these be little in comparison with those, let them hearken, who take the goods of others, who distribute their own among harlots, and kindle to themselves a double fire, both by the unrighteous income, and by the pernicious outlay.

But by "borrowing," here, he means not the compact with usury, but the use merely. And elsewhere he even amplifies it, saying that we should give to them, from whom we do not expect to receive [Luke 6:35].

4. "Ye have heard that it hath been said, thou shalt love thy neighbor, and hate thine enemy. But I say unto you, love your enemies, and pray for them which despitefully use you: bless them that curse you, do good to them that hate you. That ye may become like your Father which is in heaven; for he maketh his sun to rise on the evil and on the good, and sendeth rain on the just and on the unjust" [Luke 6:27, 28; Matt. 5:43-45].

See how he hath set the highest pinnacle on our good deeds. For this is why he teaches not only to endure a blow, but to offer the right cheek also; not only to add the cloak to the coat, but to travel also two miles with him who compels thee to go one; in order that thou mightest receive with all facility that which is much more than these. "But what," one may say, "is more than these?" Not even to count as an enemy him who is doing these things: or rather even somewhat else more than this. For he said not, "do not hate," but "love"; he said not, "do not injure," but "do good."

And if anyone should examine accurately, he will see that even to these things somewhat is added, much greater than they are. For neither did he simply command to love, but to pray.

Seest thou how many steps he hath ascended, and how he hath set us on the very summit of virtue? Nay, mark it, numbering from the beginning. A first step is, not to begin with injustice; a second, after he hath begun, to vindicate one's self by equal retaliation; a third, not to do unto him that is vexing us the same that one hath suffered, but to be quiet; a fourth, even to give one's self up to suffer wrongfully; a fifth, to give up yet more than the other, who did the wrong, wishes; a sixth, not to hate him who hath done so; a seventh, even to love him; an eighth, to do him good also; a ninth, to entreat God himself on his behalf. Seest thou, what height of self-command? Wherefore glorious too, as we see, is the reward which it hath. That is, because the thing enjoined was great, and needed a fervent soul, and much earnestness, he appoints for it also such a reward, as for none of the former. For he makes not mention here of earth, as with respect to the meek; nor of comfort and mercy, as with regard to the mourners and the merciful; nor of the kingdom of heaven; but of that which was more thrilling than all; our becoming like God, in such wise as men might become so. For he saith, "That ye may become like unto your Father which is in heaven."

And observe, I pray thee, how neither in this place, nor in the preceding parts, doth he call him his own Father, but in that instance, "God," and "a great King," when he was discoursing about oaths, and here, "their Father." And this he doth, as reserving for the proper season what he had to say touching these points.

5. Then, bringing the likeness yet closer, he saith,

"Because he maketh his sun to rise on the evil and on the good, and sendeth rain upon just and unjust" [Matt. 5:45].

"For he too, so far from hating," so he speaks, "even pours benefits on those that insult him." Yet surely in no respect is the case parallel, not only because of the surpassing nature of his benefits, but also by reason of the excellence of his dignity. For thou indeed art despised by thy fellow-slave, but he by his slave, who hath also received ten thousand benefits from him: and thou indeed givest words, in praying for him, but he, deeds, very great and marvellous, kindling the sun, and giving the annual showers. "Nevertheless, even so I grant thee to be mine equal, in such wise as it is possible for a man so to be."

Hate not then the man that doeth thee wrong, who is procuring thee such good things, and bringing thee to so great honor. Curse not him that uses thee despitefully; for so hast thou undergone the labor, but art deprived of the fruit; thou wilt bear the loss, but lose the reward; which is of the utmost folly, having borne the more grievous, not to bear what is less than it. "But how," saith one, "is it possible for this to take place?" Having seen God become man, and descend so far, and suffer so much for thy sake, dost thou still inquire and doubt, how it is possible to forgive thy fellow-servants their injuriousness? Hearest thou not him on the cross saying, "Forgive them, for they know not what they do" [Luke 23:34]? Hearest thou not Paul, when he saith, "He who is gone up on high, and is sitting on the right hand intercedeth for us" [Rom. 8:34]? Seest thou not that even after the cross, and after he had been received up, he sent the apostles unto the Jews that had slain him, to bring them his ten thousand blessings, and this, though they were to suffer ten thousand terrors at their hands?

6. But hast thou been greatly wronged? Nay, what hast thou endured like thy Lord, bound, beaten with whips, with rods, spit upon by servants, enduring death, and that death, which is of all deaths the most shameful, after ten thousand favors shown? And even if thou hast been greatly wronged, for this very cause most of all do thou do him good, that thou mayest both make thine own crown more glorious, and set

thy brother free from the worst infirmity. For so too the physicians, when they are kicked, and shamefully handled by the insane, then most of all pity them, and take measures for their perfect cure, knowing that the insult comes of the extremity of their disease. Now I bid thee too have the same mind touching them that are plotting against thee, and do thou so treat them that are injuring thee. For it is they above all that are diseased, it is they who are undergoing all the violence. Deliver him then from this grievous contumely, and grant him to let go his anger, and set him free from that grievous demon, wrath. Yea, for if we see persons possessed by devils, we weep for them; we do not seek to be ourselves also possessed.

Now let us do this too likewise with respect to them that are angry; for in truth the enraged are like the possessed; yea rather, are more wretched than they, being mad with consciousness of it. Wherefore also their frenzy is without excuse. Trample not then on the fallen, but rather pity him. For so, should we see any one troubled with bile, blinded and giddy, and straining to cast up this evil humor, we stretch forth a hand, and continue to support him through his struggles, and though we stain our garments, we regard it not, but seek one thing only, how we may set him free from this grievous distress. This then let us do with respect to the angry also, and continue to bear them up when vomiting and struggling; nor let him go, until he put from him all the bitterness. And then shall he feel toward thee the greatest thankfulness; when he is at rest, then he will know clearly from how great trouble thou hast released him.

But why do I speak of the thanks from him? for God will straightway crown thee, and will requite thee with ten thousand honors, because thou hast freed thy brother from a grievous disease; and that brother too will honor thee as a master, ever reverencing thy forbearance.

Seest thou not the women that are in travail, how they bite those that stand by, and they are not pained? or rather they are pained, but bear it bravely, and sympathize with them who are in sorrow and are torn by those pangs. These do thou too emulate, and prove not softer than women. For after these women have brought forth (for these men are more feeble minded than women), then they will know thee to be a man in comparison.

And if the things enjoined be grievous, consider that to this end Christ came, that he might implant these things in our mind, that he might render us profitable both to enemies and friends. Wherefore also he commands us to have a care of both these: of our brethren, when he saith, "If thou bring thy gift"; of our enemies, when he makes a law both to love them, and to pray for them.

7. And not only from the example they have in God, doth he urge them on to this, but also from the contrary.

"For if ye love those," saith he, "that love you, what reward have ye? do not even the publicans the same?" [Matt. 5:46]. This Paul also saith, "Ye have not yet resisted unto blood, striving against sin" [Heb. 12:4]. If then thou doest these things, thou hast taken thy stand with God; but if thou forsakest them, with the publicans. Seest thou how that the interval between the commandments is not so great as the difference between the persons? Let us not therefore infer this, "the injunction is hard"; but let us consider also the reward, and think whom we are like, if we duly perform it, and to whom equal, if we wander from it.

Thus then to our brother he commands us to be reconciled, and not to desist till we have removed the enmity: but when he is discoursing of persons generally, he subjects us no longer to this necessity, but requires only what is on our part; in this way also making the law easy. For inasmuch as he had said, "They persecuted the prophets which were before you"; lest on occasion of those very words they should be unfavorably disposed towards them, he bids them not only to endure such as do so, but even to love them.

8. Seest thou how he pulls up by the roots wrath, and sen-

sual lusts, as well as that of riches, that of glory, all that belongs to this life? For this he had done indeed from the first, but much more now. For the poor, and the meek, and the mourner, empties himself of his anger; the just and the merciful, of the lust of riches; the pure in heart is delivered from wicked lusts; he that is persecuted and suffers insults, and is evil spoken of, is practising of course entire contempt of things present, and is clear from pride and vainglory.

Having therefore loosed the hearer from these bonds, and having anointed him for the conflicts, again in another way he roots up these passions, and with increased strictness. For having begun by anger, and having cut out on every side the sinews of this passion; having said, "he that is angry with his brother," and "he that calleth fool," or "Raca," let him be punished: and "he that is offering his gift, let him not approach the table until he have done away the enmity"; and "he that hath an adversary, before he see the tribunal, let him make the enemy a friend": he makes a transition to lust again, and saith, "he that beholds with unchaste eyes, let him be punished as an adulterer"; whoso is offended by an unchaste woman, or by a man, or by any other of those belonging to him, let him cut off all these; "he that hath a woman by law of marriage, let him never cast her out, and look to another." For hereby he hath pulled up the roots of wicked lust. Then after this he restrains the love of riches, commanding neither to swear, nor to lie, nor to keep hold of the very cloak with which one may chance to be clad, but rather to give up one's coat too, to him who would have it, and one's bodily services; completely and more than completely taking away our longing for riches. Then after all these things, and the varied garland of these commandments, he goes on to say "pray for them which despitefully use you": leading us up to the very highest summit of self-control.

For as being meek is not so much as to take smiting, nor being merciful, as to give one's coat also together with one's cloak, nor being just, as to bear injury, nor being a peacemaker, as to follow even when smitten and compelled; so also to suffer persecution is not so much as to bless when persecuted. Seest thou how by degrees he leads us up into the very arches of heaven?

9. What then can we deserve, who are commanded to emulate God, and are perhaps in a way not so much as to equal the publicans? For if "to love them that love us" be the part of publicans, sinners, and heathens: when we do not even this (and we do it not, so long as we envy our brethren who are in honor), what penalty shall we not incur, commanded as we are to surpass the scribes, and taking our place below the heathens? How then shall we behold the kingdom, I pray thee? How shall we set foot on that holy threshold, who are not surpassing even the publicans? For he covertly signified, when he said, "Do not even the publicans the same?"

And this thing most especially we may admire in his teaching, that while in each instance he sets down with very great fullness the prizes of the conflicts; such as "to see God," and "to inherit the kingdom of heaven," and "to become sons of God," and "like God," and "to obtain mercy," and "to be comforted," and "the great reward": if anywhere he must needs mention things grievous, he doth this in a subdued tone. Thus in the first place, the name of hell he hath set down once only in so many sentences; and in some other instances too, it is with reserve that he corrects the hearer, and as though he were managing his discourse rather in the way of shaming than threatening him; where he saith, "do not even the publicans the same?" and, "if the salt have lost its savor"; and, "he shall be called least in the kingdom of heaven."

And there are places where he puts down the sin itself by way of punishment, leaving to the hearer to infer the grievousness of the punishment: as when he saith, "he hath committed adultery with her in his heart"; and, "he that putteth away causeth her to commit adultery"; and, "that which is more than these is of the evil one." For to them that have understanding, instead of the mention of the punishment, the very greatness of the sin is sufficient for correction.

Wherefore also he here brings forward the heathens and the publicans, by the quality of the person putting the disciple to shame. Which Paul too did, saying, "Sorrow not, even as the rest which have no hope" [I Thess. 4:13]; and, "Even as the Gentiles which know not God" [I Thess. 4:5].

And to signify that he requires nothing very overpowering, but a little more than was accustomed, he saith,

"Do not even the Gentiles the same?"

Yet nevertheless he stops not the discourse at this, but makes it end with his rewards, and those good hopes, saying,

"Be ye therefore perfect, as your Heavenly Father" [Matt. 5:48].

And he intersperses everywhere abundantly the name of the heavens, by the very place thoroughly elevating their minds. For as yet, I know not how, they were somewhat weak and dull.

10. Let us then, bearing in mind all the things which have been said, show forth great love even towards our enemies; and let us cast away that ridiculous custom, to which many of the more thoughtless give way, waiting for those that meet them to address them first.[2] Towards that which hath a great blessing, they have no zeal; but what is ridiculous, that they follow after.

Wherefore now dost thou not address him first? "Because he is waiting for this," is the reply. Nay, for this very reason most of all thou shouldest have sprung forward to him, that thou mightest win the crown. "No," saith he, "since this was his object." And what can be worse than this folly? That is, "Because this," saith he, "was his object;—to become procurer of a reward for me;—I will not put my hand to what he has thus suggested." Now if he first address thee, thou gainest nothing, even though thou accost him. But if thou be first to

[2] An interesting commentary on the collision between Christian views of personal relationship and Near Eastern etiquette.

spring forward and speak to him, thou hast made thyself profit of his pride, and hast gathered in a manner abundant fruit from his obstinacy. What is it then but the utmost folly, when we are to reap so large fruit from bare words, to give up the gain; and condemning him, to stumble at the very same thing? For if thou blamest him for this, that he first waits to be addressed by another, wherefore dost thou emulate that same thing which thou accusest? That which thou saidst was evil, why art thou to imitate the same as good? Seest thou how that nothing is more senseless than a man who associates with wickedness? Wherefore, I entreat, let us flee this evil and ridiculous practice. Yea, for ten thousand friendships hath this pestilence overthrown, many enmities hath it wrought.

For this cause then let us anticipate them. Since we who are commanded to take blows, and be compelled to journey, and to be stripped by enemies, and to bear it; what kind of indulgence should we deserve, exhibiting so great contentiousness in a mere formal address?

11. "Why," saith one, "we are despised and spit upon, the moment we have given him up this." And in order that man may not despise thee, dost thou offend God? And in order that thy frenzied fellow-servant may not despise thee, dost thou despise the Lord, who hath bestowed on thee benefits so great? Nay, if it be amiss that thine equal should despise thee, how much more that thou shouldest despise the God that made thee?

And together with this, consider that other point also; that when he despises thee, he is at that very moment employed in procuring to thee a greater reward. Since for God's sake thou submittest to it, because thou hast hearkened to his laws. And this, to what kind of honor is it not equal? to how many diadems? Be it my portion both to be insulted and despised for God's sake, rather than to be honored by all kings; for nothing, nothing is equal to this glory.

This then let us pursue, in such wise as himself commanded, and making no account of the things of men, but showing forth perfect self-restraint in all things, let us so direct our own lives. For so even now, from this very time, we shall enjoy the good things of the heavens, and of the crowns that are there, walking as angels among men, going about in the earth like the angelic powers, and abiding apart from all lust, from all turmoil.

And together with all these things we shall receive also the unutterable blessings: unto which may we all attain, by the grace and love towards man of our Lord Jesus Christ, to whom be glory, and power, and worship, with the unoriginate Father, and the Holy and Good Spirit, now and always, even forever and ever. Amen.

Homily XIX

"Take heed that ye do not your alms before men, to be seen of them."
—Matt. 6:1

HE ROOTS OUT IN WHAT REMAINS the most tyrannical passion of all, the rage and madness with respect to vainglory, which springs up in them that do right. For at first he had not at all discoursed about it; it being indeed superfluous, before he had persuaded them to do any of the things which they ought, to teach in which way they should practise and pursue them.

But after he had led them on to self-command, then he proceeds to purge away also the alloy which secretly subsists with it. For this disease is by no means of random birth; but when we have duly performed many of the commandments.

It behooved therefore first to implant virtue, and then to remove the passion which mars its fruit.

And see with what he begins, with fasting, and prayer, and almsgiving: for in these good deeds most especially it is wont to make its haunt. The Pharisee, for instance, was hereby puffed up, who saith, "I fast twice a week, I give tithes of my substance" [Luke 18:12]. And he was vainglorious too in his very prayer, making it for display. For since there was no one else present, he pointed himself out to the publican, saying, "I am not as the rest of men, nor even as this publican" [Luke 18:11].

And mark how Christ began, as though he were speaking of some wild beast, hard to catch, and crafty to deceive him who was not very watchful. Thus, "take heed," saith he, "as to your alms." So Paul also speaks to the Philippians; "Beware of dogs" [Phil. 3:2]. And with reason, for the evil beast comes in upon us secretly, and without noise puffs all away, and unobservedly carries out all that is within.

Forasmuch then as he had made much discourse about almsgiving, and brought forward God, "Who maketh his sun to rise on the evil and the good" [Matt. 5:45], and by motives from all quarters had urged them on to this, and had persuaded them to exult in the abundance of their giving; he finishes by taking away also all things that encumber this fair olive tree. For which same cause he saith, "Take heed that ye do not your alms before men," for that which was before mentioned, is "God's" almsgiving.

2. And when he had said, "not to do it before men," he added, "to be seen of them." And though it seems as if the same thing were said a second time, yet if any one give particular attention, it is not the same thing, but one is different from the other; and it hath great security, and unspeakable care and tenderness. For it may be, both that one doing alms before men may not do it to be seen of them, and again that one not doing it before men may do it to be seen of them. Wherefore it is not simply the thing, but the intent, which he both punishes and rewards. And unless such exactness were employed, this would make many more backward about the giving of alms, because it is not on every occasion altogether possible to do it secretly. For this cause, setting thee free from this restraint, he defines both the penalty and the reward not by the result of the action, but by the intention of the doer.

That is, that thou mayest not say, "What? am I then the worse, should another see?"—"it is not this," saith he, "that I am seeking, but the mind that is in thee, and the tone of what thou doest." For his will is to bring our soul altogether into frame, and to deliver it from every disease. Now having, as you see, forbidden men's acting for display, and having taught them the penalty thence ensuing, namely, to do it vainly, and for nought, he again rouses their spirits by putting them in mind of the Father, and of heaven, that not by the loss alone he might sting them, but also shame them by the recollection of him who gave them being.

"For ye have no reward," saith he, "with your Father which is in heaven" [Matt. 6:1].

Nor even at this did he stop, but proceeds yet further, by other motives also increasing their disgust. For as above he set forth publicans and heathens, by the quality of the person shaming their imitators, so also in this place the hypocrites.

"Therefore when thou doest thine alms," saith he, "do not sound a trumpet before thee, as the hypocrites do" [Matt. 6:2].

Not that they had trumpets, but he means to display the greatness of their frenzy, by the use of this figure of speech, deriding and making a show of them hereby.

And well hath he called them "hypocrites" for the mask was of mercy, but the spirit of cruelty and inhumanity. For they do it, not because they pity their neighbors, but that they themselves may enjoy credit; and this came of the utmost cruelty; while another was perishing with hunger, to be seeking vainglory, and not putting an end to his suffering.

It is not then the giving alms which is required, but the giving as one ought, the giving for such and such an end.

Having then amply derided those men, and having handled them so, that the hearer should be even ashamed of them, he again corrects thoroughly the mind which is so distempered: and having said how we ought not to act, he signifies on the other hand how we ought to act. How then ought we to do our alms?

"Let not thy left hand know," saith he, "what thy right hand doeth" [Matt. 6:3].

Here again his enigmatical meaning is not of the hands, but he hath put the thing hyperbolically.[1] As thus: "If it can be," saith he, "for thyself not to know it, let this be the object of thine endeavor; that, if it were possible, it may be concealed from the very hands that minister." It is not, as some say, that

[1] Cf. Introduction, p. 27.

we should hide it from wrong-headed men, for he hath here commanded that it should be concealed from all.

And then the reward too; consider how great it is. For after he had spoken of the punishment from the one, he points out also the honor derived from the other; from either side urging them, and leading them on to high lessons. Yea, for he is persuading them to know that God is everywhere present, and that not by our present life are our interests limited, but a yet more awful tribunal will receive us when we go hence, and the account of all our doings, and honors, and punishments: and that no one will be hid in doing anything either great or small, though he seem to be hid from men. For all this did he darkly signify, when he said,

"Thy Father which seeth in secret shall reward thee openly" [Matt. 6:4].

Setting for him a great and august assemblage of spectators, and what he desires, that very thing bestowing on him in great abundance. "For what," saith he, "dost thou wish? is it not to have some to be spectators of what is going on? Behold then, thou hast some; not angels, nor archangels, but the God of all." And if thou desire to have men also as spectators, neither of this desire doth he deprive thee at the fitting season, but rather in greater abundance affords it unto thee. For, if thou shouldest now make a display, thou wilt be able to make it to ten only, or twenty, or (we will say) a hundred persons: but if thou take pains to lie hid now, God himself will then proclaim thee in the presence of the whole universe. Wherefore above all, if thou wilt have men see thy good deeds, hide them now, that then all may look on them with the more honor, God making them manifest, and extolling them, and proclaiming them before all. Again, whereas now they that behold will rather condemn thee as vainglorious; when they see thee crowned, so far from condemning, they will even admire thee, all of them. When therefore by waiting a little, thou mayest both receive a reward, and reap greater admiration; consider what folly it is to cast thyself out of both these; and while thou art seeking thy reward from God, and while God is beholding, to summon men for the display of what is going on. Why, if display must be made of our love, to our Father above all should we make it; and this most especially, when our Father hath the power both to crown and to punish.

And let me add, even were there no penalty, it were not meet for him who desires glory, to let go this our theatre, and take in exchange that of men. For who is there so wretched, as that when the king was hastening to come and see his achievements, he would let him go, and make up his assembly of spectators of poor men and beggars? For this cause then, he not only commands to make no display, but even to take pains to be concealed: it not being at all the same, not to strive for publicity, and to strive for concealment.

3. "And when ye pray," saith he, "ye shall not be as the hypocrites, for they love to pray standing in the synagogues, and in the corners of the streets. Verily I say unto you, they have their reward" [Matt. 6:5].

"But thou, when thou prayest, enter into thy closet, and when thou hast shut thy door, pray to thy Father which is in secret" [Matt. 6:6].

These too again he calls "hypocrites," and very fitly;[2] for while they are feigning to pray to God, they are looking round after men: wearing the garb not of suppliants, but of ridiculous persons. For he, who is to do a suppliant's office, letting go all other, looks to him alone, who hath power to grant his request. But if thou leave this one, and go about wandering and casting around thine eyes everywhere, thou wilt depart with empty hands. For this was thine own will. Wherefore he said not, "such shall not receive a reward," but, "they have it out": that is, they shall indeed receive one, but from those of whom they themselves desire to have it. For God wills not this: he rather for his part was willing to bestow on men the recompense that comes from himself; but they seeking that

[2] The word "hypocrite" originally meant "playactor" and may still carry some of that connotation here in Matt. 6:5.

which is from men, can be no longer justly entitled to receive from him, for whom they have done nothing.

But mark, I pray thee, the lovingkindness of God, in that he promises to bestow on us a reward, even for those good things which we ask of him.

Having then discredited them, who order not this duty as they ought, both from the place and from their disposition of mind, and having shown that they are very ridiculous: he introduces the best manner of prayer, and again gives the reward, saying, "Enter into thy closet."

"What then," it may be said, "ought we not to pray in church?" Indeed we ought by all means, but in such a spirit as this. Because everywhere God seeks the intention of all that is done. Since even if thou shouldest enter into thy closet, and having shut the door, shouldest do it for display, the doors will do thee no good.

It is worth observing in this case also, how exact the definition, which he made when he said, "That they may appear unto men." So that even if thou shut the doors, this he desires thee duly to perform, rather than the shutting of the doors, even to shut the doors of the mind. For as in everything it is good to be freed from vainglory, so most especially in prayer. For if even without this, we wander and are distracted, when shall we attend unto the things which we are saying, should we enter in having this disease also? And if we who pray and beseech attend not, how do we expect God to attend?

4. But yet some there are, who after such and so earnest charges, behave themselves so unseemly in prayer, that even when their person is concealed, they make themselves manifest to all by their voice, crying out disorderly, and rendering themselves objects of ridicule both by gesture and voice. Seest thou not that even in a market place, should anyone come up doing like this, and begging clamorously, he will drive away him whom he is petitioning; but if quietly, and with the proper gesture, then he rather wins over him that can grant the favor?

Let us not then make our prayer by the gesture of our body,

nor by the loudness of our voice, but by the earnestness of our mind: neither with noise and clamor and for display, so as even to disturb those that are near us, but with all modesty, and with contrition in the mind, and with inward tears.

But art thou pained in mind, and canst not help crying aloud? yet surely it is the part of one exceedingly pained to pray and entreat even as I have said. Since Moses too was pained, and prayed in this way and was heard; for this cause also God said unto him, "Wherefore criest thou unto me" [Exod. 14:15]. And Hannah too again, her voice not being heard, accomplished all she wished, forasmuch as her heart cried out [I Sam. 1:13]. But Abel prayed not only when silent, but even when dying, and his blood sent forth a cry more clear than a trumpet [Gen. 4:10].

Do thou also then groan, even as that holy one, I forbid it not. "Rend," as the prophet commanded [Joel 2:13], "thine heart, and not thy garments." Out of deeps call upon God, for it is said, "Out of the depths have I cried to Thee, O Lord" [Ps. 130:1]. From beneath, out of the heart, draw forth a voice, make thy prayer a mystery. Seest thou not that even in the houses of kings all tumult is put away, and great on all sides is the silence? Do thou also therefore, entering as into a palace—not that on the earth, but what is far more awful than it, that which is in heaven,—show forth great seemliness. Yea, for thou art joined to the choirs of angels, and art in communion with archangels, and art singing with the seraphim. And all these tribes show forth much goodly order, singing with great awe that mystical strain, and their sacred hymns to God, the King of all. With these then mingle thyself, when thou art praying, and emulate their mystical order.[3]

For not unto men art thou praying, but to God, who is everywhere present, who hears even before the voice, who knows the secrets of the mind. If thou so pray, great is the reward thou shalt receive.

[3] An evident reference to the liturgy, in which angels, archangels, and seraphim, "and all the company of heaven" led the church in its worship.

"For thy Father," saith he, "who seeth in secret, shall reward thee openly" [Matt. 6:6].

He said not, "shall freely give thee," but, "shall reward thee"; yea, for he hath made himself a debtor to thee, and even from this hath honored thee with great honor. For because he himself is invisible, he would have thy prayer be so likewise.

5. Then he speaks even the very words of the prayer.

"When ye pray," saith he, "use no vain repetitions, even as the heathen do" [Matt. 6:7].

You see that when he was discoursing of almsgiving, he removed only that mischief which comes of vainglory, and added nothing more; neither did he say whence one should give alms; as from honest labor, and not from rapine nor covetousness: this being abundantly acknowledged among all. And also before that, he had thoroughly cleared up this point, when he blessed them "that hunger after righteousness."

But touching prayer, he adds somewhat over and above; "not to use vain repetitions." And as there he derides the hypocrites, so here the heathen; shaming the hearer everywhere most of all by the vileness of the persons. For since this, in most cases, is especially biting and stinging, I mean our appearing to be likened to outcast persons; by this topic he dissuades them; calling frivolousness, here, by the name of "vain repetition": as when we ask of God things unsuitable, kingdoms, and glory, and to get the better of enemies, and abundance of wealth, and in general what does not at all concern us.

"For he knoweth," saith he, "what things ye have need of" [Matt. 6:8].

And herewith he seems to me to command in this place, that neither should we make our prayers long; long, I mean, not in time, but in the number and length of the things mentioned. For perseverance indeed in the same requests is our duty: his word being, "continuing instant in prayer" [Rom. 12:12].

And he himself too, by that example of the widow, who

prevailed with the pitiless and cruel ruler, by the continuance of her intercession [Luke 18:1-5]; and by that of the friend, who came late at night time, and roused the sleeper from his bed [Luke 11:5], not for his friendship's, but for his importunity's sake; what did he, but lay down a law, that all should continually make supplication unto him? He doth not however bid us compose a prayer of ten thousand clauses, and so come to him and merely repeat it. For this he obscurely signified when he said, "They think that they shall be heard for their much speaking."

"For he knoweth," saith he, "what things ye have need of." And if he know, one may say, what we have need of, wherefore must we pray? Not to instruct him, but to prevail with him; to be made intimate with him, by continuance in supplication; to be humbled; to be reminded of thy sins.

6. "After this manner, therefore, pray ye," saith he: "Our Father, which art in heaven" [Matt. 6:9].

See how he straightway stirred up the hearer, and reminded him of all God's bounty in the beginning. For he who calls God Father, by him both remission of sins, and taking away of punishment, and righteousness, and sanctification, and redemption, and adoption, and inheritance, and brotherhood with the Only-Begotten, and the supply of the Spirit, are acknowledged in this single title. For one cannot call God Father, without having attained to all those blessings. Doubly, therefore, doth he awaken their spirit, both by the dignity of him who is called on, and by the greatness of the benefits which they have enjoyed. But when he saith, "in heaven," he speaks not this as shutting up God there, but as withdrawing him who is praying from earth, and fixing him in the high places, and in the dwellings above.

He teaches, moreover, to make our prayer common, in behalf of our brethren also. For he saith not, "my Father, which art in heaven," but, "our Father," offering up his supplications for the body in common, and nowhere looking to his own, but everywhere to his neighbor's good. And by this he at once takes away hatred, and quells pride, and casts out envy, and brings in the mother of all good things, even charity, and exterminates the inequality of human things, and shows how far the equality reaches between the king and the poor man, if at least in those things which are greatest and most indispensable, we are all of us fellows. For what harm comes of our kindred below, when in that which is on high we are all of us knit together, and no one hath aught more than another; neither the rich more than the poor, nor the master than the servant, neither the ruler than the subject, nor the king than the common soldier, nor the philosopher than the barbarian, nor the skillful than the unlearned? For to all hath he given one nobility, having vouchsafed to be called the Father of all alike.

7. When therefore he hath reminded us of this nobility, and of the gift from above, and of our equality with our brethren, and of charity; and when he hath removed us from earth, and fixed us in heaven; let us see what he commands us to ask after this. Not but, in the first place, even that saying alone is sufficient to implant instruction in all virtue. For he who hath called God Father, and a common Father, would be justly bound to show forth such a conversation, as not to appear unworthy of this nobility, and to exhibit a diligence proportionate to the gift. Yet is he not satisfied with this, but adds, also another clause, thus saying,

"Hallowed be Thy name."

Worthy of him who calls God Father, is the prayer to ask nothing before the glory of his Father, but to account all things secondary to the work of praising him. For "hallowed" is glorified. For his own glory he hath complete, and ever continuing the same, but he commands him who prays to seek that he may be glorified also by our life. Which very thing he had said before likewise, "Let your light so shine before men, that they may see your good works, and glorify your Father which is in heaven" [Matt. 5:16]. Yea, and the seraphim too, giving glory, said on this wise, "Holy, holy, holy" [Isa. 6:3; Rev. 4:8]. So that "hallowed" means this, viz.

"glorified." That is, "vouchsafe," saith he, "that we may live so purely, that through us all may glorify thee." Which thing again appertains unto perfect self-control, to present to all a life so irreprehensible, that every one of the beholders may offer to the Lord the praise due to him for this.

"Thy kingdom come" [Matt. 6:10].

And this again is the language of a right-minded child, not to be rivetted to things that are seen, neither to account things present some great matter; but to hasten unto our Father, and to long for the things to come. And this springs out of a good conscience, and a soul set free from things that are on earth. This, for instance, Paul himself was longing after every day: wherefore he also said, that "even we ourselves, who have the first-fruits of the Spirit, groan, waiting for an adoption, the redemption of our body" [Rom. 8:23]. For he who hath this fondness, can neither be puffed up by the good things of this life, nor abashed by its sorrows; but as though dwelling in the very heavens, is freed from each sort of irregularity.

"Thy will be done in earth, as it is in heaven."

Behold a most excellent train of thought! in that he bade us indeed long for the things to come, and hasten towards that sojourn; and, till that may be, even while we abide here, so long to be earnest in showing forth the same conversation as those above. For ye must long, saith he, for heaven, and the things in heaven; however, even before heaven, he hath bidden us make the earth a heaven and do and say all things, even while we are continuing in it, as having our conversation there; insomuch that these too should be objects of our prayer to the Lord. For there is nothing to hinder our reaching the perfection of the powers above, because we inhabit the earth; but it is possible even while abiding here, to do all, as though already placed on high. What he saith therefore is this: "As there all things are done without hindrance, and the angels are not partly obedient and partly disobedient, but in all things yield and obey (for he saith, 'Mighty in strength, performing his word' [Ps. 103:20]); so vouchsafe that we men may not do thy will by halves, but perform all things as thou willest."

Seest thou how he hath taught us also to be modest, by making it clear that virtue is not of our endeavors only, but also of the grace from above? And again, he hath enjoined each one of us, who pray, to take upon himself the care of the whole world. For he did not at all say, "Thy will be done" *in me*, or *in us*, but everywhere on the earth; so that error may be destroyed, and truth implanted, and all wickedness cast out, and virtue return, and no difference in this respect be henceforth between heaven and earth. "For if this come to pass," saith he, "there will be no difference between things below and above, separated as they are in nature; the earth exhibiting to us another set of angels."

8. "Give us this day our daily bread" [Matt. 6:11].

What is "daily bread"? That for one day.[4]

For because he had said thus, "Thy will be done in earth as it is in heaven," but was discoursing to men encompassed with flesh, and subject to the necessities of nature, and incapable of the same impassibility with the angels:—while he enjoins the commands to be practised by us also, even as they perform them; he condescends likewise, in what follows, to the infirmity of our nature. Thus, "perfection of conduct," saith he, "I require as great, not however freedom from passions; no, for the tyranny of nature permits it not: for it requires necessary food." But mark, I pray thee, how even in things that are bodily, that which is spiritual abounds. For it is neither for riches, nor for delicate living, nor for costly raiment, nor for any other such thing, but for bread only, that he hath commanded us to make our prayer. And for "daily bread," so as not to "take thought for the morrow" [Matt. 6:34]. Because of this he added, "*daily* bread," that is, bread for one day.

And not even with this expression is he satisfied, but adds another too afterwards, saying, "Give us *this day*"; so that we may not, beyond this, wear ourselves out with the care of the

[4] On the contrast between Chrysostom's exegesis of the Greek word *epiousios* and Origen's exegesis, cf. Introduction, p. 18.

following day. For that day, the interval before which thou knowest not whether thou shalt see, wherefore dost thou submit to its cares?

This, as he proceeded, he enjoined also more fully, saying, "Take no thought for the morrow." He would have us be on every hand unencumbered and winged for flight, yielding just so much to nature as the compulsion of necessity requires of us.

9. Then forasmuch as it comes to pass that we sin even after the washing of regeneration [Titus 3:5], he, showing his love to man to be great even in this case, commands us for the remission of our sins to come unto God who loves man, and thus to say,

"Forgive us our debts, as we also forgive our debtors" [Matt. 6:12].

Seest thou surpassing mercy? After taking away so great evils, and after the unspeakable greatness of his gift, if men sin again, he counts them such as may be forgiven. For that this prayer belongs to believers, is taught us both by the laws of the church, and by the beginning of the prayer. For the uninitiated could not call God Father.[5] If then the prayer belongs to believers, and they pray, entreating that sins may be forgiven them, it is clear that not even after the laver is the profit of repentance taken away. Since, had he not meant to signify this, he would not have made a law that we should so pray. Now he who both brings sins to remembrance, and bids us ask forgiveness, and teaches how we may obtain remission, and so makes the way easy; it is perfectly clear that he introduced this rule of supplication, as knowing, and signifying, that it is possible even after the font to wash ourselves from our offenses; by reminding us of our sins, persuading us to be modest; by the command to forgive others, setting us free from all revengeful passion; while by promising in return for this to pardon us also, he holds out good hopes, and instructs us to

[5] For the distinction between "initiated" and "uninitiated," see also p. 89, n. 10 and Introduction, p. 8.

have high views concerning the unspeakable mercy of God toward man.

But what we should most observe is this, that whereas in each of the clauses he had made mention of the whole of virtue, and in this way had included also the forgetfulness of injuries (for so, that "his name be hallowed," is the exactness of a perfect conversation; and that "his will be done," declares the same thing again; and to be able to call God "Father," is the profession of a blameless life; in all which things had been comprehended also the duty of remitting our anger against them that have transgressed): still he was not satisfied with these, but meaning to signify how earnest he is in the matter, he sets it down also in particular, and after the prayer, he makes mention of no other commandment than this, saying thus:

"For if ye forgive men their trespasses, your heavenly Father also will forgive you" [Matt. 6:14].

So that the beginning is of us, and we ourselves have control over the judgment that is to be passed upon us. For in order that no one, even of the senseless, might have any complaint to make, either great or small, when brought to judgment; on thee, who art to give account, he causes the sentence to depend; and "in what way soever thou hast judged for thyself, in the same," saith he, "do I also judge thee." And if thou forgive thy fellow-servant, thou shalt obtain the same favor from me; though indeed the one be not equal to the other. For thou forgivest in thy need, but God, having need of none: thou, thy fellow-slave; God, his slave: thou liable to unnumbered charges; God, being without sin. But yet even thus doth he show forth his lovingkindness towards man.

Since he might indeed, even without this, forgive thee all thine offenses; but he wills thee hereby also to receive a benefit; affording thee on all sides innumerable occasions of gentleness and love to man, casting out what is brutish in thee, and quenching wrath, and in all ways cementing thee to him who is thine own member.

For what canst thou have to say? that thou hast wrongfully endured some ill of thy neighbor? (For these only are trespasses, since if it be done with justice, the act is not a trespass.) But thou too art drawing near to receive forgiveness for such things, and for much greater. And even before the forgiveness, thou hast received no small gift, in being taught to have a human soul, and in being trained to all gentleness. And herewith a great reward shall also be laid up for thee elsewhere, even to be called to account for none of thine offenses.

What sort of punishment then do we not deserve, when after having received the privilege, we betray our salvation? And how shall we claim to be heard in the rest of our matters, if we will not, in those which depend on us, spare our own selves?

10. "And lead us not into temptation; but deliver us from the evil one: for thine is the kingdom, and the power, and the glory, for ever. Amen" [Matt. 6:13].

Here he teaches us plainly our own vileness, and quells our pride, instructing us to deprecate all conflicts, instead of rushing upon them. For so both our victory will be more glorious, and the devil's overthrow more to be derided. I mean, that as when we are dragged forth, we must stand nobly; so when we are not summoned, we should be quiet, and wait for the time of conflict; that we may show both freedom from vainglory, and nobleness of spirit.

And he here calls the devil "the wicked one," commanding us to wage against him a war that knows no truce, and implying that he is not such by nature. For wickedness is not of those things that are from nature, but of them that are added by our own choice. And he is so called pre-eminently, by reason of the excess of his wickedness, and because he, in no respect injured by us, wages against us implacable war. Wherefore neither said he, "deliver us from the wicked ones," but, "from the wicked one"; instructing us in no case to entertain displeasure against our neighbors, for what wrongs soever we may suffer at their hands, but to transfer our enmity from these to him, as being himself the cause of all our wrongs.

Having then made us anxious as before conflict, by putting us in mind of the enemy, and having cut away from us all our remissness; he again encourages and raises our spirits, by bringing to our remembrance the King under whom we are arrayed, and signifying him to be more powerful than all. "For thine," saith he, "is the kingdom, and the power, and the glory."

Doth it not then follow, that if his be the kingdom, we should fear no one, since there can be none to withstand, and divide the empire with him? For when he saith, "Thine is the kingdom," he sets before us even him, who is warring against us, brought into subjection, though he seem to oppose, God for a while permitting it. For in truth he too is among God's servants, though of the degraded class, and those guilty of offense; and he would not dare set upon any of his fellow-servants, had he not first received license from above. And why say I, "his fellow-servants?" Not even against swine did he venture any outrage, until He himself allowed him [Luke 8:32]; nor against flocks, nor herds, until he had received permission from above [Job 1:12].

"And the power," saith he. Therefore, manifold as thy weakness may be, thou mayest of right be confident, having such a one to reign over thee, who is able fully to accomplish all, and that with ease, even by thee.

"And the glory, for ever. Amen." Thus he not only frees thee from the dangers that are approaching thee, but can make thee also glorious and illustrious. For as his power is great, so also is his glory unspeakable, and they are all boundless, and no end of them. Seest thou how he hath by every means anointed his Champion, and hath framed him to be full of confidence?

11. Then, as I said before, meaning to signify, that of all things he most loathes and hates bearing malice, and most of

all accepts the virtue which is opposite to that vice; he hath after the prayer also again put us in mind of this same point of goodness; both by the punishment set, and by the reward appointed, urging the hearer to obey this command.

"For if ye forgive men," saith he, "your heavenly Father will also forgive you. But if ye forgive not, neither will he forgive you" [Matt. 6:14, 15].

With this view he hath again mentioned heaven also, and their Father; to abash the hearer by this topic likewise; that he of all people, being of such a Father, should be made a wild beast of; and summoned as he is to heaven, should cherish an earthly and ordinary sort of mind. Since not by grace only, you see, ought we to become his children, but also by our works. And nothing makes us so like God, as being ready to forgive the wicked and wrong doers; even as indeed he had taught before, when he spake of his "making the sun to shine on the evil and on the good" [Matt. 5:45].

For this same cause again in every one of the clauses he commands us to make our prayers common, saying, "Our Father," and "Thy will be done in earth as it is in heaven," and "Give *us* the bread, and forgive *us* our debts," and "lead *us* not into temptation," and "deliver *us*"; everywhere commanding us to use this plural word, that we may not retain so much as a vestige of anger against our neighbor.

How great punishment then must they deserve, who after all this, so far from themselves forgiving, do even entreat God for vengeance on their enemies, and diametrically as it were transgress this law; and this while he is doing and contriving all, to hinder our being at variance one with another? For since love is the root of all that is good, he removing from all sides whatever mars it, brings us together, and cements us to each other. For there is not, there is not one, be he father, or mother, or friend, or what you will, who so loved us as the God who created us. And this, above all things, both his daily benefits and his precepts make manifest. But if thou tell me of the pains, and of the sorrows, and of the evils of life; consider in how many things thou offendest him every day, and thou wilt no longer marvel, though more than these evils should come upon thee, but if thou shouldest enjoy any good, then thou wilt marvel, and be amazed. But as it is, we look upon the calamities that come upon us, but the offenses, whereby we offend daily, we consider not; therefore we are perplexed. Since if we did but reckon up with strictness our sins of one day only, in that case we should know well how great evils we must be liable to.

And to let pass the other misdoings of which we have been guilty, each one for himself, and to speak of what have been committed this day; although of course I know not in what each of us may have sinned, yet such is the abundance of our misdoings, that not even he who knew all exactly would be able to choose from among these only. Which of us, for instance, hath not been careless in his prayers? Which hath not been insolent, or vainglorious? Who hath not spoken evil of his brother, hath not admitted a wicked desire, hath not looked with unchaste eyes, hath not remembered things with hostile feeling, even till he made his heart swell?

And if while we are in church, and in a short time we have become guilty of so great evils; what shall be when we are gone out from hence? If in the harbor the waves are so high, when we are gone forth into the channel of wickedness, the forum I mean, and to public business, and our cares at home, shall we indeed be able so much as to know ourselves again?

But yet from our so great and so many sins, God hath given us a short and easy way of deliverance, and one that is free from all toil. For what sort of toil is it to forgive him that hath grieved us? Nay, it is a toil not to forgive, but to keep up our enmity: even as to be delivered from the anger, both works in us a great refreshment, and is very easy to him that is willing. For there is no sea to be crossed, nor long journey to be travelled, nor summits of mountains to be passed over, nor money to be spent, no need to torment thy body; but it suffices to be willing only, and all our sins are done away.

But if so far from forgiving him thyself, thou makest intercession to God against him, what hope of salvation wilt thou then have, if at the very time when thou oughtest rather to appease God, even then thou provokest him; putting on the garb of a suppliant, but uttering the cries of a wild beast, and darting out against thyself those shafts of the wicked one? Wherefore Paul also, making mention of prayer, required nothing so much as the observance of this commandment; for he saith, "lifting up holy hands without wrath and doubting" [I Tim. 2:8]. And if when thou hast need of mercy, not even then wilt thou let go thine anger, but art rather exceedingly mindful of it, and that, although thou knowest thou art thrusting the sword into thyself; when will it be possible for thee to become merciful, and to spew out the evil venom of this wickedness?

But if thou hast not yet seen this outrageousness in its full extent, suppose it happening among men, and then thou wilt perceive the excess of the insolence. As thus: should one approach thee who are a man, seeking to obtain mercy, and then, in the midst of his lying on the ground, should see an enemy, and leaving off to supplicate thee, begin to beat him; wouldest thou not make thyself more angry with him? This do thou consider as taking place with regard to God also. For so thou likewise, making supplication unto God, leavest thy supplication in the midst, and smitest thine enemy with thy words, and insultest the laws of God. Him who made a law to dismiss all anger, thou art summoning against those that have vexed thee, and requiring him to do things contrary to his own commandments. Is it not enough for thee in the way of revenge, that thou thyself transgressest the law of God, but entreatest thou him likewise to do so? What? hath he forgotten what he commanded? What? is he a man who spake these things? It is God, who knows all things, and whose will is, that his own laws be kept with the utmost exactness, and who, so far from doing these things which thou art requiring of him, doth even regard thee who sayest these things, merely because thou sayest them, with aversion and hatred and exacts of thee the most extreme penalty. How then seekest thou to obtain of him things, from which he very seriously bids thee refrain?

Yet some there are, who have come to such a point of brutishness, as not only to make intercession against their enemies, but even to curse their children, and to taste, if only it might be, of their very flesh; or rather they are even tasting thereof. For tell me not this, that thou hast not fixed thy teeth in the body of him that vexed thee; since thou hast done, at least as far as concerned thee, what is much more grievous; in claiming that wrath from above should fall upon him, and that he should be delivered over to undying punishment, and be overthrown with his whole house.

Why, what sort of bites are as ferocious as this? what kind of weapons as bitter? Not so did Christ instruct thee; not so did he command thee to stain thy mouth with blood. Nay, mouths made bloody with human flesh are not so shocking as tongues like these.

How then wilt thou salute thy brother? how wilt thou touch the sacrifice? how taste the Lord's blood, when thou hast so much venom upon thy mind? Since when thou sayest, "Rend him in pieces, and overthrow his house, and destroy all," when thou art imprecating on him ten thousand deaths, thou art in nothing different from a murderer, or rather from a wild beast that devours men.

Let us cease then from this disease and madness, and that kindliness which he commanded let us show forth towards them that have vexed us: that we may become like "our Father which is in heaven." And we shall cease therefrom, if we call to mind our own sins; if we strictly search out all our misdeeds at home, abroad, and in the market, and in church.

12. For if for nothing else, surely for our disrespectfulness here we are worthy to undergo the utmost punishment. For when prophets are chanting, and apostles singing hymns, and God is discoursing, we wander without, and bring in upon us

a turmoil of worldly business. And we do not afford to the laws of God so great stillness, even as the spectators in the theatres to the emperor's letters, keeping silence for them. For there, when these letters are being read, deputies at once, and governors, and senate, and people, stand all upright, with quietness hearkening to the words. And if amid that most profound silence anyone should suddenly leap up and cry out, he suffers the utmost punishment, as having been insolent to the emperor. But here, when the letters from heaven are being read, great is the confusion on all sides. And yet both he who sent the letters is much greater than this our king, and the assembly more venerable: for not men only, but angels too are in it; and these triumphs, of which the letters bear us the good tidings, are much more awful than those on earth. Wherefore not men only, but angels also and archangels; both the nations of heaven, and all we on the earth, are commanded to give praise. For, "Bless the Lord," it is said, "all his works" [Ps. 103:22]. Yea, for his are no small achievements, rather they surpass all speech, and thought, and understanding of man.

And these things the prophets proclaim every day, each of them in a different way publishing this glorious triumph. For one saith, "Thou hast gone up on high, thou hast led captivity captive, and hast received gifts amongst men" [Ps. 68:18]. And, "The Lord strong and mighty in battle" [Ps. 24:8]. And another saith, "He shall divide the spoils of the strong" [Isa. 53:12]. For indeed to this purpose he came, that he might "preach deliverance to captives, and recovery of sight to the blind" [Isa. 61:1; Luke 4:19].

And raising aloud the cry of victory over death, he said, "Where, O Death, is thy victory? Where, O Grave, is thy sting?" [Hos. 13:14; I Cor. 15:55]. And another again, declaring glad tidings of the most profound peace, said, "They shall beat their swords into ploughshares, and their spears into pruning hooks" [Isa. 2:4; Mic. 4:3]. And while one calls on Jerusalem, saying, "Rejoice greatly, O daughter of Sion, for lo! thy King cometh to thee meek, riding upon an ass, and a young colt" [Zech. 9:9]; another proclaims his second coming also, saying on this wise, "The Lord, whom ye seek, will come, and who will abide the day of his coming?" [Mal. 3:1, 2]. "Leap ye as calves set free from bonds" [Mal. 4:2]. And another again, amazed at such things, said, "This is our God; there shall none other be accounted of in comparison of him" [Bar. 3:36].

Yet, nevertheless, while both these and many more sayings than these are being uttered, while we ought to tremble, and not so much as account ourselves to be on the earth; still, as though in the midst of a forum, we make an uproar and disturbance, and spend the whole time of our solemn assembly in discoursing of things which are nothing to us.

When therefore both in little things, and in great, both in hearing, and in doing, both abroad, and at home, in the church, we are so negligent; and together with all this, pray also against our enemies: whence are we to have any hope of salvation, adding to so great sins yet another grievous enhancement, and equivalent to them all, even this unlawful prayer?

Have we then hereafter any right to marvel, if aught befall us of the things which are unexpected and painful? whereas we ought to marvel when no such thing befalls us. For the former is in the natural order of things, but the latter were beyond all reason and expectation. For surely it is beyond reason, that they who are become enemies of God, and are provoking him to anger, should enjoy sunshine and showers, and all the rest; who being men surpass the barbarity of wild beasts, setting themselves one against another, and by the biting of their neighbors staining their own tongues with blood: after the spiritual table, and his so great benefits, and his innumerable injunctions.

Therefore, considering these things, let us cast up that venom; let us put an end to our enmities, and let us make the prayers that become such as we are. Instead of the brutality of devils, let us take upon us the mildness of angels; and in whatsoever things we may have been injured, let us, considering our own case, and the reward appointed us for this commandment, soften our anger; let us assuage the billows, that we may both pass through the present life calmly, and when we have departed thither, may find our Lord such as we have been towards our fellow-servants. And if this be a heavy and fearful thing, let us make it light and desirable; and let us open the glorious gates of confidence towards him; and what we had not strength to effect by abstaining from sin, that let us accomplish by becoming gentle to them who have sinned against us (for this surely is not grievous, nor burdensome); and let us by doing kindnesses to our enemies, lay up beforehand much mercy for ourselves.

For so both during this present life all will love us, and above all others, God will both befriend and crown us, and will count us worthy of all the good things to come; unto which may we all attain, by the grace and love towards man of our Lord Jesus Christ, to whom be glory and might for ever and ever. Amen.

Homily XX

"And when ye fast, be not as the hypocrites, of a sad countenance. For they disfigure their faces, that they may appear unto men to fast." —*Matt. 6:16*

HERE IT WERE WELL TO SIGH aloud, and to wail bitterly: for not only do we imitate the hypocrites, but we have even surpassed them. For I know, yea I know many, not merely fasting and making a display of it, but neglecting to fast and yet wearing the masks of them that fast, and cloaking themselves with an excuse worse than their sin.

For "I do this," say they, "that I may not offend the many." What sayest thou? There is a law of God which commands these things, and dost thou talk of offense? And thinkest thou that in keeping it thou art offending, in transgressing it, delivering men from offense? And what can be worse than this folly?

Wilt thou not leave off becoming worse than the very hypocrites, and making thine hypocrisy double? And when thou considerest the great excess of this evil, wilt thou not be abashed at the force of the expression now before us? In that he did not say, "they act a part," merely, but willing also to touch them more deeply, he saith, "For they disfigure their faces"; that is, they corrupt, they mar them.

But if this be a disfiguring of the face, to appear pale for vainglory, what should we say concerning the women who corrupt their faces with colorings and paintings to the ruin of the unchaste sort of young men? For while those harm themselves only, these women harm both themselves and them who behold them. Wherefore we should fly both from the one pest and from the other, keeping at distance enough and to spare. For so he not only commanded to make no display, but even to seek to be concealed. Which thing he had done before likewise.

And whereas in the matter of almsgiving, he did not put it simply, but having said, "Take heed not to do it before men," he added, "to be seen of them"; yet concerning fasting and prayer, he made no such limitation. Why could this have been? Because for almsgiving to be altogether concealed is impossible, but for prayer and fasting, it is possible.

As therefore, when he said, "Let not thy left hand know what thy right hand doeth," it was not of hands that he was speaking, but of the duty of being strictly concealed from all; and as when he commanded us to enter into our closet, not there alone absolutely, nor there primarily, did he command us to pray, but he covertly intimated the same thing again; so likewise here, in commanding us "to be anointed," he did not enact that we positively must anoint ourselves; for then we should all of us be found transgressors of this law; and above all, surely, they who have taken the most pains to keep it, the societies of the monks, who have taken up their dwelling on the mountains. It was not this then that he enjoined, but, forasmuch as the ancients had a custom to anoint themselves continually, when they were taking their pleasure and rejoicing (and this one may see clearly from David [II Sam. 12:20] and from Daniel [Dan. 10:3]); he said that we were to anoint ourselves, not that we should positively do this, but that by all means we might endeavor, with great strictness, to hide this our acquisition. And to convince thee that so it is, he himself, when by action exhibiting what he enjoined in words, having fasted forty days, and fasted in secret, did neither anoint nor wash himself: nevertheless, though he did not these things, he most assuredly fulfilled the whole without vainglory. It is this then that he enjoins on us likewise, both bringing before us the hypocrites, and by a twice repeated charge dissuading the hearers.

And somewhat else he signified by this name, this of hypocrites,[1] I mean. That is, not only by the ridiculousness of the thing, nor by its bringing an extreme penalty, but also by showing that such deceit is but for a season, doth he withdraw us from that evil desire. For the actor seems glorious just so long as the audience is sitting; or rather not even then in the sight of all. For the more part of the spectators know who it is, and what part he is acting. However, when the audience is broken up, he is more clearly discovered to all. Now this, you see, the vainglorious must in all necessity undergo. For even here they are manifest to the majority, as not being that which they appear to be, but as wearing a mask only; but much more will they be detected hereafter, when all things appear "naked and open" [Heb. 4:13].

And by another motive again he withdraws them from the hypocrites, by showing that his injunction is light. For he doth not make the fast more strict, nor command us to practise more of it, but not to lose the crown thereof. So that what seems hard to bear, is common to us and to the hypocrites, for they also fast; but that which is lightest, namely, not to lose the reward after our labors, "this is what I command," saith he; adding nothing to our toils, but gathering our wages for us with all security, and not suffering us to go away unrewarded, as they do. Nay, they will not so much as imitate them that wrestle in the Olympic games, who although so great a multitude is sitting there, and so many princes, desire to please but one, even him who adjudges the victory amongst them; and this, though he be much their inferior. But thou, though thou hast a twofold motive for displaying the victory to Him, first, that he is the person to adjudge it, and also, that he is beyond comparison superior to all that are sitting in the theatre,—thou art displaying it to others, who so far from profiting, do privily work thee the greatest harm.

However, I do not forbid even this, saith he. Only, if thou art desirous to make a show to men, also, wait, and I will

[1] Cf. p. 134, n. 2.

bestow on thee this too in fuller abundance, and with great profit. For as it is, this quite breaks thee off from the glory which is with me, even as to despise these things unites thee closely; but then shalt thou enjoy all in entire security; having, even before that last, no little fruit to reap in this world also, namely, that thou hast trodden under foot all human glory, and art freed from the grievous bondage of men, and art become a true worker of virtue. Whereas now, as long at least as thou art so disposed, if thou shouldest be in a desert, thou wilt be deserted by all thy virtue, having none to behold thee. This is to act as one insulting virtue itself, if thou art to pursue it not for its own sake, but with an eye to the ropemaker, and the brazier, and the common people of the baser sort, that the bad and they that are far removed from virtue may admire thee. And thou art calling the enemies of virtue to the display and the sight thereof, as if one were to choose to live continently, not for the excellency of continence, but that he might make a show before prostitutes. Thou also, it would seem, wouldest not choose virtue, but for the sake of virtue's enemies; whereas thou oughtest indeed to admire her on this very ground, that she hath even her enemies to praise her,—yet to admire her (as is meet), not for others, but for her own sake. Since we too, when we are loved not for our own, but for others' sake, account the thing an insult. Just so I bid thee reckon in the case of virtue as well, and neither to follow after her for the sake of others, nor for men's sake to obey God; but men for God's sake. Since if thou do the contrary, though thou seem to follow virtue, thou hast provoked equally with him who follows her not. For just as he disobeyed by not doing, so thou by doing unlawfully.

2. "Lay not up for yourselves treasures upon earth" [Matt. 6:19].

Thus, after he hath cast out the disease of vainglory, and not before, he seasonably introduces his discourse of voluntary poverty. For nothing so trains men to be fond of riches, as the fondness for glory. This, for instance, is why men devise those herds of slaves, and that swarm of eunuchs, and their horses with trappings of gold, and their silver tables, and all the rest of it, yet more ridiculous; not to satisfy any wants, nor to enjoy any pleasure, but that they may make a show before the multitude.

Now above he had only said, that we must show mercy; but here he points out also how great mercy we must show, when he saith, "Lay not up treasure." For it not being possible at the beginning to introduce all at once his discourse on contempt of riches, by reason of the tyranny of the passion, he breaks it up into small portions, and having set free the hearer's mind, instills it therein, so as that it shall become acceptable. Wherefore, you see, he said first, "Blessed are the merciful"; and after this, "Agree with thine adversary"; and after that again, "If anyone will sue thee at the law and take thy coat, give him thy cloak also"; but here, that which is much greater than all these. For there his meaning was, "if thou see a law-suit impending, do this; since to want and be freed from strife, is better than to possess and strive"; but here, supposing neither adversary nor any one at law with thee, and without all mention of any other such party, he teaches the contempt of riches itself by itself, implying that not so much for their sake who receive mercy, as for the giver's sake, he makes these laws: so that though there be no one injuring us, or dragging us into a court of justice, even so we may despise our possessions, bestowing them on those that are in need.

And neither here hath he put the whole, but even in this place it is gently spoken; although he had in the wilderness shown forth to a surpassing extent his conflicts in that behalf [Matt. 4:9, 10]. However he doth not express this, nor bring it forward; for it was not yet time to reveal it; but for a while he searches out for reasons, maintaining the place of an adviser rather than a lawgiver, in his sayings on this subject.

For after he had said, "Lay not up treasures upon the earth," he added, "where moth and rust doth corrupt, and where thieves break through and steal."

For the present he signifies the hurtfulness of the treasure here, and the profit of what is there, both from the place, and from the things which mar it. And neither at this point doth he stop, but adds also another argument.

And first, what things they most fear, from these he urges them. For "of what art thou afraid?" saith he: "lest thy goods should be spent, if thou give alms? Nay, then give alms, and so they will not be spent; and, what is more, so far from being spent, they will actually receive a greater increase; yea, for the things in heaven are added unto them."

However, for a time he saith it not, but puts it afterwards. But for the present, what had most power to persuade them, that he brings forward, namely, that the treasure would thus remain for them unspent.

And on either hand he attracts them. For he said not only, "If thou give alms, it is preserved": but he threatened also the opposite thing, that if thou give not, it perishes.

And see his unspeakable prudence. For neither did he say, "Thou dost but leave them to others"; since this too is pleasant to men: He alarms them however on a new ground, by signifying that not even this do they obtain: since though men defraud not, there are those which are sure to defraud, "the moth" and "the rust." For although this mischief seem very easy to restrain, it is nevertheless irresistible and uncontrollable, and devise what thou wilt, thou wilt be unable to check this harm.

"What then, doth moth make away with the gold?" Though not moth, yet thieves do. "What then, have all been despoiled?" Though not all, yet the more part.

3. On this account then he adds another argument, which I have already mentioned, saying,

"Where the man's treasure is, there is his heart also" [Matt. 6:21].

For though none of these things should come to pass, saith

he, thou wilt undergo no small harm, in being nailed to the things below, and in becoming a slave instead of a freeman, and casting thyself out of the heavenly things, and having no power to think on aught that is high, but all about money, usuries and loans, and gains, and ignoble traffickings. Than this what could be more wretched? For in truth such an one will be worse off than any slave, bringing upon himself a most grievous tyranny, and giving up the chiefest thing of all, even the nobleness and the liberty of man. For how much soever anyone may discourse unto thee, thou wilt not be able to hear any of those things which concern thee, whilst thy mind is nailed down to money; but bound like a dog to a tomb, by the tyranny of riches, more grievously than by any chain, barking at all that come near thee, thou hast this one employment continually, to keep for others what thou hast laid up. Than this what can be more wretched?

However, forasmuch as this was too high for the mind of his hearers, and neither was the mischief within easy view of the generality, nor the gain evident, but there was need of a spirit of more self-command to perceive either of these; first, he hath put it after those other topics, which are obvious, saying, "Where the man's treasure is, there is his heart also"; and next he makes it clear again, by withdrawing his discourse from the intellectual to the sensible, and saying,

"The light of the body is the eye" [Matt. 6:22].

What he saith is like this: Bury not gold in the earth, nor do any other such thing, for thou dost but gather it for the moth, and the rust, and the thieves. And even if thou shouldest entirely escape these evils, yet the enslaving of thine heart, the nailing it to all that is below, thou wilt not escape: "For wheresoever thy treasure may be, there is thine heart also." As then, laying up stores in heaven, thou wilt reap not this fruit only, the attainment of the rewards for these things, but from this world thou already receivest thy recompense, in getting into harbor there, in setting thine affections on the things that are there, and caring for what is there (for where thou hast laid up thy treasures, it is most clear thou transferrest thy mind also); so if thou do this upon earth, thou wilt experience the contrary.

But if the saying be obscure to thee, hear what comes next in order.

"The light of the body is the eye; if therefore thine eye be single, thy whole body shall be full of light. But if thine eye be evil, thy whole body shall be full of darkness. But if the light that is in thee be darkness, how great is the darkness!" [Matt. 6:22, 23].

He leads his discourse to the things which are more within the reach of our senses. I mean, forasmuch as he had spoken of the mind as enslaved and brought into captivity, and there were not many who could easily discern this, he transfers the lesson to things outward, and lying before men's eyes, that by these the others also might reach their understanding. Thus, "If thou knowest not," saith he, "what a thing it is to be injured in mind, learn it from the things of the body; for just what the eye is to the body, the same is the mind to the soul." As therefore thou wouldest not choose to wear gold, and to be clad in silken garments, thine eyes withal being put out, but accountest their sound health more desirable than all such superfluity (for, shouldest thou lose this health or waste it, all thy life besides will do thee no good): for just as when the eyes are blinded, most of the energy of the other members is gone, their light being quenched; so also when the mind is depraved, thy life will be filled with countless evils:—as therefore in the body this is our aim, namely, to keep the eye sound, so also the mind in the soul. But if we mutilate this, which ought to give light to the rest, by what means are we to see clearly any more? For as he that destroys the fountain, dries up also the river, so he who hath quenched the understanding hath confounded all his doings in this life. Wherefore he saith, "If the light that is in thee be darkness, how great is the darkness!"

For when the pilot is drowned, and the candle is put out,

and the general is taken prisoner; what sort of hope will there be, after that, for those that are under command?

Thus then, omitting now to speak of the plots to which wealth gives occasion, the strifes, the suits (these indeed he had signified above, when he said, "The adversary shall deliver thee to the judge, and the judge to the officer"); and setting down what is more grievous than all these, as sure to occur, he so withdraws us from the wicked desire. For to inhabit the prison is not nearly so grievous, as for the mind to be enslaved by this disease; and the former is not sure to happen, but the other is connected as an immediate consequent with the desire of riches. And this is why he puts it after the first, as being a more grievous thing, and sure to happen.

For God, he saith, gave us understanding, that we might chase away all ignorance, and have the right judgment of things, and that using this as a kind of weapon and light against all that is grievous or hurtful, we might remain in safety. But we betray the gift for the sake of things superfluous and useless.

For what is the use of soldiers arrayed in gold, when the general is dragged along a captive? what the profit of a ship beautifully equipped, when the pilot is sunk beneath the waves? what the advantage of a well-proportioned body, when the sight of the eyes is stricken out? As therefore, should anyone cast into sickness the physician (who should be in good health, that he may end our diseases), and then bid him lie on a silver couch, and in a chamber of gold, this will nothing avail the sick persons; even so, if thou corrupt the mind (which hath power to put down our passions), although thou set it by a treasure, so far from doing it any good, thou hast inflicted the very greatest loss, and hast harmed thy whole soul.

4. Seest thou how by those very things, through which most especially men everywhere affect wickedness, even by these most of all he deters them from it, and brings them back to virtue? "For with what intent dost thou desire riches?" saith

he; "is it not that thou mayest enjoy pleasure and luxury? Why now, this above all things thou wilt fail to obtain thereby, it will rather be just contrary." For if, when our eyes are stricken out, we perceive not any pleasant thing, because of such our calamity; much more will this be our case in the perversion and maiming of the mind.

Again, with what intent dost thou bury it in the earth? That it may be kept in safety? But here too again it is the contrary, saith he.

And thus, as in dealing with him that for vainglory fasts and gives alms and prays, by those very things which he most desires he had allured him not to be vainglorious:—"for with what intent," saith he, "dost thou so pray and give alms? for love of the glory that may be had from men? then do not pray thus," saith he, "and so thou shalt obtain it in the day that is to come":—so he hath taken captive the covetous man also, by those things for which he was most earnest. Thus: "what wouldest thou?" saith he, "to have thy wealth preserved, and to enjoy pleasure? Both these things I will afford thee in great abundance, if thou lay up thy gold in that place, where I bid thee."

It is true that hereafter he displayed more clearly the evil effect of this on the mind, I mean, when he made mention of the thorns [Matt. 13:22]; but for the present, even here he hath strikingly intimated the same, by representing him as darkened who is beside himself in this way.

And as they that are in darkness see nothing distinct, but if they look at a rope, they suppose it to be a serpent, if at mountains and ravines, they are dead with fear; so these also: what is not alarming to them that have sight, that they regard with suspicion. Thus among other things they tremble at poverty: or rather not at poverty only, but even at any trifling loss. Yea, and if they should lose some little matter, those who are in want of necessary food do not so grieve and bewail themselves as they. At least many of the rich have come even to the halter, not enduring such ill fortune: and to be insulted also, and to be despitefully used, seems to them so intolerable, that even because of this again many have actually torn themselves from this present life. For to everything wealth had made them soft, except to the waiting on it. Thus, when it commands them to do service unto itself, they venture on murders, and stripes, and revilings, and all shame. A thing which comes of the utmost wretchedness; to be of all men most effeminate, where one ought to practise self-command, but where more caution was required, in these cases again to become more shameless and obstinate. Since in fact the same kind of thing befalls them, as one would have to endure who had spent all his goods on unfit objects. For such an one, when the time of necessary expenditure comes on, having nothing to supply it, suffers incurable evils, forasmuch as all that he had hath been ill spent beforehand.

And as they that are on the stage, skilled in those wicked arts, do in them go through many things strange and dangerous, but in other necessary and useful things none so ridiculous as they; even so is it with these men likewise. For so such as walk upon a stretched rope, making a display of so much courage, should some great emergency demand daring or courage, they are not able, neither do they endure even to think of such a thing. Just so they likewise that are rich, daring all for money, for self-restraint's sake endure not to submit to anything, be it small or great. And as the former practise both a hazardous and fruitless business; even so do these undergo many dangers and downfalls, but arrive at no profitable end. Yea, they undergo a twofold darkness, both having their eyes put out by the perversion of their mind, and being by the deceitfulness of their cares involved in a great mist. Wherefore neither can they easily so much as see through it. For he that is in darkness, is freed from the darkness by the mere appearance of the sun; but he that hath his eyes mutilated not even when the sun shines; which is the very case of these men: not even now that the Sun of Righteousness hath shone out, and is admonishing, do they hear, their wealth having closed their eyes. And so they have a twofold darkness to undergo, part from themselves, part from disregard to their teacher.

5. Let us then give heed unto him exactly, that though late we may at length recover our sight. And how may one recover sight? If thou learn how thou wast blinded. How then wast thou blinded? By thy wicked desire. For the love of money, like an evil humor which hath collected upon a clear eyeball, hath caused the cloud to become thick.

But even this cloud may be easily scattered and broken, if we will receive the beam of the doctrine of Christ; if we will hear him admonishing us, and saying, "Lay not up for yourselves treasures upon earth."

"But," saith one, "what avails the hearing to me, as long as I am possessed by the desire?" Now in the first place, there will be power in the continual hearing to destroy even the desire. Next, if it continue to possess thee, consider that this thing is not really so much as a desire. For what sort of desire is this, to be in grievous bondage, and to be subject to a tyranny, and to be bound on all sides, and to dwell in darkness, and to be full of turmoil, and to endure toils without profit, and to keep thy wealth for others, and often for thy very enemies? with what sort of desire do these things agree? or rather of what flight and aversion are they not worthy? What sort of desire, to lay up treasure in the midst of thieves? Nay, if thou dost at all desire wealth, remove it where it may remain safe and unmolested. Since what you are now doing is the part of one desiring, not riches, surely, but bondage, and affront, and loss, and continual vexation. Yet thou, were any one among men on earth to show thee a place beyond molestation, though he lead thee out into the very desert, promising security in the keeping of thy wealth,—thou art not slow nor backward; thou hast confidence in him, and puttest out thy goods there; but when it is God instead of men who makes thee this promise, and when he sets before thee not the desert, but heaven, thou acceptest the contrary. Yet surely, how manifold soever be their security below, thou canst never become free from the care of them. I mean, though thou lose them not, thou wilt never be delivered from anxiety lest thou lose. But there thou wilt undergo none of these things: and mark, what is yet more, thou dost not only bury thy gold, but plantest it. For the same is both treasure and seed; or rather it is more than either of these. For the seed remains not forever, but this abides perpetually. Again, the treasure germinates not, but this bears thee fruits which never die.

6. But if thou tellest me of the time, and the delay of the recompense, I too can point out and tell how much thou receivest back even here: and besides all this, from the very things of this life, I will try to convict thee of making this excuse to no purpose. I mean, that even in the present life thou providest many things which thou art not thyself to enjoy; and should any one find fault, thou pleadest thy children, and their children, and so thinkest thou hast found palliation enough for thy superfluous labors. For when in extreme old age thou art building splendid houses, before the completion of which (in many instances) thou wilt have departed; when thou plantest trees, which will bear their fruit after many years; when thou art buying properties and inheritances, the ownership of which thou wilt acquire after a long time, and art eagerly busy in many other such things, the enjoyment whereof thou wilt not reap; is it indeed for thine own sake, or for those to come after, that thou art so employed? How then is it not the utmost folly, here not at all to hesitate at the delay of time; and this though thou art by this delay to lose all the reward of thy labors: but there, because of such waiting to be altogether torpid; and this, although it bring thee the greater gain, and although it convey not thy good things on to others, but procure the gifts for thyself.

But besides this, the delay itself it not long; nay, for those things are at the doors, and we know not but that even in our own generation all things which concern us may have their accomplishment, and that fearful day may arrive, setting before us the awful and incorruptible tribunal. Yea, for the more part of the signs are fulfilled, and the gospel moreover hath been preached in all parts of the world, and the predictions of wars, and of earthquakes, and of famines, have come to pass, and the interval is not great.

But is it that thou dost not see any signs? Why, this self-same thing is a very great sign. For neither did they in Noah's time see any presages of that universal destruction, but in the midst of their playing, eating, marrying, doing all things to which they were used, even so they were overtaken by that fearful judgment. And they too in Sodom in like manner, living in delight, and suspecting none of what befell them, were consumed by those lightnings, which then came down upon them.

Considering then all these things, let us betake ourselves unto the preparation for our departure hence.

For even if the common day of the consummation never overtake us, the end of each one is at the doors, whether he be old or young; and it is not possible for men after they have gone hence, either to buy oil any more, or to obtain pardon by prayers, though he that entreats be Abraham [Luke 16:24], or Noah, or Job, or Daniel [Ezek. 14:14].

While then we have opportunity, let us store up for ourselves beforehand much confidence, let us gather oil in abundance, let us remove all into heaven, that in the fitting time, and when we most need them, we may enjoy all: by the grace and love towards man of our Lord Jesus Christ, to whom be the glory, and the might, now and always, and forever and ever. Amen.

Homily XXI

"No man can serve two masters, for either he will hate the one and love the other, or else he will hold to one and despise the other." —*Matt. 6:24*

SEEST THOU HOW BY DEGREES[1] HE withdraws us from the things that now are, and at greater length introduces what he hath to say, touching voluntary poverty, and casts down the dominion of covetousness?

For he was not contented with his former sayings, many and great as they were, but he adds others also, more and more alarming.

For what can be more alarming than what he now saith, if indeed we are for our riches to fall from the service of Christ? or what more to be desired, if indeed, by despising wealth, we shall have our affection towards him and our charity perfect? For what I am continually repeating, the same do I now say likewise, namely, that by both kinds he presses the hearer to obey his sayings; both by the profitable, and by the hurtful; much like an excellent physician, pointing out both the disease which is the consequence of neglect, and the good health which results from obedience.

See, for instance, what kind of gain he signifies this to be, and how he establishes the advantage of it by their deliverance from the contrary things. Thus, "wealth," saith he, "hurts you not in this only, that it arms robbers against you, nor in that it darkens your mind in the most intense degree, but also in that it casts you out of God's service, making you captive of lifeless riches, and in both ways doing you harm, on the one hand,

[1] See our Introduction, p. 26.

by causing you to be slaves of what you ought to command; on the other, by casting you out of God's service, whom, above all things, it is indispensable for you to serve." For just as in the other place, he signified the mischief to be twofold, in both laying up here, "where moth corrupteth," and in not laying up there, where the watch kept is impregnable; so in this place, too, he shows the loss to be twofold, in that it both draws off from God, and makes us subject to mammon.

But he sets it not down directly, rather he establishes it first upon general considerations, saying thus; "No man can serve two masters": meaning here two that are enjoining opposite things; since, unless this were the case, they would not even be two. For so, "the multitude of them that believed were of one heart and of one soul" [Acts 4:32], and yet were they divided into many bodies; their unanimity however made the many one.

Then, as adding to the force of it, he saith, "so far from serving, he will even hate and abhor": "For either he will hate the one," saith he, "and love the other, or else he will hold to the one and despise the other." And it seems indeed as if the same thing were said twice over; he did not however choose this form without purpose, but in order to show that the change for the better is easy. I mean, lest thou shouldest say, "I am once for all made a slave; I am brought under the tyranny of wealth," he signifies that it is possible to transfer one's self, and that as from the first to the second, so also from the second one may pass over to the first.

2. Having thus, you see, spoken generally, that he might persuade the hearer to be an uncorrupt judge of his words, and to sentence according to the very nature of the things; when he hath made sure of his assent, then, and not till then, he discovers himself. Thus he presently adds,

"Ye cannot serve God and mammon."

Let us shudder to think what we have brought Christ to say; with the name of God, to put that of gold. But if this be shocking, its taking place in our deeds, our preferring the tyranny of gold to the fear of God, is much more shocking.

"What then? Was not this possible among the ancients?" By no means. "How then," saith one, "did Abraham, how did Job obtain a good report?" Tell me not of them that are rich, but of them that serve riches. Since Job also was rich, but he served not mammon, but possessed it and ruled over it, and was a master, not a slave. Therefore he so possessed all those things, as if he had been the steward of another man's goods; not only not extorting from others, but even giving up his own to them that were in need. And what is more, when he had them they were no joy to him: so he also declared, saying, "If I did so much as rejoice when my wealth waxed great" [Job 31:25]: wherefore neither did he grieve when it was gone. But they that are rich are not now such as he was, but are rather in a worse condition than any slave, paying as it were tribute to some grievous tyrant. Because their mind is as a kind of citadel occupied by the love of money, which from thence daily sends out unto them its commands full of all iniquity, and there is none to disobey. Be not therefore thus over subtle. Nay, for God hath once for all declared and pronounced it a thing impossible for the one service and the other to agree. Say not thou, then, "it is possible." Why, when the one master is commanding thee to spoil by violence, the other to strip thyself of thy possessions; the one to be chaste, the other to commit fornication; the one to be drunken and luxurious, the other to keep the belly in subjection; the one again to despise the things that are, the other to be rivetted to the present; the one to admire marbles, and walls, and roofs, the other to contemn these, but to honor self-restraint: how is it possible that these should agree?

Now he calls mammon here "a master," not because of its own nature, but on account of the wretchedness of them that bow themselves beneath it. So also he calls the belly a god [Phil. 3:19], not from the dignity of such a mistress, but from the wretchedness of them that are enslaved: it being a thing worse than any punishment, and enough, before the punishment, in the way of vengeance on him who is involved in it. For what condemned criminals can be so wretched, as they who having God for their Lord, do from that mild rule desert to this grievous tyranny, and this when their act brings after it so much harm even here? For indeed their loss is unspeakable by so doing: there are suits, and molestation, and strifes, and toils, and a blinding of the soul; and what is more grievous than all, one falls away from the highest blessings; for such a blessing it is to be God's servant.

3. Having now, as you see, in all ways taught the advantage of contemning riches, as well for the very preservation of the riches, as for the pleasure of the soul, and for acquiring self-command, and for the securing of godliness; he proceeds to establish the practicability of this command. For this especially pertains to the best legislation, not only to enjoin what is expedient, but also to make it possible. Therefore he also goes on to say,

"Take no thought for your life, what ye shall eat."

That is, lest they should say, "What then? if we cast all away, how shall we be able to live?" At this objection, in what follows, he makes a stand, very seasonably. For as surely as if at the beginning he had said, "Take no thought," the word would have seemed burdensome; so surely, now that he hath shown the mischief arising out of covetousness, his admonition coming after is made easy to receive. Wherefore neither did he now simply say, "Take no thought," but added the reason, and so enjoined this. After having said, "Ye cannot serve God and mammon," he added, "therefore I say unto you, take no thought. Therefore," for what? Because of the unspeakable loss. For the hurt you receive is not in riches only, rather the wound is in the most vital parts, and in that which is the overthrow of your salvation; casting you as it does out from God, who made you, and careth for you, and loveth you.

"Therefore I say unto you, take no thought." Thus, after he hath shown the hurt to be unspeakable, then and not before he makes the commandment stricter; in that he not only bids us cast away what we have, but forbids to take thought even for our necessary food, saying, "Take no thought for your soul, what ye shall eat." Not because the soul needs food, for it is incorporeal; but he spake according to the common custom. For though it needs not food, yet can it not endure to remain in the body, except that be fed. And in saying this, he puts it not simply so, but here also he brings up arguments, some from those things which we have already, and some from other examples.

From what we have already, thus saying:

"Is not the soul more than meat, and the body more than the raiment?" [Matt. 6:25].

He therefore that hath given the greater, how shall he not give the less? He that hath fashioned the flesh that is fed, how shall he not bestow the food? Wherefore neither did he simply say, "Take no thought what ye shall eat," or "wherewithal ye shall be clothed"; but, "for the body," and, "for the soul": forasmuch as from them he was to make his demonstrations, carrying on his discourse in the way of comparison. Now the soul he hath given once for all, and it abides such as it is; but the body increases every day. Therefore pointing out both these things, the immortality of the one, and the frailty of the other, he subjoins and says,

"Which of you can add one cubit unto his stature?" [Matt. 6:27].

Thus, saying no more of the soul, since it receives not increase, he discoursed of the body only; hereby making manifest this point also, that not the food increases it, but the providence of God. Which Paul showing also in other ways, said, "So then, neither is he that planteth anything, neither he that watereth; but God that giveth the increase" [I Cor. 3:7].

From what we have already, then, He urges us in this way: and from examples of other things, by saying, "Behold the fowls of the air" [Matt. 6:26]. Thus, lest any should say, "we do good by taking thought," he dissuades them both by that which is greater, and by that which is less; by the greater, i.e., the soul and the body; by the less, i.e., the birds. For if of the things that are very inferior he hath so much regard, how shall he not give unto you? saith he. And to them on this wise, for as yet it was an ordinary multitude: but to the devil not thus; but how? "Man shall not live by bread alone, but by every word that proceedeth out of the mouth of God" [Matt. 4:4]. But here he makes mention of the birds, and this in a way greatly to abash them; which sort of thing is of very great value for the purpose of admonition.

4. However, some of the ungodly have come to so great a pitch of madness, as even to attack his illustration. Because, say they, it was not meet for one strengthening moral principle, to use natural advantages as incitements to that end.[2] For to those animals, they add, this belongs by nature. What then shall we say to this? That even though it is theirs by nature, yet possibly we too may attain it by choice. For neither did he say, "behold how the birds fly," which were a thing impossible to man; but that they are fed without taking thought, a kind of thing easy to be achieved by us also, if we will. And this they have proved, who have accomplished it in their actions.

Wherefore it were meet exceedingly to admire the consideration of our Lawgiver, in that, when he might bring forward his illustration from among men, and when he might have spoken of Moses and Elias and John, and others like them, who took no thought; that he might touch them more to the quick, he made mention of the irrational beings. For had he spoken of those righteous men, these would have been able to say, "We are not yet become like them." But now by passing them over in silence, and bringing forward the fowls of the air, he hath cut off from them every excuse, imitating in this place also the old law. Yea, for the old covenant likewise sends to the bee, and to the ant [Prov. 6:6-8], and to the turtle, and to the swallow [Jer. 8:7]. And neither is this a small

[2] As part of their abhorrence of creation, some Gnostics even questioned the use of natural analogies for "spiritual" truths; cf. Introduction, p. 11.

sign of honor, when the same sort of things, which those animals possess by nature, those we are able to accomplish by an act of our choice. If then he take so great care of them which exist for our sakes, much more of us; if of the servants, much more of the master. Therefore he said, "Behold the fowls," and he said not, "for they do not traffic, nor make merchandise," for these were among the things that were earnestly forbidden. But what? "they sow not, neither do they reap." "What then?" saith one, "must we not sow?" He said not, "we must not sow," but "we must not *take thought*"; neither that one ought not to work, but not to be low-minded, nor to rack one's self with cares. Since he bade us also be nourished, but not in "taking thought."

Of this lesson David also lays the foundation from old time, saying enigmatically on this wise, "Thou openest thine hand, and fillest every living thing with bounty" [Ps. 145:16]; and again, "To him that giveth to the beasts their food, and to the young ravens that call upon him" [Ps. 147:9].

"Who then," it may be said, "have not taken thought?" Didst thou not hear how many of the righteous I adduced? Seest thou not with them Jacob, departing from his father's house destitute of all things? Dost thou not hear him praying and saying, "If the Lord give me bread to eat and raiment to put on?" [Gen. 28:20] which was not the part of one taking thought, but of one seeking all of God. This the apostles also attained, who cast away all, and took no thought: also, the "five thousand," and the "three thousand" [Acts 4:4; 2:41].

5. But if thou canst not bear, upon hearing so high words, to release thyself from these grievous bonds, consider the unprofitableness of the thing, and so put an end to thy care. For "Which of you by taking thought" (saith he) "can add one cubit unto his stature" [Matt. 6:27].

Seest thou how by that which is evident, he hath manifested that also which is obscure? Thus, "As unto thy body," saith he, "thou wilt not by taking thought be able to add, though it be ever so little; so neither to gather food; think as thou mayest otherwise."

Hence it is clear that not our diligence, but the providence of God, even where we seem to be active, effects all. So that, were he to forsake us, no care, nor anxiety, nor toil, nor any other such thing, will ever appear to come to anything, but all will utterly pass away.

Let us not therefore suppose his injunctions are impossible: for there are many who duly perform them, even as it is. And if thou knowest not of them, it is nothing marvellous, since Elias too supposed he was alone, but was told, "I have left unto myself seven thousand men" [I Kings 19:18; Rom. 11:4]. Whence it is manifest that even now there are many who show forth the apostolical life;[3] like as the "three thousand" then, and the "five thousand" [Acts 2:41; 4:4]. And if we believe not, it is not because there are none who do well, but because we are far from so doing. So that just as the drunkard would not easily believe, that there exists any man who doth not taste even water (and yet this hath been achieved by many solitaries in our time); nor he who connects himself with numberless women, that it is easy to live in virginity; nor he that extorts other men's goods, that one shall readily give up even his own: so neither will those, who daily melt themselves down with innumerable anxieties, easily receive this thing.

Now as to the fact, that there are many who have attained unto this, we might show it even from those, who have practised this self-denial even in our generation.

But for you, just now, it is enough to learn not to covet, and that almsgiving is a good thing; and to know that you must impart of what ye have. For these things if thou wilt duly perform, beloved, thou wilt speedily proceed to those others also.

6. For the present therefore let us lay aside our excessive

[3] From the context it seems plausible, though not certain, that "the apostolical life" was a synonym for "the monastic life."

sumptuousness, and let us endure moderation, and learn to acquire by honest labor all that we are to have: since even the blessed John, when he was discoursing with those that were employed upon the tribute, and with the soldiery, enjoined them "to be content with their wages" [Luke 3:14]. Anxious though he were to lead them on to another, and a higher self-command, yet since they were still unfit for this, he speaks of the lesser things. Because, if he had mentioned what are higher than these, they would have failed to apply themselves to them, and would have fallen from the others.

For this very reason we too are practising you in the inferior duties. Yes, because as yet, we know, the burden of voluntary poverty is too great for you, and the heaven is not more distant from the earth, than such self-denial from you. Let us then lay hold, if it be only of the lowest commandments, for even this is no small encouragement. And yet some amongst the heathens have achieved even this, though not in a proper spirit, and have stripped themselves of all their possessions.[4] However, we are contented in your case, if alms are bestowed abundantly by you; for we shall soon arrive at those other duties too, if we advance in this way. But if we do not so much as this, of what favor shall we be worthy, who are hidden to surpass those under the old law, and yet show ourselves inferior to the philosophers among the heathens? What shall we say, who when we ought to be angels and sons of God, do not even quite maintain our being as men? For to spoil and to covet comes not of the gentleness of men, but of the fierceness of wild beasts; nay, worse than wild beasts are the assailers of their neighbor's goods. For to them this comes by nature, but we who are honored with reason, and yet are falling away unto that unnatural vileness, what indulgence shall we receive?

Let us then, considering the measures of that discipline

[4] Perhaps a reference to Diogenes and to the Cynics, who had been praised by another student of Libanius at Antioch, the emperor Julian.

which is set before us, press on at least to the middle station, that we may both be delivered from the punishment which is to come, and proceeding regularly, may arrive at the very summit of all good things; unto which may we all attain, by the grace and love towards man of our Lord Jesus Christ, to whom be glory and dominion for ever and ever. Amen.

Homily XXII

"Consider the lilies of the field, how they grow; they toil not, neither do they spin. And yet I say unto you, that even Solomon in all his glory was not arrayed like one of these."
—Matt. 6:28, 29

HAVING SPOKEN OF OUR NECESSARY food, and having signified that not even for this should we take thought, he passes on in what follows to that which is more easy. For raiment is not so necessary as food.

Why then did he not make use here also of the same example, that of the birds, neither mention to us the peacock, and the swan, and the sheep? for surely there were many such examples to take from thence. Because he would point out how very far the argument may be carried both ways: both from the vileness of the things that partake of such elegance, and from the munificence vouchsafed to the lilies, in respect of their adorning. For this cause, when he hath decked them out, he doth not so much as call them lilies any more, but "grass of the field" [Matt. 6:30]. And he is not satisfied even with this name, but again adds another circumstance of vileness, saying, "which today is." And he said not, "and tomorrow is not," but what is much baser yet, "is cast into the oven." And he said not, "clothe," but "so clothe."

Seest thou everywhere how he abounds in amplifications and intensities? And this he doth, that he may touch them home: and therefore he hath also added, "shall he not much more clothe you?" For this too hath much emphasis: the force of the word, "you," being no other than to indicate covertly the great value set upon our race, and the concern shown for it; as though he had said, "*you,* to whom he gave a soul, for whom he fashioned a body, for whose sake he made all the things that are seen, for whose sake he sent prophets, and gave the law, and wrought those innumerable good works; for whose sake he gave up his only begotten Son."

And not till he hath made his proof clear, doth he proceed also to rebuke them, saying, "O ye of little faith." For this is the quality of an adviser: he doth not admonish only, but reproves also, that he may awaken men the more to the persuasive power of his words.

Hereby he teaches us not only to take no thought, but not even to be dazzled at the costliness of men's apparel. Why, such comeliness is of grass, such beauty of the green herb: or rather, the grass is even more precious than such apparelling. Why then pride thyself on things, whereof the prize rests with the mere plant, with a great balance in its favor?

And see how from the beginning he signifies the injunction to be easy; by the contraries again, and by the things of which they were afraid, leading them away from these cares. Thus, when he had said, "Consider the lilies of the field," he added, "they toil not": so that in desire to set us free from toils, did he give these commands. In fact, the labor lies, not in taking no thought, but in taking thought for these things. And as in saying, "they sow not," it was not the sowing that he did away with, but the anxious thought; so in saying, "they toil not, neither do they spin," he put an end not to the work, but to the care.

But if Solomon was surpassed by their beauty, and that not once nor twice, but throughout all his reign:—for neither can one say, that at one time he was clothed with such apparel, but after that he was so no more; rather not so much as on one day did he array himself so beautifully: for this Christ declared by saying, "in all his reign": and if it was not that he was surpassed by this flower, but vied with that, but he gave place to all alike (wherefore He also said, "as one of these": for such as between the truth and the counterfeit, so great is the interval between those robes and these flowers):—if then he acknowledged his inferiority, who was more glorious than all kings that ever were: when wilt thou be able to surpass, or rather to approach even faintly to such perfection of form?

After this he instructs us, not to aim at all at such ornament. See at least the end thereof; after its triumph "it is cast into the oven": and if of things mean, and worthless, and of no great use, God hath displayed so great care, how shall he give up thee, of all living creatures the most important?

Wherefore then did he make them so beautiful? That he might display his own wisdom and the excellency of his power; that from everything we might learn his glory. For not "the heavens only declare the glory of God" [Ps. 19:1], but the earth too; and this David declared when he said, "Praise the Lord, ye fruitful trees, and all cedars" [Ps. 148:9]. For some by their fruits, some by their greatness, some by their beauty, send up praise to him who made them: this too being a sign of great excellency of wisdom, when even upon things that are very vile (and what can be viler than that which today is, and tomorrow is not?) he pours out such great beauty. If then to the grass he hath given that which it needs not (for what doth the beauty thereof help to the feeding of the fire?) how shall he not give unto thee that which thou needest? If that which is the vilest of all things, he hath lavishly adorned, and that as doing it not for need, but for munificence, how much more will he honor thee, the most honorable of all things, in matters which are of necessity.

2. Now when, as you see, he had demonstrated the greatness of God's providential care, and they were in what follows to be rebuked also, even in this he was sparing, laying to their charge not want, but poverty, of faith. Thus, "if God" saith he, "so clothe the grass of the field, much more you, O ye of little faith" [Matt. 6:30].

And yet surely all these things he himself works. For "all things were made by him, and without him was not so much as one thing made" [John 1:3]. But yet he nowhere as yet makes mention of himself: it being sufficient for the time, to indicate his full power, that he said at each of the commandments, "Ye have heard that it hath been said to them of old time, but I say unto you."

Marvel not then, when in subsequent instances also he conceals himself, or speaks something lowly of himself: since for the present he had but one object, that his word might prove such as they would readily receive, and might in every way demonstrate that he was not a sort of adversary of God, but of one mind, and in agreement with the Father.

Which accordingly he doth here also; for through so many words as he hath spent he ceases not to set him before us, admiring his wisdom, his providence, his tender care extending through all things, both great and small. Thus, both when he was speaking of Jerusalem, he called it "the city of the Great King" [Matt. 5:35]; and when he mentioned heaven, he spake of it again as "God's throne" [Matt. 5:34]; and when he was discoursing of his economy in the world, to him again he attributes it all, saying, "he maketh his sun to rise on the evil and on the good, and sendeth rain on the just and on the unjust" [Matt. 5:45]. And in the prayer too he taught us to say, his "is the kingdom and the power and the glory." And here in discoursing of his providence, and signifying how even in little things he is the most excellent of artists, he saith, that "he clothes the grass of the field." And nowhere doth he call him his own Father, but theirs; in order that by the very honor he might reprove them, and that when he should call him his Father, they might no more be displeased.

Now if for bare necessaries one is not to take thought, what pardon can we deserve, who take thought for things expensive? Or rather, what pardon can they deserve, who do even without sleep, that they may take the things of others?

3. "Therefore take no thought, saying, what shall we eat? or, what shall we drink? or wherewithal shall we be clothed? For after all these things do the nations of the world seek" [Matt. 6:31, 32; Luke 12:30].

Seest thou how again he hath both shamed them the more,

and hath also shown by the way, that he had commanded nothing grievous nor burdensome? As therefore when he said, "If ye love them which love you," it is nothing great which ye practise, for the very Gentiles do the same; by the mention of the Gentiles he was stirring them up to something greater: so now also he brings them forward to reprove us, and to signify that it is a necessary debt which he is requiring of us. For if we must show forth something more than the Scribes or Pharisees, what can we deserve, who so far from going beyond these, do even abide in the mean estate of the Gentiles, and emulate their littleness of soul?

He doth not however stop at the rebuke, but having by this reproved and roused them, and shamed them with all strength of expression, by another argument he also comforts them, saying, "For your heavenly Father knoweth that ye have need of all these things." He said not, "God knoweth," but, "your Father knoweth"; to lead them to a greater hope. For if he be a Father, and such a Father, he will not surely be able to overlook his children in extremity of evils; seeing that not even men, being fathers, bear to do so.

And he adds along with this yet another argument. Of what kind then is it? That "ye have need" of them. What he saith is like this. What! are these things superfluous, that he should disregard them? Yet not even in superfluities did he show himself wanting in regard, in the instance of the grass: but now are these things even necessary. So that what thou considerest a cause for thy being anxious, this I say is sufficient to draw thee from such anxiety. I mean, if thou sayest, "Therefore I must needs take thought, because they are necessary"; on the contrary, I say, "Nay, for this self-same reason take no thought, because they are necessary." Since were they superfluities, not even then ought we to despair, but to feel confident about the supply of them; but now that they are necessary, we must no longer be in doubt. For what kind of father is he, who can endure to fail in supplying to his children even necessaries? So that for this cause again God will most surely bestow them.

For indeed he is the artificer of our nature, and he knows perfectly the wants thereof. So that neither canst thou say, "He is indeed our Father, and the things we seek are necessary, but he knows not that we stand in need of them." For he that knows our nature itself, and was the framer of it, and formed it such as it is; evidently he knows its need also better than thou, who art placed in want of them: it having been by his decree, that our nature is in such need. He will not therefore oppose himself to what he hath willed, first subjecting it of necessity to so great want, and on the other hand again depriving it of what it wants, and of absolute necessaries.

Let us not therefore be anxious, for we shall gain nothing by it, but tormenting ourselves. For whereas he gives both when we take thought, and when we do not, and more of the two, when we do not; what dost thou gain by thy anxiety, but to exact of thyself a superfluous penalty? Since one on the point of going to a plentiful feast, will not surely permit himself to take thought for food; nor is he that is walking to a fountain anxious about drink. Therefore seeing we have a supply more copious than either any fountain, or innumerable banquets made ready, the providence of God; let us not be beggars, nor little minded.

4. For together with what hath been said, he puts also yet another reason for feeling confidence about such things, saying,

"Seek ye the kingdom of heaven, and all these things shall be added unto you" [Matt. 6:33].

Thus when he had set the soul free from anxiety, then he made mention also of heaven. For indeed he came to do away with the old things, and to call us to a greater country. Therefore he doeth all, to deliver us from things unnecessary, and from our affection for the earth. For this cause he mentioned the heathens also, saying that "the Gentiles seek after these things"; they whose whole labor is for the present life, who have no regard for the things to come, nor any thought of heaven. But to you not these present are the chief things, but other than these. For we were not born for this end, that we should eat and drink and be clothed, but that we might please God, and attain unto the good things to come. Therefore as things here are secondary in our labor, so also in our prayers let them be secondary. Therefore he also said, "Seek ye the kingdom of heaven, and all these things shall be added unto you."

And he said not, "shall be given," but "shall be added," that thou mightest learn, that the things present are no great part of his gifts, compared with the greatness of the things to come. Accordingly, he doth not bid us so much as ask for them, but while we ask for other things, to have confidence, as though these also were added to those. Seek then the things to come, and thou wilt receive the things present also; seek not the things that are seen, and thou shalt surely attain unto them. Yea, for it is unworthy of thee to approach thy Lord for such things. And thou, who oughtest to spend all thy zeal and thy care for those unspeakable blessings, dost greatly disgrace thyself by consuming it on the desire of transitory things.

"How then?" saith one, "did he not bid us ask for bread?" Nay, he added, "daily," and to this again, "this day," which same thing in fact he doth here also. For he said not, "Take no thought," but, "Take no thought for the morrow," at the same time both affording us liberty, and fastening our soul on those things that are more necessary to us.

For to this end also he bade us ask even those, not as though God needed reminding by us, but that we might learn that by his help we accomplish whatever we do accomplish, and that we might be made more his own by our continual prayer for these things.

Seest thou how by this again he would persuade them, that they shall surely receive the things present? For he that bestows the greater, much more will he give the less. "For not for this end," saith he, "did I tell you not to take thought nor to ask, that ye should suffer distress, and go about naked, but in order that ye might be in abundance of these things also":

and this, you see, was suited above all things to attract them to him. So that like as in almsgiving, when deterring them from making a display to men, he won upon them chiefly by promising to furnish them with it more liberally;—"for thy Father," saith he, "who seeth in secret, shall reward thee openly" [Matt. 6:4]—even so here also, in drawing them off from seeking these things, this is his persuasive topic, that he promises to bestow it on them, not seeking it, in greater abundance. Thus, to this end, saith he, do I bid thee not seek, not that thou mayest not receive, but that thou mayest receive plentifully; that thou mayest receive in the fashion that becomes thee, with the profit which thou oughtest to have; that thou mayest not, by taking thought, and distracting thyself in anxiety about these, render thyself unworthy both of these, and of the things spiritual; that thou mayest not undergo unnecessary distress, and again fall away from that which is set before thee.

5. "Take therefore no thought for the morrow: for sufficient unto the day is the evil thereof": that is to say, the affliction, and the bruising thereof [Matt. 6:34]. Is it not enough for thee, to eat thy bread in the sweat of thy face? Why add the further affliction that comes of anxiety, when thou art on the point to be delivered henceforth even from the former toils?

By "evil" here he means, not wickedness, far from it, but affliction, and trouble, and calamities; much as in another place also he saith, "Is there evil in a city, which the Lord hath not done?" [Amos 3:6] not meaning rapines, nor injuries, nor anything like these, but the scourges which are borne from above. And again, "I" saith he, "make peace, and create evils" [Isa. 45:7]: For neither in this place doth he speak of wickedness, but of famines, and pestilences, things accounted evil by most men: the generality being wont to call these things evil. Thus, for example, the priests and prophets of those five lordships, when having yoked the kine to the ark, they let them go without their calves [I Sam. 6:7], gave the name of "evil" to those heaven-sent plagues, and the dismay and anguish which thereby sprang up within them.

This then is his meaning here also, when he saith, "sufficient unto the day is the evil thereof." For nothing so pains the soul, as carefulness and anxiety. Thus did Paul also, when urging to celibacy, give counsel, saying, "I would have you without carefulness" [I Cor. 7:32].

But when he saith, "the morrow shall take thought for itself," he saith it not, as though the day took thought for these things, but forasmuch as he had to speak to a people somewhat imperfect, willing to make what he saith more expressive, he personifies the time,[1] speaking unto them according to the custom of the generality.

And here indeed he advises, but as he proceeds, he even makes it a law, saying, "provide neither gold nor silver, nor scrip for your journey" [Matt. 10:9, 10]. Thus, having shown it all forth in his actions, then after that he introduces the verbal enactment of it more determinately, the precept too having then become more easy of acceptance, confirmed as it had been previously by his own actions. Where then did he confirm it by his actions? Hear him saying, "The Son of Man hath not where to lay his head" [Matt. 8:20]. Neither is he satisfied with this only, but in his disciples also he exhibits his full proof of these things, by fashioning them too in like manner, yet not suffering them to be in want of anything.

But mark his tender care also, how he surpasses the affection of any father. Thus, "This I command," saith he, "for nothing else, but that I may deliver you from superfluous anxieties. For even if today thou hast taken thought for tomorrow, thou wilt also have to take thought again tomorrow. Why then what is over and above? Why force the day to receive more than the distress which is allotted to it, and together with its own troubles add to it also the burden of the following day; and this, when there is no chance of thy lightening the other by the addition so taking place, but thou art merely to exhibit thyself as coveting superfluous troubles?" Thus, that he may

[1] Chrysostom refers here to the figure of speech called in Greek *prosōpopoiia*.

reprove them the more, he doth all but give life to the very time, and brings it in as one injured, and exclaiming against them for their causeless despite. Why, thou hast received the day, to care for the things thereof. Wherefore then add unto it the things of the other day also? Hath it not then burden enough in its own anxiety? Why now, I pray, dost thou make it yet heavier? Now when the Lawgiver saith these things, and he that is to pass judgment on us, consider the hopes that he suggests to us, how good they are; he himself testifying, that this life is wretched and wearisome, so that the anxiety even of the one day is enough to hurt and afflict us.

6. Nevertheless, after so many and so grave words, we take thought for these things, but for the things in heaven no longer: rather we have reversed his order, on either side fighting against his sayings. For mark; "Seek ye not the things, present," saith he, "at all"; but we are seeking these things for ever: "seek the things in heaven," saith he; but those things we seek not so much as for a short hour, but according to the greatness of the anxiety we display about the things of the world, is the carelessness we entertain in things spiritual; or rather even much greater. But this doth not prosper forever; neither can this be forever. What if for ten days we think scorn? if for twenty? if for an hundred? must we not of absolute necessity depart, and fall into the hands of the Judge?

"But the delay hath comfort." And what sort of comfort, to be every day looking for punishment and vengeance? Nay, if thou wouldest have some comfort from this delay, take it by gathering for thyself the fruit of amendment after repentance. Since if the mere delay of vengeance seem to thee a sort of refreshment, far more is it gain not to fall into the vengeance. Let us then make full use of this delay, in order to have a full deliverance from the dangers that press upon us. For none of the things enjoined is either burdensome or grievous, but all are so light and easy, that if we only bring a genuine purpose of heart, we may accomplish all, though we be chargeable with countless offenses. For so Manasses had perpetrated innumerable pollutions, having both stretched out his hands against the saints, and brought abominations into the temple, and filled the city with murders, and wrought many other things beyond excuse; yet nevertheless after so long and so great wickedness, he washed away from himself all these things [II Chron. 33:1-20; II Kings 21:1-18]. How and in what manner? By repentance, and consideration.

For there is not, yea, there is not any sin, that doth not yield and give way to the power of repentance, or rather to the grace of Christ. Since if we would but only change, we have him to assist us. And if thou art desirous to become good, there is none to hinder us; or rather there is one to hinder us, the devil, yet hath he no power, so long as thou choosest what is best, and so attractest God to thine aid. But if thou art not thyself willing, but startest aside, how shall he protect thee? Since not of necessity or compulsion, but of thine own will, he wills thee to be saved. For if thou thyself, having a servant full of hatred and aversion for thee, and continually going off, and fleeing away from thee, wouldest not choose to keep him, and this though needing his services; much less will God, who doeth all things not for his own profit, but for thy salvation, choose to retain thee by compulsion; as on the other hand, if thou show forth a right intention only, he would not choose ever to give thee up, no, not whatever the devil may do. So that we are ourselves to blame for our own destruction. Because we do not approach, nor beseech, nor entreat him, as we ought: but even if we do draw nigh, it is not as persons who have need to receive, neither is it with the proper faith, nor as making demand, but we do all in a gaping and listless way.

7. And yet God would have us demand things of him, and for this accounts himself greatly bound to thee. For he alone of all debtors, when the demand is made, counts it a favor, and gives what we have not lent him. And if he should see him pressing earnestly that makes the demand, he pays down even what he hath not received of us; but if sluggishly, he too keeps on making delays; not through unwillingness to give,

but because he is pleased to have the demand made upon him by us. For this cause he told thee also the example of that friend, who came by night, and asked a loaf [Luke 11:5-8]; and of the judge that feared not God, nor regarded men [Luke 18:1-8]. And he stayed not at similitudes, but signified it also in his very actions, when he dismissed that Phoenician woman, having filled her with his great gift [Matt. 15:21-28; Mark 7:24-30]. For through her he signified, that he gives to them that ask earnestly, even the things that pertain not to them. "For it is not meet," saith he, "to take the children's bread, and to give it unto the dogs." But for all that he gave, because she demanded of him earnestly. But by the Jews he showed, that to them that are careless, he gives not even their own. They accordingly received nothing, but lost what was their own. And while these, because they asked not, did not receive so much as their very own; she, because she assailed him with earnestness, had power to obtain even what pertained to others, and the dog received what was the children's. So great a good is importunity. For though thou be a dog, yet being importunate, thou shalt be preferred to the child being negligent: for what things affection accomplishes not, these, all of them, importunity did accomplish. Say not therefore, "God is an enemy to me, and will not hearken." He doth straightway answer thee, continually troubling him, if not because thou art his friend, yet because of thine importunity. And neither the enmity, or the unseasonable time, nor anything else becomes an hindrance. Say not, "I am unworthy, and do not pray"; for such was the Syrophoenician woman too. Say not, "I have sinned much, and am not able to entreat him whom I have angered"; for God looks not at the desert, but at the disposition. For if the ruler that feared not God, neither was ashamed of men, was overcome by the widow, much more will he that is good be won over by continual entreaty.

So that though thou be no friend, though thou be not demanding thy due, though thou hast devoured thy Father's substance, and have been a long time out of sight, though without honor, though last of all, though thou approach him angry, though much displeased; be willing only to pray, and to return, and thou shalt receive all, and shall quickly extinguish the wrath and the condemnation (cf. Luke 15:11-32).

But, "behold, I pray," saith one, "and there is no result." Why, thou prayest not like those; such I mean as the Syrophoenician woman, the friend that came late at night, and the widow that is continually troubling the judge, and the son that consumed his father's goods. For didst thou so pray, thou wouldest quickly obtain. For though despite have been done unto him, yet is he a Father; and though he have been provoked to anger, yet is he fond of his children; and one thing only doth he seek, not to take vengeance for our affronts, but to see thee repenting and entreating him. Would that we were warmed in like measure, as those bowels are moved to the love of us. But this fire seeks a beginning only, and if thou afford it a little spark, thou kindlest a full flame of beneficence. For not because he hath been insulted, is he sore vexed, but because it is thou who art insulting him, and so becoming frenzied. For if we being evil, when our children molest us, grieve on their account; much more is God, who cannot so much as suffer insult, sore vexed on account of thee, who hast committed it. If we, who love by nature, much more he, who is kindly affectioned beyond nature. "For though," saith he, " a woman should forget the fruits of her womb, yet will I not forget thee" [Isa. 49:15].

8. Let us therefore draw nigh unto him, and say, "Truth, Lord; for even the dogs eat of the crumbs which fall from their masters' table" [Matt. 15:27]. Let us draw nigh "in season, out of season": or rather, one can never draw nigh out of season, for it is unseasonable not to be continually approaching. For of him who desires to give it is always seasonable to ask: yea, as breathing is never out of season, so neither is praying unseasonable, but rather not praying. Since as we need this breath, so do we also the help that comes from him; and if we be willing, we shall easily draw him to us. And the prophet,

to manifest this, and to point out the constant readiness of his beneficence, said, "We shall find him prepared as the morning" [Hos. 6:3]. For as often as we may draw nigh, we shall see him awaiting our movements. And if we fail to draw from out of his ever-springing goodness, the blame is all ours. This, for example, was his complaint against certain Jews, when he said, "My mercy is as a morning cloud, and as the early dew it goeth away" [Hos. 6:4]. And his meaning is like this; "I indeed have supplied all my part, but ye, as a hot sun coming over scatters both the cloud and the dew, and makes them vanish, so have ye by your great wickedness restrained the unspeakable Beneficence."

Which also itself again is an instance of providential care: that even when he sees us unworthy to receive good, he withholds his benefits, lest he render us careless. But if we change a little, even but so much as to know that we have sinned, he gushes out beyond the fountains, he is poured forth beyond the ocean; and the more thou receivest, so much the more doth he rejoice; and in this way is stirred up again to give us more. For indeed he accounts it as his own wealth, that we should be saved, and that he should give largely to them that ask. And this, it may seem, Paul was declaring when he said, that he is "rich unto all and over all that call upon him" [Rom. 10:12]. Because when we pray not, then he is wroth; when we pray not, then doth he turn away from us. For this cause "he became poor, that he might make us rich" [II Cor. 8:9]; for this cause he underwent all those sufferings, that he might incite us to ask.

Let us not therefore despair, but having so many motives and good hopes, though we sin every day, let us approach him, entreating, beseeching, asking the forgiveness of our sins. For thus we shall be more backward to sin for the time to come; thus shall we drive away the devil, and shall call forth the lovingkindness of God, and attain unto the good things to come, by the grace and love towards man of our Lord Jesus Christ, to whom be glory and might forever and ever. Amen.

Homily XXIII

"Judge not, that ye be not judged." —*Matt. 7:1*

WHAT THEN? OUGHT WE NOT TO blame them that sin? Because Paul also saith this self-same thing: or rather, there too it is Christ, speaking by Paul, and saying, "Why dost thou judge thy brother? And thou, why dost thou set at nought thy brother?" [Rom. 14:10] and, "Who art thou that judgest another man's servant?" [Rom. 14:4]. And again, "Therefore judge nothing before the time, until the Lord come" [I Cor. 4:5].

How then doth he say elsewhere, "Reprove, rebuke, exhort," [II Tim. 4:2] and, "Them that sin rebuke before all" [I Tim. 5:20]? And Christ too to Peter, "Go and tell him his fault between thee and him alone, and if he neglect to hear, add to thyself another also; and if not even so doth he yield, declare it to the church likewise" [Matt. 18:15-17]? And how hath he set over us so many to reprove; and not only to reprove, but also to punish? For him that hearkens to none of these, he hath commanded to be "as a heathen man and a publican" [Matt. 18:17]. And how gave he them the keys also? since if they are not to judge, they will be without authority in any matter, and in vain have they received the power to bind and to loose.

And besides, if this were to obtain, all would be lost alike, whether in churches, or in states, or in houses. For except the master judge the servant, and the mistress the maid, and the father the son, and friends one another, there will be an increase of all wickedness. And why say I, friends? unless we judge our enemies, we shall never be able to put an end to our enmity, but all things will be turned upside down.

What then can the saying be? Let us carefully attend, lest the medicines of salvation, and the laws of peace, be accounted by any man laws of overthrow and confusion. First of all, then, even by what follows, he hath pointed out to them that have understanding the excellency of this law, saying, "Why beholdest thou the mote that is in thy brother's eye, but considerest not the beam that is in thine own eye?" [Matt. 7:3].

But if to many of the less attentive, it seem yet rather obscure, I will endeavor to explain it from the beginning. In this place, then, as it seems at least to me, he doth not simply command us not to judge any of men's sins, neither doth he simply forbid the doing of such a thing, but to them that are full of innumerable ills, and are trampling upon other men for trifles. And I think that certain Jews too are here hinted at, for that while they were bitter accusing their neighbors for small faults, and such as came to nothing, they were themselves insensibly committing deadly sins. Herewith towards the end also he was upbraiding them, when he said, "Ye bind heavy burdens, and grievous to be borne, but ye will not move them with your finger" [Matt. 23:4], and, "ye pay tithe of mint and anise, and have omitted the weightier matters of the law, judgment, mercy, and faith" [Matt. 23:23].

Well then, I think that these are comprehended in his invective; that he is checking them beforehand as to those things, wherein they were hereafter to accuse his disciples. For although his disciples had been guilty of no such sin, yet in them were supposed to be offenses; as, for instance, not keeping the sabbath, eating with unwashen hands, sitting at meat with publicans; of which he saith also in another place, "Ye which strain at the gnat, and swallow the camel" [Matt. 23:24]. But yet it is also a general law that he is laying down on these matters.

And the Corinthians [I Cor. 4:5] too Paul did not absolutely command not to judge, but not to judge their own superiors, and upon grounds that are not acknowledged; not absolutely to refrain from correcting them that sin. Neither indeed was he then rebuking all without distinction, but disciples doing so to their teachers were the object of his reproof; and they who, being guilty of innumerable sins, bring an evil report upon the guiltless.

This then is the sort of thing which Christ also in this place intimated; not intimated merely, but guarded it too with a great terror, and the punishment from which no prayers can deliver.

2. "For with what judgment ye judge," saith he, "ye shall be judged" [Matt. 7:2].

That is, "it is not the other," saith Christ, "that thou condemnest, but thyself, and thou art making the judgment-seat dreadful to thyself, and the account strict." As then in the forgiveness of our sins the beginnings are from us, so also in this judgment, it is by ourselves that the measures of our condemnation are laid down. You see, we ought not to upbraid nor trample upon them, but to admonish; not to revile, but to advise; not to assail with pride, but to correct with tenderness. For not him, but thyself, dost thou give over to extreme vengeance, by not sparing him, when it may be needful to give sentence on his offenses.

Seest thou, how these two commandments are both easy, and fraught with great blessings to the obedient, even as of evils on the other hand, to the regardless? For both he that forgives his neighbor, hath freed himself first of the two from the grounds of complaint, and that without any labor; and he that with tenderness and indulgence inquires into other men's offenses, great is the allowance of pardon, which he hath by his judgment laid up beforehand for himself.

"What then!" say you: "if one commit fornication, may I not say that fornication is a bad thing, nor at all correct him that is playing the wanton?" Nay, correct him, but not as a foe, nor as an adversary exacting a penalty, but as a physician providing medicines. For neither did Christ say, "stay not him that is sinning," but "judge not"; that is, be not bitter in pronouncing sentence.

And besides, it is not of great things (as I have already observed), nor of things prohibited, that this is said, but of those which are not even counted offenses. Wherefore he said also,

"Why beholdest thou the mote that is in thy brother's eye?" [Matt. 7:3].

Yea, for many now do this; if they see but a monk wearing an unnecessary garment, they produce against him the law of our Lord [Matt. 10:10], while they themselves are extorting without end, and defrauding men every day. If they see him but partaking rather largely of food, they become bitter accusers, while they themselves are daily drinking to excess and surfeiting: not knowing, that besides their own sins, they do hereby gather up for themselves a greater flame, and deprive themselves of every plea. For on this point, that thine own doings must be strictly inquired into, thou thyself hast first made the law, by thus sentencing those of thy neighbor. Account it not then to be a grievous thing, if thou art also thyself to undergo the same kind of trial.

"Thou hypocrite, first cast out the beam out of thine own eye" [Matt. 7:5].

Here his will is to signify the great wrath, which he hath against them that do such things. For so, wheresoever he would indicate that the sin is great, and the punishment and wrath in store for it grievous, he begins with a reproach. As then unto him that was exacting the hundred pence, he said in his deep displeasure, "Thou wicked servant, I forgave thee all that debt" [Matt. 18:32]; even so here also, "Thou hypocrite." For not of protecting care comes such a judgment, but of ill will to man; and while a man puts forward a mask of benevolence, he is doing a work of the utmost wickedness, causing reproaches without ground, and accusations, to cleave unto his neighbors, and usurping a teacher's rank, when he is not worthy to be so much as a disciple. On account of this he called him "hypocrite." For thou, who in other men's doings art so bitter, as to see even the little things; how hast thou become so remiss in thine own, as that even the great things are hurried over by thee?

"First cast out the beam out of thine own eye."

Seest thou, that he forbids not judging, but commands to cast out first the beam from thine eye, and then to set right the doings of the rest of the world? For indeed each one knows his own things better than those of others; and sees the greater rather than the less; and loves himself more than his neighbor. Wherefore, if thou doest it out of guardian care, I bid thee care for thyself first, in whose case the sin is both more certain and greater. But if thou neglect thyself, it is quite evident that neither dost thou judge thy brother in care for him, but in hatred, and wishing to expose him. For what if he ought to be judged? it should be by one who commits no such sin, not by thee.

Thus, because he had introduced great and high doctrines of self-denial, lest any man should say, it is easy so to practise it in words; he willing to signify his entire confidence, and that he was not chargeable with any of the things that had been mentioned, but had duly fulfilled all, spake this parable. And that, because he too was afterwards to judge, saying, "Woe unto you, Scribes and Pharisees, hypocrites" [Matt. 13:13]. Yet was not he chargeable with what hath been mentioned; for neither did he pull out a mote, nor had he a beam on his eyes, but being clean from all these, he so corrected the faults of all. "For it is not at all meet," saith he, "to judge others, when one is chargeable with the same things." And why marvel at his establishing this law, when even the very thief knew it upon the cross, saying to the other thief, "Dost not thou fear God, seeing we are in the same condemnation" [Luke 23:40, 41]; expressing the same sentiments with Christ?

But thou, so far from casting out thine own beam, dost not even see it, but another's mote thou not only seest, but also judgest, and essayest to cast it out; as if anyone seized with a grievous dropsy, or indeed with any other incurable disease, were to neglect this, and find fault with another who was neglecting a slight swelling. And if it be an evil not to see one's own sins, it is a twofold and threefold evil to be even sitting in judgment on others, while men themselves, as if past feeling, are bearing about beams in their own eyes: since no beam is so heavy as sin.

His injunction therefore in these words is as follows, that he who is chargeable with countless evil deeds, should not be a bitter censor of other men's offenses, and especially when these are trifling. He is not overthrowing reproof nor correction, but forbidding men to neglect their own faults, and exult over those of other men.

For indeed this was a cause of men's going unto great vice, bringing in a twofold wickedness. For he, whose practice it had been to slight his own faults, great as they were, and to search bitterly into those of others, being slight and of no account, was spoiling himself two ways: first, by thinking lightly of his own faults; next, by incurring enmities and feuds with all men, and training himself every day to extreme fierceness, and want of feeling for others.

3. Having then put away all these things, by this his excellent legislation, he added yet another charge, saying,

"Give not that which is holy unto the dogs, neither cast ye your pearls before swine" [Matt. 7:6].

"Yet surely further on," it will be said, "he commanded, 'What ye have heard in the ear, that preach ye upon the housetops'" [Matt. 10:27]. But this is in no wise contrary to the former. For neither in that place did he simply command to tell all men, but to whom it should be spoken, to them he bade speak with freedom [Matt. 10:28]. And by "dogs" here he figuratively described them that are living in incurable ungodliness, and affording no hope of change for the better; and by "swine," them that abide continually in an unchaste life, all of whom he hath pronounced unworthy of hearing such things. Paul also, it may be observed, declared this when he said, "But a natural man receiveth not the things of the Spirit, for they are foolishness unto him" [I Cor. 2:14]. And in many other places too he saith that corruption of life is the cause of men's not receiving the more perfect doctrines. Wherefore he commands not to open the doors to them; for indeed they become more insolent after learning. For as to the well-disposed and intelligent, things appear venerable when revealed, so to the insensible, when they are unknown rather. "Since then from their nature, they are not able to learn them, let the thing be hidden," saith he, "that at least for ignorance they may reverence them. For neither doth the swine know at all what a pearl is. Therefore since he knows not, neither let him see it, lest he trample under foot what he knows not."

For nothing results, beyond greater mischief to them that are so disposed when they hear; for both the holy things are profaned by them, not knowing what they are; and they are the more lifted up and armed against us. For this is meant by, "lest they trample them under their feet, and turn again and rend you."

Nay, "surely," saith one, "they ought to be so strong as to remain equally impregnable after men's learning them, and not to yield to other people occasions against us." But it is not the things that yield it, but that these men are swine; even as when the pearl is trampled under foot, it is not so trampled, because it is really contemptible, but because it fell among swine.

And full well did he say, "turn again and rend you": for they feign gentleness, so as to be taught: then after they have learnt, quite changing from one sort to another, they jeer, mock and deride us, as deceived persons. Therefore Paul also said to Timothy, "Of whom be thou ware also; for he hath greatly withstood our words" [II Tim. 4:15]; and again in another place, "From such turn away" [II Tim. 3:5], and, "A man that is an heretic, after the first and second admonition, reject" [Titus 3:10].

It is not, you see, that those truths furnish them with armor, but they become fools in this way of their own accord, being filled with more willfulness. On this account it is no small gain for them to abide in ignorance, for so they are not such entire scorners. But if they learn, the mischief is twofold. For neither will they themselves be at all profited thereby, but rather the more damaged, and to thee they will cause endless difficulties.

Let them hearken, who shamelessly associate with all, and make the awful things contemptible. For the mysteries we too therefore celebrate with closed doors, and keep out the uninitiated, not for any weakness of which we have convicted our rites, but because the many are as yet imperfectly prepared for them.[1] For this very reason he himself also discoursed much unto the Jews in parables, "because they seeing saw not." For this, Paul likewise commanded "to know how we ought to answer every man" [Col. 4:6].

4. "Ask, and it shall be given you; seek, and ye shall find; knock, and it shall be opened unto you" [Matt. 7:7].

For inasmuch as he had enjoined things great and marvellous, and had commanded men to be superior to all their passions, and had led them up to heaven itself, and had enjoined them to strive after the resemblance, not of angels and archangels, but (as far as was possible) of the very Lord of all; and had bidden his disciples not only themselves duly to perform all this, but also to correct others, and to distinguish between the evil and them that are not such, the dogs and them that are not dogs (although there be much that is hidden in men):—that they might not say, "these things are grievous and intolerable" (for indeed in the sequel Peter did utter some such things, saying, "Who can be saved?" and again, "If the case of the man be so, it is not good to marry" [Matt. 19:25, 10]): in order therefore that they might not now likewise say so; as in the first place even by what had gone before he had proved it all to be easy, setting down many reasons one upon another, of power to persuade men: so after all he adds also the pinnacle of all facility, devising as no ordinary relief to our toils, the assistance derived from persevering prayers.

[1] Cf. Introduction, p. 8.

Thus, we are not ourselves, saith he, to strive alone, but also to invoke the help from above: and it will surely come and be present with us, and will aid us in our struggles, and make all easy. Therefore he both commanded us to ask, and pledged himself to the giving.

However, not simply to ask did he command us, but with much assiduity and earnestness. For this is the meaning of "seek." For so he that seeks, putting all things out of his mind, is taken up with that alone which is sought, and forms no idea of any of the persons present. And this which I am saying they know, as many as have lost either gold, or servants, and are seeking diligently after them.

By "seeking," then, he declared this; by "knocking," that we approach with earnestness and a glowing mind.

Despond not therefore, O man, nor show less of zeal about virtue, than they do of desire for wealth. For things of that kind thou hast often sought and not found, but nevertheless, though thou know this, that thou art not sure to find them, thou puttest in motion every mode of search; but here, although having a promise that thou wilt surely receive, thou dost not show even the smallest part of that earnestness. And if thou dost not receive straightway, do not even thus despair. For to this end he said, "knock," to signify that even if he should not straightway open the door, we are to continue there.

5. And if thou doubt my affirmation, at any rate believe his example.

"For what man is there of you," saith he, "whom if his son ask bread, will he give him a stone?" [Matt. 7:9].

Because, as among men, if thou keep on doing so, thou art even accounted troublesome, and disgusting: so with God, when thou doest not so, then thou dost more entirely provoke him. And if thou continue asking, though thou receive not at once, thou surely wilt receive. For to this end was the door shut, that he may induce thee to knock; to this end he doth not straightway assent, that thou mayest ask. Continue then to do these things, and thou wilt surely receive. For that thou mightest not say, "What then if I should ask and not receive?" He hath blocked up thy approach with that similitude, again framing arguments, and by those human things urging us to be confident on these matters; implying by them that we must not only ask, but ask what we ought.

"For which of you is there, a father, of whom if his son shall ask bread, will he give him a stone?" So that if thou receive not, thy asking a stone is the cause of thy not receiving. For though thou be a son, this suffices not for thy receiving: rather this very thing even hinders thy receiving, that being a son, thou askest what is not profitable.

Do thou also therefore ask nothing worldly, but all things spiritual, and thou wilt surely receive. For so Solomon [I Kings 3:10-14; II Chron. 1:11, 12], because he asked what he ought, behold how quickly he received. Two things now, you see, should be in him that prays, asking earnestly, and asking what he ought: "since ye too," saith he, "though ye be fathers, wait for your sons to ask: and if they should ask of you anything inexpedient, ye refuse the gifts; just as, if it be expedient, ye consent and bestow it." Do thou too, considering these things, not withdraw until thou receive; until thou have found, retire not; relax not thy diligence, until the door be opened. For if thou approach with this mind, and say, "Except I receive, I depart not"; thou wilt surely receive, provided thou ask such things, as are both suitable for him of whom thou askest to give, and expedient for thee the petitioner. But what are these? To seek the things spiritual, all of them; to forgive them that have trespassed, and so to draw nigh asking forgiveness; "to lift up holy hands without wrath and doubting" [I Tim. 2:8]. If we thus ask, we shall receive. As it is, surely our asking is a mockery, and the act of drunken rather than of sober men.

"What then," saith one, "if I ask even spiritual things, and do not receive?" Thou didst not surely knock with earnestness; or thou madest thyself unworthy to receive; or didst quickly leave off.

"And wherefore," it may be inquired, "did he not say, what things we ought to ask?" Nay verily, he hath mentioned them all in what precedes, and hath signified for what things we ought to draw nigh. Say not then, "I drew nigh, and did not receive." For in no case is it owing to God that we receive not, God who loves us so much as to surpass even fathers, to surpass them as far as goodness doth this evil nature.

"For if ye, being evil, know how to give good gifts unto your children, how much more your heavenly Father" [Matt. 7:11].

Now this he said, not to bring an evil name on man's nature, nor to condemn our race as bad; but in contrast to his own goodness he calls paternal tenderness evil, so great is the excess of his love to man.

Seest thou an argument unspeakable, of power to arouse to good hopes even him that hath become utterly desperate?

Now here indeed he signifies his goodness by means of our fathers, but in what precedes by the chief among his gifts, by the "soul," by the body. And nowhere doth he set down the chief of all good things, nor bring forward his own coming:—for he who thus made speed to give up his Son to the slaughter, "how shall he not freely give us all things?"—because it had not yet come to pass. But Paul indeed sets it forth, thus saying, "He that spared not his own Son, how shall he not also with him freely give us all things" [Rom. 8:32]. But his discourse with them is still from the things of men.

6. After this, to indicate that we ought neither to feel confidence in prayer, while neglecting our own doings; nor, when taking pains, trust only to our own endeavors; but both to seek after the help from above, and contribute withal our own part; he sets forth the one in connection with the other. For so after much exhortation, he taught also how to pray, and when he had taught how to pray, he proceeded again to his exhortation concerning what we are to do; then from that again to the necessity of praying continually, saying, "Ask,"

and "seek," and "knock." And thence again, to the necessity of being also diligent ourselves.

"For all things," saith he, "whatsoever ye would that men should do to you, do ye also to them" [Matt. 7:12].

Summing up all in brief, and signifying, that virtue is compendious, and easy, and readily known of all men.

And he did not merely say, "All things whatsoever ye would," but, "Therefore all things whatsoever ye would." For this word, "therefore," he did not add without purpose, but with a concealed meaning: "if ye desire," saith he, "to be heard, together with what I have said, do these things also." What then are these? "Whatsoever ye would that men should do to you." Seest thou how he hath hereby also signified that together with prayer we need exact conversation? And he did not say, "whatsoever things thou wouldest to be done unto thee of God, those do unto thy neighbor"; lest thou should say, "But how is it possible? He is God and I am man": but, "whatsover thou wouldest to be done unto thee of thy fellow servant, these things do thou also thyself show forth towards thy neighbor." What is less burdensome than this? what fairer?

Then the praise also, before the rewards, is exceeding great.

"For this is the law and the prophets."

Whence it is evident, that virtue is according to our nature; that we all, of ourselves, know our duties; and that it is not possible for us ever to find refuge in ignorance.

7. "Enter ye in at the strait gate, for wide is the gate and broad is the way that leadeth to destruction, and many there be which go in thereat: and strait is the gate and narrow is the way which leadeth unto life, and few there be that find it" [Matt. 7:13, 14].

And yet after this he said, "My yoke is easy, and my burden is light" [Matt. 11:30]. And in what he hath lately said also, he intimated the same: how then doth he here say it is strait and confined? In the first place, if thou attend, even here he points to it as very light, and easy, and accessible. "And how," it may be said, "is the narrow and confined way easy?" Because it is a way and a gate; even as also the other, though it be wide, though spacious, is also a way and a gate. And of these there is nothing permanent, but all things are passing away, both the pains and the good things of life.

And not only herein is the part of virtue easy, but also by the end again it becomes yet easier. For not the passing away of our labors and toils, but also their issuing in a good end (for they end in life) is enough to console those in conflict. So that both the temporary nature of our labors, and the perpetuity of our crowns, and the fact that the labors come first, and the crowns after, must prove a very great relief in our toils. Wherefore Paul also called their affliction "light"; not from the nature of the events, but because of the mind of the combatants, and the hope of the future. "For our light affliction," saith he, "worketh an eternal weight of glory, while we look not at the things which are seen, but at the things which are not seen" [II Cor. 4:17, 18]. For if to sailors the waves and the seas, to soldiers their slaughters and wounds, to husbandmen the winters and the frosts, to boxers the sharp blows, be light and tolerable things, all of them, for the hope of those rewards which are temporary and perishing; much more when heaven is set forth, and the unspeakable blessings, and the eternal rewards, will no one feel any of the present hardships. Or if any account it, even thus, to be toilsome, the suspicion comes of nothing but their own remissness.

See, at any rate, how he on another side also makes it easy, commanding not to hold intercourse with the dogs, nor to give one's self over to the swine, and to "beware of the false prophets"; thus on all accounts causing men to feel as if in real conflict. And the very fact too of calling it narrow contributed very greatly towards making it easy; for it wrought on them to be vigilant. As Paul then, when he saith, "We wrestle not against flesh and blood" [Eph. 6:12], doth so not to cast down, but to rouse up the spirits of the soldiers: even so he also, to shake the travellers out of their sleep, called the way rough. And not in this way only did he work upon men to be vigilant, but also by adding, that it contains likewise many to supplant them; and, what is yet more grievous, they do not even attack openly, but hiding themselves; for such is the race of the false prophets. "But look not to this," saith he, "that it is rough and narrow, but where it ends; nor that the opposite is wide and spacious, but where it issues."

And all these things he saith, thoroughly to awaken our alacrity; even as elsewhere also he said, "Violent men take it by force" [Matt. 11:12]. For whoever is in conflict, when he actually sees the judge of the lists marvelling at the painfulness of his efforts, is the more inspirited.

Let it not then bewilder us, when many things spring up hence, that turn to our vexation. For the way is strait, and the gate narrow, but not the city. Therefore must one neither look for rest here, nor there expect any more aught that is painful.

Now in saying, "Few there be that find it," here again he both declared the carelessness of the generality, and instructed his hearers not to regard the felicities of the many, but the labors of the few. For the more part, saith he, so far from walking this way, do not so much as make it their choice: a thing of most extreme criminality. But we should not regard the many, nor be troubled thereat, but emulate the few; and, by all means equipping ourselves, should so walk therein.

For besides that it is strait, there are also many to overthrow us in the way that leads thither. Wherefore he also added,

8. "Beware of false prophets, for they will come to you in sheep's clothing, but inwardly they are ravening wolves" [Matt. 7:15]. Behold together with the dogs and swine another kind of ambush and conspiracy, far more grievous than that. For those are acknowledged and open, but these shaded over. For which cause also, while from those he commanded to hold off, these he charged men to watch with exact care, as though it were not possible to see them at the first approach. Wherefore he also said, "beware"; making us more exact to discern them.

Then, lest when they had heard that it was narrow and strait, and that they must walk on a way opposite to the many, and must keep themselves from swine and dogs, and together with these from another more wicked kind, even this of wolves; lest, I say, they should sink down at this multitude of vexations, having both to go a way contrary to most men, and therewith again to have such anxiety about these things: he reminded them of what took place in the days of their fathers, by using the term, "false prophets," for then also no less did such things happen. Be not now, I pray you, troubled (so he speaks), for nothing new nor strange is to befall you. Since for all truth the devil is always secretly substituting its appropriate deceit.

And by the figure of "false prophets," here, I think he shadows out not the heretics[2] but them that are of a corrupt life, yet wear a mask of virtue; whom the generality are wont to call by the name of impostors. Wherefore he also said further,

"By their fruits ye shall know them" [Matt. 7:16].

For amongst heretics one may often find actual goodness, but amongst those whom I was mentioning, by no means.

"What then," it may be said, "if in these things too they counterfeit?" "Nay, they will be easily detected; for such is the nature of this way, in which I commanded men to walk, painful and irksome; but the hypocrite would not choose to take pains, but to make a show only; wherefore also he is easily convicted." Thus, inasmuch as he had said, "there be few that find it," he clears them out again from among those, who find it not, yet feign so to do, by commanding us not to look to them that wear the masks only, but to them who in reality pursue it.

"But wherefore," one may say, "did he not make them manifest, but set us on the search for them?" That we might watch, and be ever prepared for conflict, guarding against our disguised as well as against our open enemies: which kind in-

[2] Both Irenaeus *Against Heresies* i. pr. and Tertullian *On Prescription against Heresies* 4 had applied this passage to heretics.

deed Paul also was intimating, when he said, that "by their good words they deceive the hearts of the simple" [Rom. 16:18]. Let us not be troubled therefore, when we see many such even now. Nay, for this too Christ foretold from the beginning.

And see his gentleness: how he said not, "Punish them," but, "Be not hurt by them," "Do not fall amongst them unguarded." Then that thou mightest not say, "it is impossible to distinguish that sort of men," again he states an argument from a human example, thus saying,

"Do men gather grapes of thorns, or figs of thistles? even so every good tree bringeth forth good fruit, but the corrupt tree bringeth forth evil fruit. A good tree cannot bring forth evil fruit, neither can a corrupt tree bring forth good fruit" [Matt. 7:16-18].

Now what he saith is like this: they have nothing gentle nor sweet; it is the sheep only so far as the skin; wherefore also it is easy to discern them. And lest thou shouldest have any the least doubt, he compares it to certain natural necessities, in matters which admit of no result but one. In which sense Paul also said, "The carnal mind is death; for it is not subject to the law of God, neither indeed can be" [Rom. 8:6, 7].

And if He states the same thing twice, it is not tautology.[3] But, lest anyone should say, "Though the evil tree bear evil fruit, it bears also good, and makes the distinction difficult, the crop being twofold": "This is not so," saith he, "for it bears evil fruit only, and never can bear good: as indeed in the contrary case also."

"What then? Is there no such thing as a good man becoming wicked? And the contrary again takes place, and life abounds with many such examples."

But Christ saith not this, that for the wicked there is no way to change, or that the good cannot fall away, but that so long as he is living in wickedness, he will not be able to bear good fruit. For he may indeed change to virtue, being evil;

[3] Cf. Introduction, p. 27.

but while continuing in wickedness, he will not bear good fruit.

What then? did not David, being good, bear evil fruit? Not continuing good, but being changed; since, undoubtedly, had he remained always what he was, he would not have brought forth such fruit. For nor surely while abiding in the habit of virtue, did he commit what he committed.

Now by these words he was also stopping the mouths of those who speak evil at random, and putting a bridle on the lips of all calumniators. I mean, whereas many suspect the good by reason of the bad, he by this saying hath deprived them of all excuse. "For thou canst not say, 'I am deceived and beguiled'; since I have given thee exactly this way of distinguishing them by their works, having added the injunction to go to their actions, and not to confound all at random."

9. Then forasmuch as he had not commanded to punish, but only to beware of them, he, at once both to comfort those whom they vex, and to alarm and change them, set up as a bulwark against them the punishment they should receive at his hands, saying,

"Every tree that bringeth not forth good fruit is hewn down, and cast into the fire" [Matt. 7:19].

Then, to make the saying less grievous, he added.

"Wherefore by their fruits ye shall know them" [Matt. 7:20].

That he might not seem to introduce the threatening as his leading topic, but to be stirring up their mind in the way of admonition and counsel.

Here he seems to me to be hinting at the Jews also, who were exhibiting such fruits. Wherefore also he reminded them of the sayings of John, in the very same terms delineating their punishment. For he too said the very same, making mention to them of an "axe," and of a "tree cut down," and of "unquenchable fire."

And though it appear indeed to be some single judgment, the being burnt up, yet if one examine carefully, these are two punishments. For he that is burnt is also cast of course out of God's kingdom; and this latter punishment is more grievous than the other. Now I know indeed that many tremble only at hell, but I affirm the loss of that glory to be a far greater punishment than hell. And if it be not possible to exhibit it such in words, this is nothing marvellous. For neither do we know the blessedness of those good things, that we should on the other hand clearly perceive the wretchedness ensuing on being deprived of them; since Paul, as knowing these things clearly, is aware, that to fall from Christ's glory is more grievous than all. And this we shall know at that time, when we shall fall into the actual trial of it.

But may this never be our case, O thou only-begotten Son of God, neither may we ever have any experience of this irremediable punishment. For how great an evil it is to fall from those good things, cannot indeed be accurately told: nevertheless, as I may be able, I will labor and strive by an example to make it clear to you, though it be but in some small degree.

Let us then imagine a wondrous child, having besides his virtue the dominion of the whole world, and in all respects so virtuous, as to be capable of bringing all men to the yearning of a father's affection. What then do you think the father of this child would not gladly suffer, not to be cast out of his society? And what evil, small or great, would he not welcome, on condition of seeing and enjoying him? Now let us reason just so with respect to that glory also. For no child, be he never so virtuous, is so desirable and lovely to a father, as the having our portion in those good things, and "to depart and be with Christ" [Phil. 1:23].

No doubt hell, and punishment, is a thing not to be borne. Yet though one suppose ten thousand hells, he will utter nothing like what it will be to fail of that blessed glory, to be hated of Christ, to hear "I know you not" [Matt. 25:12], to be accused for not feeding him when we saw him an hungered [Matt. 25:42]. Yea, better surely to endure a thousand thunderbolts, than to see that face of mildness turning away from us, and that eye of peace not enduring to look upon us. For if he, while I was an enemy, and hating him, and turning from him, did in such wise follow after me, as not to spare even himself, but to give himself up unto death: when after all this I do not vouchsafe to him so much as a loaf in his hunger, with what kind of eyes shall I ever again behold him?

But mark even here his gentleness; in that he doth not at all speak of his benefits, nor say; "Thou hast despised him that hath done thee so much good": neither doth he say, "Me, who brought thee from that which is not into being, who breathed into thee a soul, and set thee over all things on earth, who for thy sake made earth, and heaven, and sea, and air, and all things that are, who had been dishonored by thee, yea accounted of less honor than the devil, and did not even so withdraw himself, but had innumerable thoughts for thee after it all; who chose to become a slave, who was beaten with rods and spit upon, who was slain, who died the most shameful death, who also on high makes intercession for thee, who freely gives thee his Spirit, who vouchsafes to thee a kingdom, who makes thee such promises, whose will it is to be unto thee head, and bridegroom, and garment, and house, and root, and meat, and drink, and shepherd, and king, and who hath taken thee to be brother, and heir, and joint-heir with himself; who hath brought thee out of darkness into the dominion of light." These things, I say, and more than these he might speak of, but he mentions none of these; but what? only the sin itself.

Even here he shows his love, and indicates the yearning which he hath toward thee: not saying, "Depart into the fire prepared for you," but "prepared for the devil." And before he tells them what wrongs they had done, and neither so doth he endure to mention all, but a few. And before these he calls the other sort, those who have done well, to signify from this too that he is blaming them unjustly.

What amount of punishment, then, is so grievous as these words? For if anyone seeing but a man who was his benefactor an hungered, would not neglect him; or if he should neglect him, being upbraided with it, would choose rather to sink into the earth than to hear of it in the presence of two or three friends; what will be our feelings, on hearing these words in the presence of the whole world; such as he would not say even then, were he not earnestly accounting for his own doings? For that not to upbraid did he bring these things forward, but in self-defense, and for the sake of showing, that not without ground nor at random was he saying, "depart from me"; this is evident from his unspeakable benefits. For if he had been minded to upbraid, he would have brought forwards all these, but now he mentions only what treatment he had received.

10. Let us therefore, beloved, fear the hearing these words. Life is not a plaything: or rather our present life is a plaything, but the things to come are not such; or perchance our life is not a plaything only, but even worse than this. For it ends not in laughter, but rather brings exceeding damage on them who are not minded to order their own ways strictly. For what, I pray thee, is the difference between children who are playing at building houses, and us when we are building our fine houses? what again between them making out their dinners, and us in our delicate fare? None, but just that we do it at the risk of being punished. And if we do not yet quite perceive the poverty of what is going on, no wonder, for we are not yet become men; but when we are become so, we shall know that all these things are childish.

For so those other things too, as we grow to manhood, we laugh to scorn; but when we are children we account them to be worth anxiety; and while we are gathering together potsherds and mire we think no less of ourselves than they who are erecting their great circuits of walls. Nevertheless they straightway perish and fall down, and not even when standing can they be of any use to us, as indeed neither can those fine houses. For the citizen of heaven they cannot receive, neither can he bear to abide in them, who hath his country above; but as we throw down these with our feet, so he too those by his high spirit. And as we laugh at the children, weeping at that overthrow, even so these also, when we are bewailing it all, do not laugh only, but weep also: because both their bowels are compassionate, and great is the mischief thence arising.

Let us therefore become men. How long are we to crawl on the earth, priding ourselves on stones and stocks? How long are we to play? And would we played only! But now we even betray our own salvation; and as children when they neglect their learning, and practise themselves in these things at their leisure, suffer very severe blows; even so we too, spending all our diligence herein, and having then our spiritual lessons required of us in our works, and not being able to produce them, shall have to pay the utmost penalty. And there is none to deliver us; though he be father, brother, what you will. But while these things shall all pass away, the torment ensuing upon them remains immortal and unceasing; which sort of thing indeed takes place with respect to the children as well, their father destroying their childish toys altogether for their idleness, and causing them to weep incessantly.

11. And to convince thee that these things are such, let us bring before us wealth, that which more than anything seems to be worthy of our pains, and let us set against it a virtue of the soul (which soever thou wilt), and then shalt thou see most clearly the vileness thereof. Let us, I say, suppose there are two men (and I do not now speak of injuriousness, but as yet of honest wealth); and of these two, let the one get together money, and sail on the sea, and till the land, and find many other ways of merchandise (although I know not quite, whether, so doing, he can make honest gains); nevertheless let it be so, and let it be granted that his gains are gotten with honesty; that he buys fields, and slaves, and all such things, and suppose no injustice connected therewith. But let the other one, possessing as much, sell fields, sell houses, and vessels of gold and silver, and give to the poor; let him supply the necessitous, heal the sick, free such as are in straits, some

let him deliver from bonds, others let him release that are in mines, these let him bring back from the noose, those, who are captives, let him rescue from their punishment. Of whose side then would you be? And we have not as yet spoken of the future, but as yet of what is here. Of whose part then would ye be? his that is gathering gold, or his that is doing away with calamities? with him that is purchasing fields, or him who is making himself a harbor of refuge for the human race? him that is clothed with much gold, or him that is crowned with innumerable blessings? Is not the one like some angel come down from heaven for the amendment of the rest of mankind; but the other not so much as like a man, but like some little child that is gathering all together vainly and at random?

But if to get money honestly be thus absurd, and of extreme madness; when not even the honesty is there, how can such a man choose but be more wretched than any? I say, if the absurdity be so great; when hell is added thereto, and the loss of the kingdom, how great wailings are due to him, both living and dead?

12. Or wilt thou that we take in hand some other part also of virtue? Let us then introduce again another man, who is in power, commanding all, invested with great dignity, having a gorgeous herald, and girdle, and lictors, and a large company of attendants. Doth not this seem great, and meet to be called happy? Well then, against this man again let us set another, him that is patient of injuries, and meek, and lowly, and long suffering; and let this last be despitefully used, be beaten, and let him bear it quietly, and bless them that are doing such things.

Now which is the one to be admired, I pray thee? he that is puffed up, and inflamed, or he that is self-subdued? Is not the one again like the powers above, that are so free from passion, but the other like a blown bladder, or a man who hath the dropsy, and great inflammation? The one like a spiritual physician, the other, a ridiculous child that is puffing out his cheeks?

For why dost thou pride thyself, O man? Because thou art borne on high in a chariot? Because a yoke of mules is drawing thee? And what is this? Why, this one may see befalling mere logs of wood and stones. Is it that thou art clothed with beautiful garments? But look at him that is clad with virtue for garments, and thou wilt see thyself to be like withering hay, but him like a tree that bears marvellous fruit, and affords much delight to the beholders. For thou art bearing about food for worms and moths, who, if they should set upon thee, will quickly strip thee bare of this adorning (for truly garments and gold and silver, are the one, the spinning of worms; the other earth and dust, and again become earth and nothing more): but he that is clothed with virtue hath such raiment, as not only worms cannot hurt, but not even death itself. And very naturally; for these virtues of the soul have not their origin from the earth, but are a fruit of the Spirit; wherefore neither are they subject to the mouths of worms. Nay, for these garments are woven in heaven, where is neither moth, nor worm, nor any other such thing.

Which then is better, tell me? To be rich, or to be poor? To be in power, or in dishonor? In luxury, or in hunger? It is quite clear; to be in honor, and enjoyment, and wealth. Therefore, if thou wouldest have the things and not the names, leave the earth and what is here, and find thee a place to anchor in heaven: for what is here is a shadow, but all things that are immovable, steadfast, and beyond any assault.

Let us therefore choose them with all diligent care, that we may be delivered from the turmoil of the things here, and having sailed into that calm harbor, may be found with our lading abundant, and with that unspeakable wealth of almsgiving; unto which God grant we may all attain, by the grace and love towards man of our Lord Jesus Christ, to whom be the glory and the might, world without end. Amen.

Homily XXIV

"Not every one that saith unto me, Lord, Lord, shall enter into the kingdom of heaven, but he that doeth the will of my Father which is in heaven." —*Matt. 7:21*

WHEREFORE SAID HE NOT, "but he that doeth my will"? Because for the time it was a great gain for them to receive even this first; yea it was very great, considering their weakness. And moreover he intimated the one also by the other. And withal this may be mentioned, that in fact there is no other will of the Son besides that of the Father.

And here he seems to me to be censuring the Jews chiefly, laying as they did the whole stress upon the doctrines, and taking no care of practice. For which Paul also blames them, saying, "Behold thou art called a Jew, and restest in the law, and makest thy boast of God, and knowest his will" [Rom. 2:17-18]: but thou art nothing advantaged thereby, so long as the manifestation by life and by works is not there.

But he himself staid not at this, but said also what was much more: that is,

"Many will say to me in that day, Lord, Lord, have we not prophesied in thy name?" [Matt. 7:22]. For "not only," saith he, "is he that hath faith, if his life be neglected, cast out of heaven, but though, besides his faith, he have wrought many signs, yet if he have done nothing good, even this man is equally shut out from that sacred porch." "For many will say unto me in that day, Lord, Lord, have we not prophesied in thy name?" Seest thou how he secretly brings in himself also here and afterwards, having now finished his whole exhortation? how he implies himself to be judge? For that punishment awaits such as sin, he hath signified in what precedes; and now who it is that punishes, he here proceeds to unfold.

And he said not openly, I am he, but, "Many will say unto me"; making out again the same thing. Since were he not the judge, how could he have told them,

"And then will I profess unto them, depart from me, I never knew you" [Matt. 7:23]?

"Not only in the time of the judgment, but not even then, when ye were working miracles," saith he. Therefore he said also to his disciples, "Rejoice not, that the devils are subject unto you, but because your names are written in heaven" [Luke 10:20]. And everywhere he bids us practise great care of our way of life. For is it not possible for one living rightly, and freed from all the passions, ever to be overlooked; but though he chance to be in error, God will quickly draw him over to the truth.

But there are some who say, "they made this assertion falsely"; and this is their account why such men are not saved. Nay then it follows that his conclusion is the contrary of what he intends. For surely his intention is to make out that faith is of no avail without works. Then, enhancing it, he added miracles also, declaring that not only faith, but the exhibiting even of miracles, avails nothing for him who works such wonders without virtue. Now if they had not wrought them, how could this point have been made out here? And besides, they would not have dared, when the judgment was come, to say these things to his face: and the very reply too, and their speaking in the way of question, implies their having wrought them: I mean, that they, having seen the end contrary to their expectation, and after they had been here admired among all for their miracles, beholding themselves there with nothing but punishment awaiting them;—as amazed and marvelling they say, "Lord, have we not prophesied in thy name?" how then dost thou turn from us now? What means this strange and unlooked-for end?

2. But though they marvel because they are punished after

working such miracles, yet do not thou marvel. For all the grace was of the free gift of him that gave it, but they contributed nothing on their part; wherefore also they are justly punished, as having been ungrateful and without feeling towards him that had so honored them as to bestow his grace upon them though unworthy.

"What then," saith one, "did they perform such things while working iniquity?" Some indeed say that it was not at the time when they did these miracles that they also committed iniquity, but that they changed afterwards, and wrought their iniquity. But if this be so, a second time the point at which he is laboring fails to be established. For what he took pains to point out is this, that neither faith nor miracles avail where practise is not: to which effect Paul also said, "Though I have faith, so that I could remove mountains, and understand all mysteries, and all knowledge, and have not charity, I am nothing" [I Cor. 13:2]. "Who then are these men?" you ask. Many of them that believed received gifts such as he that was casting out devils [Mark 9:38; Luke 9:49], and was not with him; such as Judas; for even he too, wicked as he was, had a gift. And in the Old Testament also this may be found, in that grace hath oftentimes wrought upon unworthy persons, that it might do good to others. That is, since all men were not meet for all things, but some were of a pure life, not having so great faith, and others just the contrary; by these sayings, while he urges the one to show forth much faith, the others too he was summoning by this his unspeakable gift to become better men. Wherefore also with great abundance did he bestow that grace. For "we wrought," it is said, "many mighty works." But "then will I profess unto them, I knew you not." For "now indeed they suppose they are my friends; but then shall they know, that not as to friends did I give to them."

And why marvel if he hath bestowed gifts on men that have believed on him, though without life suitable to their faith, when even on those who have fallen from both these, he is unquestionably found working? For so Balaam was an alien both from faith and from a truly good life; nevertheless grace wrought on him for the service of other men. And Pharaoh too was of the same sort: yet for all that even to him He signified the things to come. And Nebuchadnezzar was very full of iniquity; yet to him again He revealed what was to follow after many generations [Dan. 3]. And again to the son of this last, though surpassing his father in iniquity, He signified the things to come, ordering a marvellous and great dispensation [Dan. 5]. Accordingly because then also the beginnings of the gospel were taking place, and it was requisite that the manifestation of its power should be abundant, many even of the unworthy used to receive gifts. Howbeit, from those miracles no gain accrued to them; rather they are the more punished. Wherefore unto them did he utter even that fearful saying, "I never knew you"; there being many for whom his hatred begins already even here; whom he turns away from, even before the judgment.

Let us fear therefore, beloved; and let us take great heed to our life, neither let us account ourselves worse off, in that we do not work miracles now. For that will never be any advantage to us, as neither any disadvantage in our not working them, if we take heed to all virtue. Because for the miracles we ourselves are debtors, but for our life and our doings we have God our debtor.

3. Having now, you see, finished all, having discoursed accurately of all virtue, and pointed out the pretenders to it, of divers kinds, both such as for display fast and make prayers, and such as come in the sheep's hide; and them too that spoil it, whom he also called swine and dogs: he proceeds to signify how great is the profit of virtue even here, and how great the mischief of wickedness, by saying,

"Whosoever therefore heareth these sayings of mine, and doeth them, shall be likened unto a wise man" [Matt. 7:24].

As thus: What they shall suffer who do not (although they work miracles), ye have heard; but ye should know also what such as obey all these sayings shall enjoy; not in the world to come only, but even here. "For whosoever," saith he, "heareth these sayings of mine, and doeth them, shall be likened to a wise man."

Seest thou how he varies his discourse; at one time saying, "Not every one that saith unto me, Lord, Lord," and revealing himself; at another time, "he that doeth the will of my Father"; and again, bringing in himself as judge, "For many will say to me in that day, Lord, Lord, have we not prophesied in thy name, and I will say, I know you not." And here again he indicates himself to have the power over all, this being why he said, "Whosoever heareth these sayings of mine."

Thus whereas all his discourse had been touching the future; of a kingdom, and an unspeakable reward and consolation, and the like; his will is, out of things here also to give them their fruits, and to signify how great is the strength of virtue even in the present life. What then is this her strength? To live in safety, to be easily subdued by no terror, to stand superior to all that despitefully use us. To this what can be equal? For this, not even he that wears the diadem can provide for himself, but that man who follows after virtue. For he alone is possessed of it in full abundance: in the ebb and flow of the things present he enjoys a great calm. The truly marvellous thing being this, that not in fair weather, but when the storm is vehement, and the turmoil great, and the temptations continual, he cannot be shaken ever so little.

"For the rain descended," saith he, "the floods came, the winds blew, and beat upon that house; and it fell not: for it was founded upon the rock" [Matt. 7:25].

By "rain" here, and "floods," and "winds," he is expressing metaphorically the calamities and afflictions that befall men; such as false accusations, plots, bereavements, deaths, loss of friends, vexations from strangers, all the ills in our life that any one could mention. "But to none of these," saith he, "doth such a soul give way; and the cause is, it is founded on the rock." He calls the stedfastness of his doctrine a rock; because in truth his commands are stronger than any rock, setting one above all the waves of human affairs. For he who keeps these things strictly, will not have the advantage of men only when they are vexing him, but even of the very devils plotting against him. And that it is not vain boasting so to speak, Job is our witness, who received all the assaults of the devil, and stood unmoveable; and the apostles too are our witnesses, for that when the waves of the whole world were beating against them, when both nations and princes, both their own people and strangers, both the evil spirits, and the devil, and every engine was set in motion, they stood firmer than a rock, and dispersed it all.

And now, what can be happier than this kind of life? For this, not wealth, not strength of body, not glory, not power, nor ought else will be able to secure, but only the possession of virtue. For there is not, nay there is not another life we may find free from all evils, but this alone. And ye are witnesses, who know the plots in king's courts, the turmoils and the troubles in the houses of the rich.[1] But there was not among the apostles any such thing.

What then? Did no such thing befall them? Did they suffer no evil at any man's hand? Nay, the marvel is this above all things, that they were indeed the object of many plots, and many storms burst upon them, but their soul was not overset by them, nor thrown into despair, but with naked bodies they wrestled, prevailed, and triumphed.

Thou then likewise, if thou be willing to perform these things exactly, shalt laugh all ills to scorn. Yea, for if thou be but strengthened with such philosophy as is in these admonitions, nothing shall be able to hurt thee. Since in what is he to harm thee, who is minded to lay plots? Will he take away thy money? Well, but before their threatening thou wast commanded to despise it, and to abstain from it so exceedingly, as not so much as even to ask any such thing of thy Lord.

[1] On the significance of this observation for the situation of the church at the end of the fourth century, cf. Introduction, p. 7.

But doth he cast thee into prison? Why, before thy prison, thou wast enjoined so to live, as to be crucified even to all the world. But doth he speak evil? Nay, from this pain also Christ hath delivered thee, by promising thee without toil a great reward for the endurance of evil, and making thee so clear from the anger and vexation hence arising, as even to command thee to pray for them. But doth he banish thee and involve thee in innumerable ills? Well, he is making the crown more glorious for thee. But doth he destroy and murder thee? Even hereby he profits thee very greatly, procuring for thee the rewards of the martyrs, and conducting thee more quickly into the untroubled haven, and affording thee matter for a more abundant recompense, and contriving for thee to make a gain of the universal penalty. Which thing indeed is most marvellous of all, that the plotters, so far from injuring at all, do rather make the objects of their despite more approved. To this what can be comparable? I mean, to the choice of such a mode of life as this, and no other, is.

Thus whereas he had called the way strait and narrow; to soothe our labors on this side also, he signifies the security thereof to be great, and great the pleasure; even as of the opposite course great is the unsoundness, and the detriment. For as virtue even from things here was signified by him to have her rewards, so vice also her penalties. For what I am ever saying, that I will say now also: that in both ways he is everywhere bringing about the salvation of his hearers, on the one hand by zeal for virtue, on the other by hatred of vice. Thus, because there would be some to admire what he said, while they yield no proof of it by their works, he by anticipation awakens their fears, saying, Though the things spoken be good, hearing is not sufficient for security, but there is need also of obedience in actions, and the whole lies chiefly in this. And here he ends his discourse, leaving the fear at its height in them.

For as with regard to virtue, not only from the things to come did he urge them (speaking of a kingdom, and of heaven, and an unspeakable reward, and comfort, and the unnumbered good things): but also from the things present, indicating the firm and immoveable quality of the Rock; so also with respect to wickedness, not from the expected things only doth he excite their fears (as from the tree that is cut down, and the unquenchable fire, and the not entering into the kingdom, and from his saying, "I know you not"): but also from the things present, the downfall, I mean, in what is said of the house.

4. Wherefore also he made his argument more expressive, by trying its force in a parable; for it was not the same thing to say, "The virtuous man shall be impregnable, but the wicked easily subdued," as to suppose a rock, and a house, and rivers, and rain, and wind, and the like.

"And every one," saith he, "that heareth these sayings of mine, and doeth them not, shall be likened to a foolish man, which built his house upon the sand" [Matt. 7:26].

And well did he call this man "foolish": for what can be more senseless than one building a house on the sand, and while he submits to the labor, depriving himself of the fruit and refreshment, and instead thereof undergoing punishment? For that they too, who follow after wickedness, do labor, is surely manifest to everyone: since both the extortioner, and the adulterer, and the false accuser, toil and weary themselves much to bring their wickedness to effect; but so far from reaping any profit from these their labors, they rather undergo great loss. For Paul too intimated this when he said, "He that soweth to his flesh, shall of his flesh reap corruption" [Gal. 6:8]. To this man are they like also, who build on the sand; as those that are given up to fornication, to wantonness, to drunkenness, to anger, to all the other things.

Such an one was Ahab, but not such Elias (since when we have put virtue and vice along side of one another, we shall know more accurately the difference): for the one had built upon the rock, the other on the sand; wherefore though he were a king, he feared and trembled at the prophet, at him that had only his sheepskin. Such were the Jews but not the apostles; and so though they were few and in bonds, they exhibited the steadfastness of the rock; but those, many as they were, and in armor, the weakness of the sand. For so they said, "What shall we do to these men?" [Acts 4:16]. Seest thou those in perplexity, not who are in the hands of others, and bound, but who are active in holding down and binding? And what can be more strange than this? Hast thou hold of the other, and art yet in utter perplexity? Yes, and very naturally. For inasmuch as they had built all on the sand, therefore also were they weaker than all. For this cause also they said again, "What do ye, seeking to bring this man's blood upon us?" [Acts 5:28]. What saith he? Dost thou scouch, and art thou in fear? entreatest thou despitefully, and art in dismay? Dost thou judge, and yet tremble? So feeble is wickedness.

But the apostles not so, but how? "We cannot but speak the things which we have seen and heard" [Acts 4:20]. Seest thou a noble spirit? seest thou a rock laughing waves to scorn? seest thou a house unshaken? And what is yet more marvellous; so far from turning cowards themselves at the plots formed against them, they even took more courage, and cast the others into greater anxiety. For so he that smites adamant, is himself the one smitten; and he that kicks against the pricks, is himself the one pricked, the one on whom the severe wounds fall: and he who is forming plots against the virtuous, is himself the one in jeopardy. For wickedness becomes so much the weaker, the more it sets itself in array against virtue. And as he who wraps up fire in a garment, extinguishes not the flame, but consumes the garment; so he that is doing despite to virtuous men, and oppressing them, and binding them, makes them more glorious, but destroys himself. For the more ills thou sufferest, living righteously, the stronger art thou become; since the more we honor self-restraint, the less we need anything; and the less we need anything, the stronger we grow, and the more above all. Such a one was John; wherefore him no man pained, but he caused pain to Herod; so he that had nothing prevailed against him that ruled; and he that wore a diadem, and purple, and endless pomp, trembles, and is in fear of him that is stripped of all, and not even when beheaded could he without fear see his head. For that even after his death he had the terror of him in full strength, hear what he saith, "This is John, whom I slew" [Matt. 14:2; Luke 9:9]. Now the expression, "I slew," is that of one not exulting, but soothing his own terror, and persuading his troubled soul to call to mind, that he himself slew him. So great is the force of virtue, that even after death it is more powerful than the living. For this same cause again, when he was living, they that possessed much wealth came unto him, and said, "What shall we do?" [Luke 3:10, 14]. Is so much yours, and are ye minded to learn the way of your prosperity from him that hath nothing? the rich from the poor? the soldiers from him that hath not even a house?

Such an one was Elias too: wherefore also with the same freedom did he discourse to the people. For as the former said, "Ye generation of vipers" [Matt. 3:7]; so this latter, "How long will ye halt upon both your hips?" [I Kings 18:21]. And the one said, "Hast thou killed, and inherited?" [I Kings 21:19]; the other, "It is not lawful for thee to have thy brother Philip's wife" [Mark 6:18].

Seest thou the rock? Seest thou the sand; how easily it sinks down, how it yields to calamities? how it is overthrown, though it have the support of royalty, of number, of nobility? For them that pursue it, it makes more senseless than all.

And it doth not merely fall, but with great calamity: for "great indeed," he saith, "was the fall of it." The risk not being of trifles, but of the soul, of the loss of heaven, and those immortal blessings. Or rather even before that loss, no life so wretched as he must live that follows after this; dwelling with continual despondencies, alarms, cares, anxieties; which a certain wise man also was intimating when he said, "The wicked fleeth, when no man is pursuing" [Prov. 28:1]. For such men tremble at their shadows, suspect their friends, their enemies, their servants, such as know them, such as know them not; and before their punishment, suffer extreme punishment here. And to declare all this, Christ said, "And great was the fall of it"; shutting up these good commandments with that suitable ending, and persuading even by the things present the most unbelieving to flee from vice.

For although the argument from what is to come be vaster, yet is this of more power to restrain the grosser sort, and to withdraw them from wickedness. Wherefore also he ended with it, that the profit thereof might make its abode in them.

Conscious therefore of all these things, both the present, and the future, let us flee from vice, let us emulate virtue, that we may not labor fruitlessly and at random, but may both enjoy the security here, and partake of the glory there: unto which God grant we may all attain, by the grace and love towards man of our Lord Jesus Christ, to whom be the glory and the might forever and ever. Amen.

INDEX

INDEX

Abel, 136
Abraham, 77, 83, 110, 166, 169
Acts of the Apostles, 24
Adam, 118
Adultery, 73, 75, 81, 96-100, 102-5, 107, 113, 126, 193, 221.
Ahab, 221
Alexandrian school of exegesis, 16
Allegorical interpretation of Scripture, 13-19, 44
Almsgiving, 36, 42, 47, 60, 89, 130-32, 137, 154, 158, 162, 174, 175, 184
Ambrose, 4, 5
Ameringer, T. E., 22
Andragathius, 20
Anxiety, 181-82, 184-86, 205, 210
Antioch, 6, 9, 19, 21, 84, 99, 175
Antiochene school of exegesis, 12-15, 18, 19
Anti-Semitism, 22
Apollinarism, 15
Arianism, 10, 11, 15
Aristotle ,27, 46, 107
Armenia, 6, 7
Athanasius, 5
Augustine, 2, 5, 6, 17, 28, 29, 44, 80
Avarice, 36
Basil the Great, 5, 20
Basilides, 14
Baur, Chrysostomos, 5, 6, 12, 20, 35, 36
Beatitudes, 23, 30, 31, 50
Brilioth, Yngve, 27-28
Burney, C. F., 27
Burns, Mary Albania, 22

Cain, 87
Calumny, 51, 56-58
Campenhausen, Hans von, 13
Carpocrates, 17
Celibacy, 185
Cerdo, 80
Chalcedon, Council of, 5
Church, 50, 157, 191
Church discipline, 7, 8
Cicero, 3, 28
Circumcision, 68
Commandments (*see* Law)
Conscience, 56, 58, 93, 140
Constantine, 5, 7
Constantinople, 6, 23
Corinthians, 47, 83, 192
Covetousness, 46, 47, 137, 167, 170
Creation, 10-12, 69, 70, 74, 80

Daniel, 166
David, 44, 51, 173, 179, 207
Death, 59, 60, 150, 209, 223
De Lubac, Henri, 15
Demosthenes, 27, 28
Dibelius, Martin, 28

Dietrich, Veit, 2
Diodore of Tarsus, 15, 16
Diogenes, 175
Disciplina arcani, 8
Divorce, 103, 104
Downey, Glanville, 9, 19

Ebeling, Gerhard, 1
Elias (Elijah), 50, 172, 174, 221, 223
Enlightenment, 4
Esau, 87
Eudoxia, Empress, 6
Eusebius, 5
Evangelical counsels, 33, 34

Faith, 72, 187, 214-16
Fasting, 9, 42, 130, 153-55, 162
Festugière, A. J., 20, 34
Field, Frederick, 35
First Corinthians, 24
Forbearance, 116-18, 121, 122
Forgiveness, 44, 65, 66, 142-44, 146-48, 190, 193, 200
Fornication (*see* Adultery)

Galatians, 84
Geerlings, Jacob, 36
Genesis, 12, 16, 21
Gnosticism, 10-12, 14, 16-18, 39, 71, 101, 172
Grant, Robert M., 14, 16
Greer, Rowan A., 12
Gregory Nazianzus, 5, 20
Gregory of Nyssa, 5, 20

Haller, William, 2
Hannah, 136
Harkins, Paul W., 8
Harnack, Adolph von, 15, 80
Hermeneutics, 13, 14
Homilies against the Jews, 22
Homilies on First Corinthians, 24
Homilies on Genesis, 16, 21
Homilies on the Acts of the Apostles, 24
Homilies on the Gospel of John, 31
Humbert, J., 3
Humility, 41, 42, 52, 65, 69

Irenaeus, 17, 80, 205
Isaac, 77
Isaiah, 41, 100, 118
Ish'odad, 14
Isocrates, 28

Jacob, 77, 173
Jaubert, Annie, 16
Jerome, 5
Job, 51, 62, 76, 99, 166, 169, 219
John the Baptist, 33, 71, 172, 175, 207, 222-23
John the Evangelist, 70, 80
John, Gospel of, 15, 18
Joseph, 87, 118
Joshua, Book of, 16
Judgment, 43, 86, 143, 161, 186, 191-96, 215, 217
Justice, 46, 92, 115, 144, 157
Justification, 34
Justinian, 7
Julian, 20, 175

Kingdom of heaven, 41, 49, 75, 76, 110, 121, 126, 140, 145, 182, 183, 208, 212, 218

Law, 41-43, 49, 52, 58, 59, 66-68, 70-87, 90, 91, 96-100, 102, 103, 105, 107, 108, 110-17, 121, 124-26, 128, 130, 133, 136-38, 142, 143, 146, 148-50, 154, 157, 170, 172, 175, 185, 192-96, 199, 202, 223
Leclerq, Jean, 2
Libanius, 19, 20, 175
Literal interpretation of Scripture, 13-15, 19
Liturgy, 7-9, 24, 28, 136
Lord's Prayer, 18, 28, 32, 138-42
Love, 87, 88, 121, 134, 146, 152, 176, 181
Luke, 50
Luther, Martin, 23, 29, 34

Maat, W. A., 22
Macedonians, 47
Manassas, 186
Manichaeism, 10, 18, 39, 71, 80, 83, 101
Marcion, 14, 15, 80
Mark, Gospel of, 36
Markowicz, W. A., 21
Martyrdom, 62
Massaux, E., 30
Meinhold, Peter, 2
Mercy, 47, 49, 50, 52, 53, 60, 67, 73, 82, 103, 105, 115, 119, 121, 125, 126, 142, 148, 152, 157, 190
Miller, Perry, 2
Monasticism, 34, 154, 174
Monks, 154, 194
Monotheism, 11
Mosaic law, 11, 32, 80
Moses, 44, 50, 104, 136, 172

Nestorius, 13
Niebuhr, Reinhold, 29
Nicaea, Council of, 5, 99
New, Silva, 36
Newman, John Henry, 13, 15
New Testament, 6, 11-16, 31, 87
Noah, 166

Oath-taking, 105-13, 121
Old Testament, 6, 11-16, 36, 45, 52, 71, 80, 83, 87, 216
Olympias, 6
On the Priesthood, 6, 21, 22
Origen, 14-16, 18, 19, 141

Paredi, Angelo, 4
Pauck, Wilhelm, 1
Paul, 4, 42, 44, 45, 47, 51, 70, 72, 77, 83, 84, 87, 90, 92, 95, 101, 102, 112, 122, 124, 127, 140, 148, 171, 190-92, 196, 197, 201, 203, 206, 208, 214, 216, 221
Peace, 150
Peacemakers, 47, 49, 52, 53, 58, 73, 105, 125, 126
Perler, O., 8
Persecution, 48-52, 56, 57, 124, 126
Peter, 70, 110, 191, 198
Petit, P., 20
Philippians, 130
Philo, 13
Phinehas, 109, 110
Pius X, 5

Plutarch, 27
Poverty, 36, 59, 60, 61, 156, 162, 167, 175
Prayer, 68, 69, 89, 113, 125, 130, 134-38, 140-43, 146-48, 151, 154, 162, 180, 183, 189, 200, 201, 217
Prestige, G. L., 12
Prevost, George, 35
Pride, 42, 43, 60, 125, 127, 139, 193
Prophets, 41, 45, 49, 50, 52, 53, 71, 89, 103, 106, 118, 124, 136, 149, 178, 189
Proverbs, 15
Psalter, 15
Pseudo-Tertullian, 80
Punishment, 44, 75, 81-83, 85-89, 110-12, 115, 126, 127, 131, 133, 134, 138, 144, 149, 150, 169, 170, 186, 193, 194, 207-10, 212, 214, 215-16
Puritans, 2

Quasten, Johannes, 3, 34
Quintilian, 28

Redemption, 138
Reformation, 1, 4, 19
Reformers, 3, 19
Repentance, 142, 186, 187
Resurrection, 75
Retaliation, 114, 115, 121
Reward, 44, 45, 47-50, 52, 62, 73, 75, 77, 78, 93, 121, 124, 126, 127, 131, 133-37, 144, 146, 151, 159, 184, 218, 220
Riddle, M. B., 35
Righteousness, 46, 48, 49, 52, 53, 67, 71-74, 76, 79, 110, 138
Rörer, George, 2

Sacrifice, 41, 88, 89, 91, 149
Salvation, 56, 58, 102, 148, 170, 187, 192, 211
Schaff, Philip, 35
Schweitzer, Albert, 29
Second coming, 151
Skimina, Stanislaus, 20
Socrates (church historian), 20
Sodom, 166
Solomon, 200
Song of the Three Children, 41
Stiglmayer, J., 9
Subordinationism, 11

Temperance, 42
Tertullian, 17, 205
Theodore of Mopsuestia, 12, 15
Theodosius the Great, 7, 19
Theophilus, patriarch of Alexandria, 6
Thessalonians, 50
Timothy, 197

Usury, 60, 120, 169

Valentinus, 14
Van der Meer, F., 2
Virginity, 45, 174
Virtue, 46-48, 52-54, 57-59, 76, 94, 107, 113, 118, 130, 141, 143, 146, 156, 199, 203, 206, 211-13, 217, 220-23,

Williams, A. Lukyn, 22

THE PREACHER'S PAPERBACK LIBRARY

Volumes already published:

1. *The Servant of the Word* by H. H. Farmer. 1964.
2. *The Care of the Earth and Other University Sermons* by Joseph Sittler. 1964.
3. *The Preaching of F. W. Robertson* edited and with an Introduction by Gilbert E. Doan, Jr. 1964.
4. *A Brief History of Preaching* by Yngve Brilioth. 1965.
5. *The Living Word* by Gustaf Wingren. 1965.
6. *On Prayer* by Gerhard Ebeling. 1966.
7. *Renewal in the Pulpit*—Sermons by Younger Preachers edited and with an Introduction by Edmund A. Steimle. 1966.
8. *The Preaching of Chrysostom: Homilies on the Sermon on the Mount* edited and with an Introduction by Jaroslav Pelikan. 1967.

Further volumes are in preparation.